DEALING WITH ALCOHOL
Indigenous Usage in Australia, New Zealand and Canada

The devastating impact of alcohol on indigenous populations is well known, but debate often overlooks the broad context of the problem and the priorities of indigenous people themselves. This book has been written with the desire to improve the level of informed debate, and lead to constructive action. It aims to provide readers with a coherent explanation of alcohol misuse among indigenous peoples in Australia, New Zealand and Canada. The extensive health, economic, social and cultural consequences of misuse are described in the words of indigenous people themselves. The book finds that patterns of indigenous alcohol consumption cannot be understood in isolation from the impact of European colonialism and its continuing consequences. Its authors argue that our understanding of alcohol misuse needs to be reconceptualised and structural inequalities addressed.

Sherry Saggers is the head of the School of Social and Cultural Studies at Edith Cowan University in Western Australia. Dennis Gray manages an indigenous research program in the National Centre for Research into the Prevention of Drug Abuse at Curtin University of Technology, also in Perth, Western Australia. Both have taught and researched Aboriginal health for over 20 years. They are the authors of *Aboriginal Health and Society* (1991) and numerous articles.

*For Llewellyn Saggers-Gray,
who is always an inspiration
and who has sustained our working relationship.*

DEALING WITH ALCOHOL

Indigenous Usage in Australia, New Zealand and Canada

SHERRY SAGGERS
and
DENNIS GRAY

CAMBRIDGE
UNIVERSITY PRESS

PUBLISHED BY THE PRESS SYNDICATE OF THE UNIVERSITY OF CAMBRIDGE
The Pitt Building, Trumpington Street, Cambridge, United Kingdom

CAMBRIDGE UNIVERSITY PRESS
The Edinburgh Building, Cambridge CB2 2RU, UK http://www.cup.cam.ac.uk
40 West 20th Street, New York, NY 10011–4211, USA http://www.cup.org
10 Stamford Road, Oakleigh, Melbourne 3166, Australia

First published 1998

Printed in Australia by Brown Prior Anderson

Typeset in New Baskerville 10/12 pt

A catalogue record for this book is available from the British Library

Library of Congress Cataloguing in Publication data

Saggers, Sherry.
Dealing with alcohol: indigenous usage in Australia, New Zealand
and Canada/Sherry Saggers and Dennis Gray.
p.   cm.
Includes bibliographical references and index.
ISBN 0-521-62032-5 (alk. paper). – ISBN 0-521-62977-2 (pbk.:
alk. paper)
1. Indigenous peoples – Alcohol use. 2. Australian aborigines –
Alcohol use. 3. Maori (New Zealand people) – Alcohol use.
4. Indians of North America – Alcohol use – Canada. 5. Alcoholism –
Australia. 6. Alcoholism – New Zealand. 7. Alcoholism – Canada.
I. Gray, Dennis, 1947–   . II. Title.
HV5198.S34   1988
362.282′089–dc21   98–7278

ISBN 0 521 62032 5 hardback
ISBN 0 521 62977 2 paperback

Contents

Tables

Acknowledgements

Edith Cowan University provided Sherry Saggers with study leave and research funds to undertake work on this book. The National Centre for Research into the Prevention of Drug Abuse, Curtin University of Technology, which is funded as part of the Australian National Drug Strategy, provided time and resources for Dennis Gray to undertake research and writing. Funding for particular aspects of our research was provided by the Commonwealth Department of Health and Family Services and the Western Australian Aboriginal Affairs Department. We wish to extend our thanks to Charmaine Papertalk-Green for permission to use her poem 'Pension Day', which was originally published by Penguin Books, and to Maggie Brady for permission to make extensive quotes from her book *Giving Away the Grog*. We would also like to acknowledge the support we have received from our friends and colleagues Anne Atkinson, David Atkinson, Peter Bedford, Deirdre Bourbon, Peggy Brock, Peter d'Abbs, Helen Gray, Ed Jaggard, Clive Linklater, Brooke Morfitt-Sputore, and others too numerous to mention.

CHAPTER 1

Introduction

Speaking out

When we wrote a book on Australian Aboriginal health six years ago
(Saggers & Gray 1991) we included reference to alcohol and other
substance misuse, but did not emphasise it. There were a couple of
reasons for this. Primarily the book was about the ways in which the
political and economic position of Australian Aborigines affected their
past and present health status, and discussion of alcohol was somewhat
marginal to our focus. At least as important, though, was our concern
that discussing the harm that alcohol and other drugs causes to
Aboriginal people could contribute to racist 'blaming of the victim', a
concern shared by many Aboriginal people:

> Having introduced alcohol to Aboriginal people and then having used it as a
> weapon against them, non-Aboriginal people now blame Aborigines for their
> poverty, unemployment, and other problems, wrongly attributing the cause of
> all Aboriginal problems to their 'abuse of alcohol' (Australia, National
> Aboriginal Health Strategy Working Party 1989:197).

So why have we changed our minds about this? It is not due to the current
rush to engage in full and frank discussions of topics previously considered
too 'politically incorrect' to tackle. This manifestation of a more conservative social and political climate in Australia and elsewhere has resulted in
much ill-informed and insensitive debate, which has contributed little to
constructive relations between indigenous and non-indigenous peoples.
Rather, we have been influenced by the persuasive voices of indigenous
people, which both acknowledge the devastating dimensions of the
problem as 'too much sorry business' (Langton 1991; 1992), and demand
that the issue be faced in a manner that recognises indigenous priorities.

1

Perhaps less passionate, but no less persuasive in our decision, have been those who have documented the health and social consequences of alcohol misuse at national and local levels. Both the epidemiological evidence of the sickness and death associated with excessive consumption of alcohol and other drugs, and the anecdotal reports from health and community workers about the wider social consequences, indicate widespread recognition of the harm we are talking about. There is agreement then that the topic of indigenous alcohol and drug misuse needs informed debate and practical action.

Facing the facts: the pleasures of consumption

Any attempt to deal with the negative consequences of excessive alcohol and drug use comes up against what many parents hear from their teenage kids, but which is too often ignored by professionals:

> The most unspeakable truth for open and honest drug education is that drug use is often fun, exciting, rewarding, pleasurable, usual, risky, 'deviant', social, tough, status-full and naughty (O'Connor & Saunders 1992:169).

These are all reasons why alcohol and other drugs have been part of recorded human history and why most of us today enjoy our 'poisons' – sometimes in moderation, but often in amounts now known to be harmful to our health. Besides our own experiences, there is now a body of literature that examines the beneficial health and social effects of moderate alcohol and other drug use (Baum-Baiker 1985; Holman 1994). While some of this literature will be discussed here, for obvious reasons our focus is on excessive consumption and its deleterious effects. It should be noted, however, that some indigenous people have been critical of attempts to portray alcohol use in a positive light, because it glides over the pessimism apparent in many communities about the destructive impact of alcohol, and sometimes because of individual beliefs about dangers of alcohol taken even in moderation.

Comparative indigenous experiences

While the focus of this book is Australia, we have drawn upon experiences and literature from Canada and New Zealand for a number of reasons. A powerful illustration of the value of comparison came to us from a recent profile of native Canadians, of whom it was said:

> According to 1995 statistics, the average life expectancy of native Canadians is almost ten years less than that of the Canadian population as a whole, and this

discrepancy has not improved significantly in twenty-five years. Furthermore, native Canadians are only marginally better educated today than they were twenty-five years ago; they continue to be jailed at rates that far exceed what their population would indicate is possible. In fact, some experts suggest that a native Canadian is about three times as likely to land in a jail cell as in a high school graduating class. Aboriginal people destroy themselves at a phenomenal rate through violence, accidents and suicide. . . . As one western newspaper columnist noted in the late 1980s, in a story about a young native boy's suicide: 'We used to hang them. Now they hang themselves' (Comeau & Santin 1995:ix).

Readers from Australia and New Zealand will recognise the patterns, even though the details may differ a little. Continuing discrepancies in high school completion rates, incarceration, and life expectancy are everyday news in each country, as are the sad accounts of young and old lives lost through alcohol-related accidents and violence.

The health and other social inequalities faced by contemporary indigenous peoples in Australia, Canada and New Zealand are largely a consequence of their similar colonial and developmental histories. Each country was once part of the British Empire, and although they have separately forged independent identities, their constitutional, political and social institutions reflect their common origin. Each has remained part of the British Commonwealth, and developed economies largely dependent on primary production and extractive industries, initially for English, and later world, markets. Within this political and economic framework, indigenous peoples have largely been marginalised and excluded. This exclusion and the associated poverty are at the root of much indigenous ill health (Ehrensaft & Armstrong 1978, in Kunitz 1994:23).

The similarities, however, should not be allowed to obscure real differences between the situations of indigenous populations of these countries. At the time of British invasion, Australian Aborigines were band-level hunter-gatherers, whereas Maoris in New Zealand lived in stratified, agricultural societies. Across North America, there was considerable variation, from stratified, sedentary agricultural peoples to more egalitarian, hunter-gatherer groups (Kunitz 1994:23). Just as the indigenous populations differed, so too did the non-indigenous settlers. In Australia, which was first settled as a penal colony, convicts comprised a significant proportion of the early settlers, whereas Canada's early British settlers were mostly Anglican loyalists. In New Zealand, Australians and middle-class English formed the base of early European settlement (Hartz 1964; Kunitz 1994).

These differences among both indigenous peoples and British settlers in the three countries – as well as the relative power of the British crown at the time of first settlement – affected subsequent relationships between them, resulting in, for example, different levels of recognition of prior rights to land (Sinclair 1971, in Kunitz 1994). In each country indigenous peoples now comprise small minorities, and their ability to win economic, social and political equality has waxed and waned as a consequence of their historic similarities and differences, economic conditions at particular periods, the international political situation, and local, idiosyncratic players and contexts.

The history of alcohol and other drug problems among indigenous peoples in each of the countries is inextricably linked to their respective colonial histories. While psychoactive substances were available throughout much of North America, this was not the case in Australia. There, although there is some documentation of their use, there is no evidence that they were the cause of any long-term health or social problems. It was the lethal combination of the invading colonists, dispossession from ancestral country and hence from a sustaining economy, and subsequent years of marginalisation that appears to have contributed to the devastating impact of alcohol, in particular.

In Australia, Canada and New Zealand, early descriptions of indigenous use of alcohol are mostly negative, stressing the inability of people to 'hold their grog'. In each country, too, there are stories of the ways in which settlers used alcohol to bribe people to stay in their employment or to buy sex from indigenous women. Frontier lives in remote regions were marked by binge drinking of strong alcohol, and many researchers write of the impact of this type of socialisation on drinking styles. In Australia, working-class rural workers became used to hard, physical work in inhospitable climates. When the work was done, hard drinking followed – a pattern that was to become familiar even when the work declined, with the receding of the rural economy and the displacement of workers.

By the 1970s, the ill health of indigenous peoples had become an international concern, and governments began to direct resources to address appalling infant and maternal mortality rates. While these diseases were relatively amenable to positive intervention, more intractable were the so-called lifestyle diseases, of which substance misuse was only one. In the past two decades, indigenous people and health authorities have increasingly targeted alcohol and other drugs as primary causal agents in poor indigenous health.

Despite the efforts of government agencies, and more recent interventions by indigenous people themselves, there is little evidence to suggest that, overall, the problem of alcohol misuse is in decline. If we are to address this problem successfully, we need to consider carefully the causes of the phenomenon, and to know what interventions have been tried, the extents to which these have been successful, and the reasons for their success or failure. Comparison between countries is important because it provides us with a wider range of case studies and natural experiments. The range of materials from New Zealand and Canada that have been available to us is more limited than that from Australia. However, despite such a limitation, this book is an attempt to broaden understandings of indigenous alcohol misuse and the harm associated with it, and ultimately to reduce the burden of that harm on indigenous peoples.

The indigenous peoples of Australia, New Zealand and Canada

Until now, we have spoken loosely of the indigenous peoples of Australia, New Zealand and Canada, but who are these peoples? First, it is important to make clear that, particularly in Australia and Canada, both prior to British colonisation and currently, these indigenous populations were not homogeneous. Within them there were marked linguistic, cultural and political differences. Hence we speak of indigenous *peoples* rather than people.

Estimates of the size of the pre-colonial populations that occupied what are now Australia, New Zealand and Canada vary. However, the best estimates are: 315,000 to 750,000 for Australia; 120,000 to 150,000 for New Zealand; and 500,000 for Canada. Following British colonisation, the indigenous populations of these land areas suffered the combined assaults of introduced disease, malnutrition and starvation consequent upon the denial of access to natural resources which had been theirs, violence, and policies of assimilation. At the lowest points, these indigenous populations had declined: to 78,300 by 1933 in Australia; to 42,000 by 1896 in New Zealand; and to 102,000 by 1871 in Canada – declines of at least 75, 65 and 80 per cent respectively (Horton 1994:889, 1299; New Zealand, Te Tari Tatau, Statistics New Zealand 1997; Canada, Royal Commission on Aboriginal Peoples 1996).

Today, there is no simple answer to questions about who the indigenous peoples of Australia, New Zealand and Canada are, or the numbers of them. Different data collections and bureaucracies use different definitions for different purposes. Thus there is considerable variation in statistical reporting. Censuses in all three countries ask people about their origins or indigenous ancestry. However, for a variety of reasons, some of those who have indigenous origins do not identify with those indigenous groups, or do so only in some situations.

In Australia, for the past 25 years, the Commonwealth Department of Aboriginal Affairs and its successor the Aboriginal and Torres Strait Islander Commission have defined Aboriginal people as those who identify themselves as being Aboriginal and who are accepted as such by the community in which they live. This broad definition replaced earlier distinctions between so-called 'full-blood' and 'part-Aboriginal' people. The censuses of both 1991 and 1996 asked of each person identified, 'Is this person of Aboriginal or Torres Strait Islander *origin*?' (emphasis added). However, the accompanying instructions on how responses were to be recorded differed, and produced differing results (Australian Bureau of Statistics 1995).

In the 1996 Australian census, those who were identified as of Aboriginal or Torres Strait Islander origin totalled 352,970 persons or two per cent of the Australian population. This was an increase of 33 per cent over the 265,371 persons identified as being of indigenous origin in the 1991 census. The proportion increased between these and previous censuses because: the birth-rate among indigenous people is higher than among non-indigenous people; a large proportion of indigenous people marry or partner a non-indigenous person, and their children are classified as being of indigenous origin; increasing numbers of people publicly identify themselves as indigenous as they discover their indigenous ancestry (as among the 'stolen children') or feel strong enough to resist the discrimination which so often accompanies such status; and the instructions which accompanied the 1996 census more clearly provided the option for some people to identify with both the Aboriginal and Torres Strait Islander categories.

The assumption is often made by users of Australian census data that those recorded as being of Aboriginal or Torres Strait Islander origin also *identify* themselves socially and culturally as Aboriginal. However, it is not clear that this is so, and it is also likely that others, because they do not identify as Aboriginal, do not acknowledge their indigenous ancestry. For these reasons Australian census data should be regarded only as a broad indication of the size of the indigenous population.

The 1996 New Zealand census:

> . . . provides for three definitions: those who have any New Zealand Maori ancestry [this is similar to the Australian question about indigenous origins]; those who identify themselves as belonging to the New Zealand Maori ethnic group only; and those who identify themselves as belonging to the New Zealand Maori ethnic group either alone or together with any other ethnic groups (New Zealand, Te Tari Tatau, Statistics New Zealand 1997:122).

In that census a total of 579,714 persons were recorded as being of Maori descent (16 per cent of the population), of whom 486,396 identified themselves with the Maori ethnic group (13.4 per cent of the population). The number of people recorded as having Maori ancestry increased from 511,278 or 15.2 per cent of the 1991 population (also a

Table 1 The indigenous populations of Australia, New Zealand and Canada, 1991 and 1996*

| Population | 1991 | | 1996 | | 1991–96 |
	No.	%	No.	%	% change
Australia[1]					
Aboriginal	238,575	1.4	314,120	1.8	31.7
Torres Strait Islander	26,884	0.2	28,774	0.2	6.9
Aboriginal & TSI	–	–	10,106	0.06	–
Other	16,505,884	98.4	17,399,859	98.0	5.4
Total	16,771,343	100.0	17,752,859	100.0	5.9
New Zealand[2]					
Maori and identify	393,102	11.7	486,396	13.4	23.7
Maori descent not					
identify	118,176	3.5	93,318	2.6	–21.0
Other	2,862,651	84.8	3,038,588	84.0	6.1
Total	3,373,929	100.0	3,618,302	100.0	7.2
Canada[3, 4]					
Status Indians	438,000	1.6			
Non-status Indians	112,600	0.4			
Métis	139,400	0.5			
Inuit	37,800	0.1			
Aboriginal not					
identify	288,535	1.1			
Other	25,977,710	96.2			
Total	26,994,045	100.0			

*Errors due to rounding
Sources: 1. Australian Bureau of Statistics (1995)
        2. New Zealand, Te Tari Tatau, Statistics New Zealand 1997
        3. Canada, Department of Indian Affairs & Northern Development 1995
        4. Canada, Royal Commission on Aboriginal Peoples 1996

rise of 13.4 per cent); and the number identifying as Maori increased from 393,102 or 11.7 per cent of the 1991 population, an increase of 23.7 per cent. These rises were accompanied by a significant decline in the number of people reporting Maori ancestry but not identifying as Maori (New Zealand, Te Tari Tatau, Statistics New Zealand 1997:122).

In Canada indigenous peoples are officially divided into four categories. Registered or status Indians are descendants of groups that entered into treaties with the British and Canadian governments. They are registered under the terms of the Indian Act 1985 with the Department of Indian Affairs and Northern Development, and are subject to various entitlements and obligations under the terms of the treaties. Non-status Indians are those whose ancestors refused to enter treaties with the British or Canadian governments, or those with whom the governments did not establish treaty relations. Métis are people of mixed Indian and non-Indian ancestry (although it should be noted that many status and non-status Indians are also of mixed origins). The fourth category of indigenous Canadians are the Inuit, who in the past were called 'Eskimo' by Europeans (Fleras & Elliott 1992:13–15; Canada, Royal Commission on Aboriginal Peoples 1996).

The 1991 Canadian census enumerated a total of 1,016,340 people of Aboriginal origin, made up of: 385,800 status Indians; 29,455 Inuit; 64,530 Métis; and 536,550 people who had at least one Aboriginal ancestor (Canada, Department of Indian Affairs and Northern Development 1995:3). However, there was significant under-enumeration of people in some categories. For example, the number of persons on the Department of Indian Affairs and Northern Development's statutory register of status Indians was 511,791 in December 1995. Also in 1991, Statistics Canada conducted the national Aboriginal People's Survey (APS), which counted 626,000 people who identified as Aboriginal (Canada, Statistics 1991). Again, however, there was some under-enumeration in the APS. In order to present a more accurate picture, at the request of the Royal Commission on Aboriginal Peoples, Statistics Canada adjusted the figure for the identity-based indigenous population of 1991 to a total of 720,000, made up of: 438,000 status Indians (still below the number on the register); 112,600 non-status Indians; 139,400 Métis; and 37,800 Inuit (Canada, Royal Commission on Aboriginal Peoples 1996). In Table 1, we present the adjusted figures for the identifying groups. Here, in the absence of any better estimate of the number of people of indigenous origin who do not identify as Aboriginal, we have subtracted the identifying population of 720,000 from the 1991 census figure of 1,016,340 persons of Aboriginal origin. On this basis, persons of indigenous origin comprised approximately 3.8 per cent of the population, with those identifying as Aboriginal making up 2.7 per cent of the population. At the time of writing, 1996 census data on ethnicity for Canada had not been released.

The *Report* of the Royal Commission on Aboriginal Peoples stated:

> There is some evidence that the population not identifying with their Aboriginal roots demonstrate socio-economic characteristics quite similar to those of Canadians as a whole, while those who do identify as Aboriginal have quite different socio-economic characteristics (1996).

While published studies are not available, our own experience and discussions with colleagues working in the field suggest that this is also true of Australia and New Zealand. For this reason, like the Canadian Royal Commission, when making comparisons we rely upon the figures for the identifying populations for New Zealand and Canada, but in their absence for Australia use the total population of those recorded as having Aboriginal or Torres Strait Islander ancestry.

Who is this book for?

The experiences of indigenous people themselves provide a powerful narrative that speaks to all who would better understand the effects of alcohol misuse on indigenous communities and their members. In our experience, students, academics, health professionals and others want to know more about the patterns of consumption and their consequences and, importantly, what is being done to address the issues. And while they want to know the facts and figures, they also want to hear the stories of those people who are living with this issue. The book will largely be read by non-indigenous people but we hope that indigenous people too will find it useful.

We hope that the book will provide readers with a coherent analysis of alcohol and other drug misuse among indigenous peoples. As will become clear, that analysis is influenced particularly by structural understandings of the problem. That is, with respect to the perennial sociological debate about the ability of individuals to act in the face of social institutions and forces outside their immediate control, we come down on the side of structural rather than ideational or cultural explanations. However, our approach tries to accord recognition to the positive ways in which indigenous people are dealing with sometimes seemingly hopeless situations. Individual and community agency is apparent in many of the case studies we examine.

Although we write about alcohol and other substances throughout the book, the focus is largely on alcohol. Epidemiologists could argue that tobacco presents a greater challenge for public health. However, our experiences in indigenous communities indicate that this is not a view shared by indigenous people who are more often concerned about the immediate negative social consequences of alcohol misuse than the long-term health effects of smoking.

Organisation of the book

In Chapter 2 we set out to answer the question, what is the harm involved in alcohol use? We do this not from the perspective of outsiders looking in, but largely in the words of indigenous people themselves. The broader context to this question is examined in the following two chapters. In Chapter 3 worldwide patterns of alcohol and drug consumption are reviewed, to demonstrate the ubiquitous nature of drug use, variations in the substances and the patterns of use, and the need to differentiate between use and misuse. This review is followed in Chapter 4 by an analysis of the historical contexts in which alcohol and other drugs were introduced to indigenous communities in Australia, New Zealand and Canada. We include here the ways in which subsequent colonial governments have sought to control the availability of substances through legislative and other means. Also examined are patterns of consumption, drinking environments and populations, and the ways in which drug and alcohol use are connected to broader social relationships.

In Chapter 5 we examine the ways in which drug and alcohol use have been theorised, discussing biological, social, cultural and eclectic theories of misuse, and their changing popularity through time. We then focus on political economy approaches and what they can and cannot explain.

Chapter 6 provides an Australian case study of the political economy of alcohol. This explores the interests of those in the liquor industry and how they have promoted and protected those interests among indigenous people. The broader context of social policies for indigenous Australians, and the ways in which they have influenced the availability of alcohol, are also discussed here.

The wide-ranging health, economic, social and cultural consequences of drug misuse are covered in Chapter 7. Hospital admissions, alcohol-related accidents and death, and details of those diseases attributable to alcohol are presented and discussed. The epidemiology of alcohol-related morbidity and mortality is just one aspect of the picture. The economic, social and cultural consequences are often more visible, and these are also examined. We include here material on the economic impact of drinking on household and community budgets; the social costs of domestic violence, child abuse and neglect; and the weakening of interest in traditional culture.

Cataloguing the harm caused by misuse of alcohol and other drugs can be a profoundly depressing process. In discussing this material it is difficult not to resort to structural theories that portray indigenous people as hapless victims of oppressive post-colonial capitalism, whose agents in the liquor industry bemoan the harm while collecting the profits. However, indigenous people in Australia and elsewhere are responding with creative programs of their own, some based on mainstream models of intervention, which include the use of existing legislation to control the availability of substances, and a variety of treatment and preventive models. Mainstream approaches to substance misuse are discussed in Chapter 8, followed by a selection of indigenous case studies of drug and alcohol programs.

The difficulty of assessing the impact of these programs is discussed in Chapter 9. How is it possible to evaluate indigenous alcohol and substance misuse programs in ways that are meaningful and valid to both the indigenous participants and the largely non-indigenous funding agencies? We suggest that the current climate of aggressive accountability is not conducive to measured analysis of the costs and benefits of programs. It is clear, though, that rigorous evaluation is an important part of the struggle to deal with drugs and alcohol. In the last chapter we try to assess why intervention programs, while locally important, have had little effect on alcohol- and drug-related harm among indigenous people. Like health status more generally, alcohol and other substance harm must be viewed in a broader context, in which many indigenous people continue to live their lives at the margins of the dominant economy and power structures.

CHAPTER 2

What's the harm?

> Couldn't sleep last night after listening yesterday. Thinking about how grog is killing people, family problems, culture dying, lost respect. Grog is a form of poison, can make a good man or woman go mad, kill, forget their kids. . . . Grog is tearing Aboriginal people apart. We don't know how to care for family now. In the old days we were family, need to look back. There are a lot of good things there. . . . Before Europeans our life was spot on. (Brother of one of those who died in custody in South Australia, speaking at Central Australian Aboriginal Congress, cited in Langton 1992:3.)

In countries such as Australia, New Zealand and Canada, many non-indigenous people cling to stereotypes in which all indigenous people misuse alcohol and are believed to be indifferent to the consequences of such misuse. However, indigenous people throughout the world are speaking out about the costs of the misuse of alcohol and other drugs – costs to individuals, families, communities and nations. Their voices are being heard in research reports, commissions of inquiry, autobiographies and fictional accounts. Throughout this book we will examine these costs and the ways they are being dealt with in detail. However, in this chapter, using examples from Australia which provide a strikingly vivid picture, we want first to explore the ways in which indigenous people themselves see the problem of what they, and many other Australians, colloquially refer to as the 'grog'.

Indigenous consumption of alcohol

Working out how much people drink is a difficult business, and we discuss the few quantitative studies that have been undertaken later in the book. Indigenous people themselves are generally quick to refute non-indigenous stereotypes of the 'drunken Aborigine' or the 'drunken

Indian'. They point out the complexity of indigenous drinking patterns and the fact that many of their people drink rather differently from non-indigenous people. While there are segments of indigenous communities where hard drinking is the norm, many indigenous people drink moderately, and – certainly in Australia – a greater proportion of them than non-indigenous Australians are either lifetime abstainers or have given up the 'grog'.

Nevertheless, as among non-indigenous people, a large proportion of indigenous people regard the consumption of alcohol as positive, and fictional accounts of Aboriginal life in Australia are full of references to this. Much of Weller's novel *The Day of the Dog* (1981), which describes the life of young Aboriginal people in urban Western Australia, shows the attraction of alcohol and the close association between sociability and drinking:

> What a magnificent day it is, thinks Doug. Relaxing in the sun, with the best girl in Perth beside him and drinking the coldest, nicest beer he has had for ages. All friends around, enjoying the laughter and talk of sunshine and drink together (Weller 1981:60).

Whether in urban Perth or fringe camps around Darwin, everyday activities for many indigenous people are defined in relation to alcohol:

> One is presented with people who neither shame-facedly admit nor reluctantly confess to the grogging proclivities of their camp's membership. Rather one comes to a community whose members roundly announce that grogging is an activity that, on the one hand, gives each person style, and, on the other, endows the collectivity with a style of life. . . . In the grogging community . . . the moral onus is reversed and it is the abstainer who must make apologies. Because they are deviant, temperate men in grogging communities are put on the defensive (Sansom 1980:48–9).

Indigenous people talk about being introduced to alcohol and a wide range of other drugs at relatively early ages. Young Aboriginal people in Albany, Western Australia, told Gray and his colleagues that they usually began drinking alcohol at about the age of 11 or 12, and many were regular users by the age of 15 (Gray *et al.* 1997:73). Though by no means typical, Chief Eli Mandamin, a native Canadian, told Boyce Richardson that he had become a full-time drinker by the age of nine (1993:191).

In another Australian account:

> Into whisky, wines, and beers. You kicked off on beer then got a little inebriated and then you drank anything that was put in front of you. Meekatharra (Western Australia) was my initial drinking started, Meekatharra. There was two guys, I was sort of bragging about my drinking prowess. These two guys, older

than me, they said 'we'll fix this fella', so they got three bottles of wine, 75 (sic) ml bottle of port. We went down the river at the back of the Meekatharra Pub/Hotel and they said 'righto there's one for you and one for me and one for me, each one drinks his own bottle'. I was just a bit over seventeen at the time, so they drank theirs and I'm sitting there and I passed the bottle around to them and they said 'no, no – you drink that, we drank ours so you drink yours'. So they waited and sat there with me until I drank it and we walked only a couple hundred yards from the river up into the street, where the Meekatharra Hotel is, and I blacked out (Lindsay N, in Brady 1995a:35).

Many indigenous Australian men, especially those who worked in rural areas, recall being introduced to heavy drinking through their working mates:

Well, the claim that we the shearers make generally, is that it relieves the tension – that was the excuse – the work tension. When you are shearing with a team it's very competitive. You're in a shed, say for instance you're in a shearing shed, you move into a place where there was maybe 6,000 to 10,000 sheep to shear and there is four of you's shearing, so you get in there and to get your number out, your tally. And so each night when you're eating, knocked off, you got into the booze to relieve all those tension. That was the excuse we had, but we loved the stuff too, don't worry about that! It was pretty good (Lindsay N, in Brady 1995a:36).

For non-indigenous middle-class people, the amounts of alcohol consumed in many Aboriginal drinking settings are prodigious. Surveys of indigenous drinkers in one community in Western Australia showed that 11.1% of the total sample said they drank 201 to 800 g of alcohol (equivalent to 13 to 54 cans of beer) on what they described as a 'typical' drinking day (Lyon 1990:39). Clearly there is some overestimation or exaggeration at the upper end of this range. Nevertheless, interviews with reformed drinkers indicate that, among some, consumption levels are particularly high:

Doug Abbott, an Arrente man of formidable proportions, said that in his drinking days he could drink half a dozen cartons himself in the course of a binge. 'I could outdrink anybody', he said. Doug Walker, another Alice Springs-born Arrente man and a drinking mate of Abbott's in his younger days, said he would drink a cask of wine [4 litres] in the morning just to get started.
    Willie Nelson, a Western Australian who came to Alice Springs in 1984, said he would down four full flagons [half-gallon jars] of wine – 'I could drink one down in three gulps and chuck it away empty' – and then go on to finish off a carton [24 cans] or two of beer. 'I reckon that's why I got so sick [with cirrhosis of the liver]', Nelson said (Lyon 1990:39).

Many indigenous people describe their drinking habits as drinking to get 'fall down drunk' (Langton 1992:17), rather than for socialising.

Drinking in binges lasting several days or weeks occurs when people have the money:

> On my payday I used to leave hundred dollar Curtis drive-in, hundred dollar in the pub, and my takeaway I used to take two cask, or four wine, smoke. I used to get up four o'clock in the morning, that's when I used to start drink. Till six o'clock, I used to go to Wallaby camp, or Wave Hill camp, to get more grog. Used to get drunk before ten. Over to the pub for one or two or three can, and then after that used to walk out, walk around in the pub, friend used to buy me a grog, more beer (Chappy Robinson, in Brady 1995a:44).

Similar patterns have been described among some indigenous communities in Canada:

> . . . by the late 1960s, drinking had reached frightening levels on the reserve (Alkali Lake in British Columbia). Outsiders called it 'Alcohol Lake'. There were drinking parties every weekend, often lasting for several days. All of the adults – and many of the children – were drinking heavily (York 1992:177).

Obviously many people have thought carefully about the ways in which alcohol is consumed, and are able to reflect on the differences between their own drinking experiences and those they see around them:

> I been watching this film, every film I used to watch? Like movie, and I watch em cowboy, how they go in and that's how I thought to meself, when they go in they have one little glass. Just have a glass and they walk out, and I thought I wish people could do that, you know? Have a little glass, well just get a glass and drink. But especially Aboriginal, you don't see them much. They can't take a glass, they want a – ! And I reckon, any sort of film you watch when they drink, they go and get a glass, they sit there for about an hour, whitefella you know, and they'd sit and talk. Aboriginals, as soon as they go in, they start swearing when they're drunk, and start arguing, start pushing each other. That's not really sensible way.
>
> I seen white fella when they drink they get a glass, they sit down and then they go out. I reckon that's the way should really drink alcohol. The proper way, not going to send them mad, because when they go mad, they end up in all sorts of problems (Duncan Bero, in Brady 1995a:94–5).

Despite what was said earlier about the positive effects of alcohol consumption, whether in novels, short stories, poetry or song, indigenous accounts of the grog are often tinged with sadness:

> Side by side we'd walk along
> To the end of Gertrude Street
> And we'd tarpaulin muster for a quart of wine
> Thick or thin, right or wrong
> In the cold and in the heat

We'd cross over Smith Street
To the end of the line

Then we'd laugh and sing do anything
To take away the pain
Try to keep it down
As it first went down
In Charcoal Lane
Spinning yarns and telling jokes
Now the wine is tasting good
cause it's getting closer and closer
To its end
Have a sip and roll some smokes
We'd smoke tailormades if we could
But we just make do with some city street blend

And we'd all chuck in
And we'd start to drink
When we had enough to do it again
But if things got tight
Then we'd have to bite for
Charcoal Lane

Up Gertrude Street we'd walk once more
With just a few cents short
And we'd stop at the Builders
To see who we could see
Then we'd bite round
Until we'd score a flagon of McWilliams Port
Enough to take away our misery
Then we'd all get drunk
Oh so drunk
And maybe a little insane

And we'd stagger home, all alone
And the next day we'd do it again
Have a reviver in Charcoal Lane
I'm a survivor of Charcoal Lane

(Archie Roach 1990, 'Charcoal Lane')

When the problems associated with misuse begin to outweigh the pleasures, friendships cemented by drinking make it very difficult to moderate or quit drinking. The pressure from family and mates to maintain the drinking lifestyle is echoed in many accounts collected by Brady (1995a):

I think the number one problem with my people is this: until they can accept mates as mates other than being drinking mates, you know, we're going to have no people left. You haven't lost nothing when you give it up, if you tackle it. And sadly to say that's the hardest part, because they'll tempt you and that's where you show the really strength you know, to say, 'look, I'm still one of you, but I'm not drinking no more' (Archie Barton, in Brady 1995a:152).

Counting the costs: the consequences of misuse

The health costs of alcohol misuse are well documented and we will examine some of these in detail later in the book. However, we all know that a gap often exists between what is known about living a healthy life and actually living one. How do indigenous people perceive the impact of drug and alcohol use for their lives? How have they conceptualised alcohol and its consequences for their lives? Again we need to examine both fictional and non-fictional accounts to get a feeling for these costs.

Alcohol and colonisation

A fictional account of the life of the indigenous leader Sandawara, by Aboriginal author Colin Johnson (now known as Mudrooroo), eloquently describes the ambivalence towards alcohol. Sandawara is a nineteenth-century guerrilla leader who is vainly attempting to resist the colonial occupation of his country in Western Australia. In this section, Sandawara allows his followers to drink alcohol taken from settlers during an earlier raid:

> He lets the liquor be passed around among his people, unaccustomed to any sort of drug. He should stop it, but hell exists deep within his mind. He has known the viciousness of the white man – thus comes despair and the desire to experience to the full a moment or two of heightened life before death.
> He drinks deeply of the whisky, feeling the warmth spreading like a fever through his numb body. The ways of the white men begin to prevail in the gorge. The natural disciplines, the obedience to the Law, passed down from the very dawn of humanity, disappear from the river flat.
> Scenes as riotous as in old England erupt in shrieks and cries of alcohol pain kicking out in spasmodic violence. . . . This is his earth, his people and the white man's hell (Johnson 1979:81–2 *Long live Sandawara*).

Here the introduction of alcohol serves as a metaphor for colonisation and all its disastrous consequences. The contemporary setting in which these consequences are expressed is evoked by poet Jack Davis:

> We are tired of the benches, our beds in the park,
> We welcome the sundown that heralds the dark.
> White Lady Methylate!
> Keep us warm and from crying.
> Hold back the hate.
> And hasten the dying.

The tribes are all gone,
The spears are all broken:
Once we had bread here,
You gave us stone

(*'Desolation'*, *in* The first-born and other poems *1970:36*).

Evidence presented to the Royal Commission into Aboriginal Deaths in Custody (1991) in Australia provides a very powerful statement about the contemporary impact of alcohol on Aboriginal lives. While not discounting the broader social and political contexts within which people live, the submission from the Aboriginal Issues Unit found that:

> from *an Aboriginal perspective* and from *the Aboriginal experience*, alcohol plays a primary role in both the reasons for detention, and for the subsequent chances of death occurring (Langton 1992:11).

Alcohol was implicated in seven of the ten Northern Territory Aboriginal deaths in custody investigated by the Royal Commission in 1989–90. However, Marcia Langton (1992) goes on to report that while Aboriginal deaths in custody were an obvious concern, the risk of dying from an alcohol-related cause outside prison was much higher. No Aboriginal women died in police custody in the Northern Territory in the period 1989–90, but more have been killed in alcohol-related violence than the total number of deaths in custody. Alcohol-related traffic accidents have claimed more Aboriginal lives in the Northern Territory than has death in custody.

There are now a number of reports that starkly document the costs Aboriginal people associate with heavy drinking – loss of jobs and driving licences, family violence and breakdown, alcohol-related deaths of family members and friends, and lives which were totally fixed on 'grog' and how to get it (Langton 1992; Lyon 1990; Brady 1995a).

Job loss

For many people, heavy drinking was closely associated with damaged reputation and decreasing ability to maintain any semblance of a normal working life:

> I had a job at school, then they give me the sack again because I used to off and on and they didn't like it that way. 'Oh you're drunk, you don't want to teach, you don't want to teach because you might teach the wrong way.' When I was working at hospital they used to tell me 'you don't want to work at hospital. That's why you give us wrong medicine. You know, that grog make you no good. You might kill people.' So when they tell me, you know, and I

said 'I'm not going to back to hospital because I'm a alcoholic woman. I'm finished. I'm not working anymore (Mrs G.D., in Brady 1995a:65).

Sometimes these losses were gradual, and drinkers spoke of the patience of family and employers. At other times lives deteriorated rapidly:

I had a good name, little bit. That grog bin, sort of, pulled me into the town. And I lost me all sort of licence, gun licence, motor car licence, you know? From the grog. Lose everything. Lose the job (Claude Manbulloo, in Brady 1995a:71).

Financial costs

Drinking requires a significant financial commitment, which diverts funds from the maintenance of households – this is especially problematic when the only income for many indigenous families is various social security payments. Ex-drinkers clearly identify the financial drain that excessive drinking causes, with all available money targeted for drinking with mates:

Oh she used to get child endowment. Just around about only $30.00 something. Not much, eh? But I used to go out with all me mate, you know. Spend all me money on the grog. You know, come back, fighting me wife. Drunk, get blind. Look for tucker. But there no tucker, no, fight me wife for the tucker. And then, we divorce. We divorce (Omar Joe, in Brady 1995a:67).

It is difficult for the members of drinkers' families to exercise any control over the money available for grog, even if the consequences are extreme for others:

What usually happens if a person is drinking they asking their wives or family to go and buy grog, and then they come back drunk and flog the wife and the kids, next day wife has a black eye, and he's got a headache, so the wife gives him a Panadol and makes sure he's all right. So what's happening is that the family is helping that person become an alcoholic, helping him 'cause when he comes drunk they put him to bed, they'll look after him, so you've got the dependent and the family is supporting the dependent (Langton 1992:18).

Drinkers and ex-drinkers alike are well aware of the financial exploitation connected to dependence on grog:

You know the man that runs the taxi he was telling me that times it costs $80 for one carton, and I said how come, cause it is about $30 in town. Cause they call the taxi out here and that's one way, it costs $25 right, and then back in, they buy the carton for $30 they are back out again so they've given him $50 and they give the hotel $30 so that's $80 for one carton (in Langton 1992:18).

Violence

Once a taboo subject, the stories of alcohol-related violence within families and communities are now heard throughout indigenous communities. Drinkers told Brady of the price wives, children and other family members had paid as a result of excessive alcohol use:

> I came back and still a heavy drinker. I used to bash my wife, I used to hit across the one floor to another floor at nighttime if she didn't have a packet of cigarettes for me (Alan Dodd, in Brady 1995a:127).

The recent video *Speak Quiet, Speak Strong* shows very clearly the relationship between family or domestic violence, child abuse, sexual assault and incest, and alcohol abuse. One woman tells her story about the husband who, when asked to return home from a drinking party, threw her into the car, drove her to a remote spot, removed her clothes and raped her, then returned her to her brother's place. Elsewhere in the documentary members of an Aboriginal night patrol surprise a man attempting to rape an apparently inebriated woman. This is everyday business for patrol members, who routinely intervene to prevent violence between drinking people.

Audrey Bolger's survey of family violence (1990) in the Northern Territory reveals many such stories. One Aboriginal woman speaks of the almost routine terror associated with her husband's drunken behaviour:

> I shut myself and the kids in the house if I know he's been drinking. He comes and knocks; I don't answer, don't open the door. Then he starts shouting, smashing and it goes on all night. In the daytime he screams at the kids, says shame things about me. His family says they'll send him out bush – they do but he comes back. I'm okay – not battered much – mostly mental – threats, hassles (Bolger 1990:27).

It is not just wives and children who bear the brunt of this violence. Drinkers and their other victims have accounts of fights and accidents which come with the grog:

> Head injuries, broken arm, accident and when they fight with white people's weapon, like knife, gun, especially knife and gun. Climb the electric pole when they're drunk (discussion with Tiwi people, in Langton 1992:19).

> One time I hit a bottle tree, right inside, just carved me front tyre off. When I woke up next morning and I seen the damage I done, I thought, I could have been dead if I could have hit it front on. And I thought to myself that's how grog get into you, you know? You even fight your friend, and you says all the silly word. And when you come sober some of them sober people tell you 'hey

you bin doing that' and you can hardly believe what you bin saying. I kept on and nearly got killed, run over by a big truck . . . And after that I thought I better steady up, so anyway I steady up drinking (Duncan Bero, in Brady 1995a:91).

Speaking out about the violence associated with alcohol misuse is not easy for indigenous people. The film *Once Were Warriors* (Communicado Film *et al.* 1994) graphically depicts the way in which heavy drinking is part of almost institutionalised violence. The book upon which the film is based was written by Maori Alan Duff (1991), who has been vilified in some quarters for his uncompromising approach to the devastation caused by alcohol in some Maori communities. The film is able to portray not only the attractions of the extended kin and social networks which provide warm sociable gatherings to urban Maori, but also the extent to which excessive amounts of alcohol contribute to escalating violence and abuse of family trust, leading even to incidents of sexual assault against women and children.

Effects on children

Less immediately visible than violence, but just as devastating, are the other consequences of alcohol and other drug abuse on children. Children recall growing up in households where getting grog was paramount, and where the everyday securities other children take for granted – food, shelter, affection – were either not present or very inconsistently given.

Sometimes the introduction of the young to alcohol itself starts very early:

The beer arrives and everyone gathers around begging for a drink. Charley sits supreme and at peace, brushing younger brothers and sisters and cousins away as though they were flies.

He rocks his little son upon his knee and feeds him the odd sip of beer. Start them off young, then they won't feel the bump so much when it comes as they get older (Weller 1981:59).

This pleasant, casual atmosphere is unpredictable, however, and easy friendships can turn violent. Often children find themselves in the firing line:

I bin thinking meself, I had too many kids. I had big mob. Five boy and four girl. All big one now. Still I don't drink. I bin worried about my future. No good I drinking, you know. I'm worried someone drunk can kill em my kids. Look after my kid properly. No good spending money la grog I been thinking about no good spending money la grog, I like to look after my kids, clothes and stuff (Duncan McDonald, in Brady 1995a:116).

Children growing up with alcohol-dependent adults all around them often themselves become alcohol-dependent. A youth worker in Alice Springs describes the life of a 'fairly typical' Aboriginal boy in that town:

The child of 'alcoholic' parents, whose father died of cirrhosis of the liver, the boy started dodging primary school at an early age. His mother was a heavy drinker, the house was usually filled with drunks, and little care was taken of the boy and his brothers and sisters. 'There was no food in the kitchen. You couldn't even pick up a towel for the shower, . . . he had no shoes, no clean clothes. He was too shamed to go to school' . . . Ultimately he dropped out. Now, he has a 'big chip on his shoulder', drinks heavily almost daily and can be very violent. Almost 17, he looks like an old man (Lyon 1990:95–6).

Sickness and early death

For many people, alcohol use is associated with continual illness, and the health consequences have led many people to finally give up the 'grog':

Then she took me up and I went in the hospital here. The doctor said 'you're sick from drinking too much'. And they had a plastic bag that shifted through my nose and a plastic bag down here and they drained it out, a bottle of moselle and beer, I think that what I was drinking. They flew me up in Darwin Hospital and I still had that tube and thing through my nose and I had that operation. My liver and kidney was really bad, and I was told from doctor not to be drinking anymore because I sick. You see, doctor told me, 'if you drink again you should have been dead' (Mrs M, in Brady 1995a:32).

For Gordon Briscoe, once a fit and very active sportsman, being constantly sick forced him to reassess his direction:

But 1980 was the time that I finished again. I decided, it took me that 12 months to try and reverse myself and get myself back on the track again, and I didn't do it with AA. I did it just by realising that my health was suffering, my back pains were getting worse, my head pains were getting worse, I wasn't able to exercise in the way that I wanted to and I could feel my bones. Used to ache like mad; my shoulders used to ache, my back used to suffer, you know and sports injuries would appear. My feet, the bones of my feet used to ache in the morning, old breaks and bruises, kicks, sprains and ligaments and bone breaks used to get worse. And I put this all down to old age, but it wasn't, it was the grog. It was that grog that did it (in Brady 1995a:158).

Early death associated with drinking is part of many indigenous people's normal experience. In many communities all the members have had relatives and friends who have died:

All my uncles died through drink. One of my aunties, my father's sister, died through the alcoholic effects. Most of my father's brothers, there were six of them, that were metho drinkers and the last fella died since I left Perth, and he was a regular metho drinker. In them days it wasn't so profound in the family situation as it is nowadays. I'm going back you know twenty to thirty years and I'm fifty seven now, and when I started was when I was seventeen, and prior to that there was some drinking in my family background. Unfortunately, I have got older sons, they went into the booze too because of my example that I set them (Lindsay N, in Brady 1995a:35).

Effects on culture

Much discussion among both indigenous and non-indigenous peoples has focused on the relationship between alcohol and culture. One view is that there is an incompatibility between indigenous ways and European 'grog':

> Well *anangu* [Aborigines] shouldn't drink! *Anangu*, grog. Because, because no history of the grog, the alcohol, you know. Long time, so people they got tradition you know, and European culture, they got tradition too you see, wine. They drink wine in wedding. You know wedding? And very important occasion, they drink. They get tradition. But *anangu* shouldn't drink, *anangu* got other tradition to look at, to look at their ways you know. They go hunting, they gotta teach their children about their ways (Keith Peters, in Brady 1995a:138).

Associated with this view is the notion that drinking or alcohol misuse leads to the 'loss' of indigenous cultures and the proliferation of social problems.

Other indigenous people do not accept the idea that their culture is 'lost' because of alcohol. Even where dispossession has been minimal and culture is perceived to be strong, alcohol exerts strong pressure. When asked what he thought about the idea that drinking by Aboriginal people was related to loss of country and culture, one man said:

> No I don't think so. I don't think so because I think they just want to drink because of what they feel about it. Like fun. And there's lot of people, thousands of people in Top End, Central Australia, that going out on alcohol, eh, even kava drinking, petrol sniffing – but still we didn't lose our culture, still got it (Chappy Robinson, in Brady 1995a:47).

In other accounts, alcohol has been absorbed into many indigenous cultures and its use has become bound up in indigenous practices of exchange and the expression of indigenous values:

> This substance has been incorporated into Aboriginal culture and is some-times accorded almost the status of ritual object when it is bound up in a traditional exchange. Also it is required by kin that others drink with them as

a matter of good etiquette and obligation in many situations, including mourning (Langton 1992:16).

Such an incorporation, it is argued, often sustains high levels of alcohol consumption and the harm that is associated with it.

For Merv Gibson, acceptance by indigenous people that their drinking behaviour embodies expression of 'traditional' social relations entails the internalisation of a myth created by white 'experts'. This myth – which romanticises indigenous misuse of alcohol and understates its consequences – now shackles indigenous people, and permits some indigenous drinkers to exploit others:

> Alcohol has become such a *particular problem* for Aboriginal people because, under the Myth, it has become an expression of *identity* and *culture* for them. For black people, to drink alcohol is to *be* an Aboriginal. Social relationships and community [are] expressed through the consumption of alcohol (Merv Gibson, in Brady 1991a:187).

> Why is such exploitation and parasitism allowed to continue? It is allowed to continue because the Myth has convinced the members of the society that it is part and parcel of Aboriginal culture and tradition . . . Jack justifies his appropriation of the family income for the purposes of buying alcohol for his cousins, as a true expression of cultural identity and as fulfilment of cultural and kinship obligations. Consuming alcohol for Jack in the way that he does is all about reinforcing kinship and cultural ties. During the course of consuming the alcohol Jack can be heard explaining his kinship ties to his fellows. . . . It is a gross denial and distortion of true Aboriginal tradition . . . (Merv Gibson, in Brady 1991a:187).

Alcohol: cause or consequence?

When considering the misuse of alcohol and associated harm, the fundamental question that arises – and one that this book seeks to answer – is whether alcohol misuse is the cause or the consequence of the social problems confronted by indigenous peoples. Those who seek a simple, unanimous answer from indigenous people themselves are bound to be disappointed. Some see the introduction of alcohol and its subsequent misuse as the root cause of the malaise and the social problems that affect many indigenous people today:

> We argue that because alcohol is a powerful addictive chemical substance, it is more causal than symptomatic. Once Aboriginal people are in the grip of alcohol they find it difficult or impossible to escape (Langton 1992:16).

Others see the misuse of alcohol as an attempt to ease the suffering imposed by European colonialism – another of the consequences of dispossession and exclusion, but one which in turn causes indigenous people to harm themselves. Yet others see it as both cause *and* consequence of the inequalities between themselves and non-indigenous people.

We believe that any adequate attempt to deal with the misuse of alcohol and its associated harm must be based on a clear understanding of the nature of the problem. Indigenous people, like non-indigenous people, are themselves grappling with this, and it is one of the issues that this book seeks to address.

CHAPTER 3

The broader context of alcohol use

Before examining indigenous use of alcohol in detail, in this chapter we want to place the use of alcohol into a broader context. Here we emphasise that alcohol is simply one of many drugs but the primary role it plays in indigenous communities in Australia, New Zealand and Canada supports our decision to concentrate on this drug, to the neglect of others which also cause harm, especially tobacco. Drugs are dealt with differently, depending upon the time, place and context. What one group of people at one time deems dangerous, another may ignore. However, whatever the variation, one thing is clear: all societies exercise some control over some drugs at some times. Examining the reasons for those controls allows us important insights into broader social and cultural values. In each of the countries we examine, drinking is an important aspect of everyday social life. Having some understanding of the ways in which consumption patterns have changed in time and place provides a more informed background to the analysis of indigenous alcohol use in the past and present.

Drugs in world history

Expressions like 'the war against drugs' illustrate contemporary attempts by some leaders and policy makers to convince society that drug taking is abnormal. The evidence, however, does not support such a view. Drug taking is ubiquitous in world history. All human societies of the past and the present have included members who have used some forms of naturally occurring, mind-altering substances – whether alcohol, cannabis, opium, coca, tobacco, cacti or mushrooms, or the more innocently regarded tea and coffee (Gossop 1993). At some times and in some places these substances have been regarded as illicit, while elsewhere they have appeared as part of everyday diets or been incorporated into traditional cultural practices.

Drugs are often conventionally defined in terms of their putative healing properties. Hence one definition is 'any chemical substance, synthetic or extracted from plant or animal tissue and of known or unknown composition, which is used as a medicant to prevent or cure disease' (from *Butterworth's Medical Dictionary*, in Gossop 1993:2). Such a definition is unsatisfactory for our purposes as it does not deal with non-medical use. Better is the definition given by Pols and Hawks, that:

> . . . a 'drug' in the broadest sense is any chemical entity or mixture of entities, other than those required for the maintenance of normal health, the administration of which alters the biological function and possible structure (1987:59).

By psychoactive drug (from *psyche*, meaning mind or spirit), we refer to:

> any chemical substance, whether of natural or synthetic origin, which can be used to alter perception, mood or other psychological states (Gossop 1993:2).

Of all the psychoactive substances, alcohol has been the most widely used in both time and place. The process of alcoholic fermentation occurs naturally when yeasts metabolise the sugars in decaying fruits, and there are various ethnographic descriptions of the consumption of such naturally occurring alcoholic beverages by hunter-gatherers. For thousands of years, the purposeful fermentation of grains and fruits by humans to make beers and wines has been widespread throughout Europe, Asia and Africa, although until the time of first European contact it was confined to a small area in the Americas and was non-existent in Australia.

Discovery of the process of distillation about a thousand years ago enabled the development of much more potent alcoholic drinks. As the distillation process became more efficient, it led to cheaper, widely available spirits. When William of Orange became King of England he put an end to the monopoly of spirits manufacture held by the London Distillers Guild. This led to an increase in the output of distilled spirits from 4 million gallons in 1694 to more than 20 million gallons in 1750 (Lewis 1992:5). Many people are aware of the gin houses of eighteenth-century England, where 'dead drunkeness' could be purchased for two pence. The British House of Commons was told in 1726:

> we have . . . observed, for some years past, the fatal effects of the frequent use of several sorts of distilled Spiritous Liquors upon great numbers of both Sexes, rendring them diseased, not fit for business, poor, a burthen to themselves and neighbours and too often the cause of weak, feeble and

distempered children, who must bee ... a charge to their country (in Royal College of Physicians 1987:1).

The outcry from the respectable led to a series of Gin Acts, which imposed restrictions on the sale of spirits. Some commentators have noted the class bias of this concern about alcohol and the public good. Hogarth's evocative depiction of the degradations of Gin Lane obscured the realities of heavy drinking among the affluent (Royal College of Physicians 1987).

Effects of drugs

People drink, smoke and take other drugs for a number of reasons, not least of which is to experience the psychoactive properties of the substances. Understanding how alcohol and other drugs affect users is not straightforward, however. Particularly influential work here has been that of Zinberg (1984), who claimed that understanding why drugs were used and how they affected the user was dependent upon three determinants, the:

> ... drug (the pharmacological action of the substance itself), set (the attitude of the person at the time of use, including his [sic] personality structure), and setting (the influence of the physical and social setting within which use occurs) (Zinberg 1984:6).

The nature of the drug (whether stimulant, depressant or hallucinogen); the purity of the substance ingested (whether 'cut' with harmless or dangerous fillers); dosage; individual characteristics of the user, such as age, sex, weight and health status; simultaneous use of other drugs; and the means by which the drug is taken (eaten, smoked, injected, inserted) will all impact on the drug-taking experience (Moss & Higgins 1986; Australia, National Campaign Against Drug Abuse 1986:10–12). Sipping two glasses of wine while enjoying a romantic dinner is obviously a very different experience to that of 'sculling' (drinking at one draught) ten 'shooters' (a combination of two or more neat spirits or liqueurs) in an hour during a hotel drinking competition. The pharmacological effects of the alcohol in the two instances would also be quite different.

A person's attitude at the time of drug taking is also known to influence the drug's effects. The best example of this principle is demonstrated by the so-called placebo effect. This refers to the psychological and physiological changes that are produced by the application of a placebo, '... a pharmacologically inert substance: starch, talc, and sugar powder' (Gossop 1993:20). That is, people who believe they are taking a particular substance with known effects will often experience those effects, even though the actual substance they have taken has no such demonstrated effects. Clinical trials using placebos have shown that about 35 per cent of patients' conditions will improve after receiving a placebo (Gossop 1993:22).

In a classic study of marijuana use, Becker showed how novice users learned of getting stoned from more experienced users, and how this 'labelling' enabled them to experience the socially and culturally appropriate effects of what previously was either an ambiguous or even unpleasant set of feelings (Becker 1953). As Mandelbaum has said of drinking:

> When a man lifts a cup, it is not only the kind of drink that is in it, the amount he is likely to take, and the circumstances under which he will do the drinking that are specified in advance for him, but also whether the contents of the cup will cheer or stupefy, whether they will induce affection or aggression, guilt or unalloyed pleasure. These and many other cultural definitions attach to the drink even before it touches the lips (Mandelbaum 1965:282).

The physical and social settings of alcohol and other drug use also affect the ways in which these are experienced. Shooting up heroin in a hotel toilet with strangers will likely produce very different feelings to injecting the same amount of heroin at home among family or trusted friends. Studies of the relationship between alcohol and violence have convincingly demonstrated the effect of particular drinking environments on levels of violence (d'Abbs 1991).

All of these factors mean that the next section on alcohol and its effects needs to be read carefully in the knowledge of the greatly varying influence that drug, set and setting may have on the experience. Another point to remember is that all drugs have both beneficial and negative effects. Like most people working in the area, we focus on the negative effects because of the acknowledged damage caused, particularly by excessive drinking, among indigenous people. But any honest assessment of alcohol misuse must also recognise the undoubted pleasure that drug taking can bring, and attempts to control misuse need to take account of the benefits that may attach to use (Moore & Gerstein 1981:21).

Alcohol

Alcohol, or, strictly speaking, ethanol (the by-product of the metabolism of yeasts in the fermentation process), is the psychoactive drug most widely used throughout the world (Heath 1983:344). Other alcohols include methyl, amyl and propyl alcohol, all of which are toxic. Of these, methyl alcohol is used sometimes in the form of methylated spirits when ethanol is either not available or too expensive, as occurs among Aboriginal heavy drinkers in parts of Australia for instance (Brady 1995a). Commercially available methylated spirits contains both ethanol and methyl alcohol, and, although it is less intoxicating than ethanol, the side effects can be much more serious, including brain damage and blindness (Gossop 1993:59).

Before listing the adverse effects of alcohol, we need to acknowledge its demonstrated and reputed benefits. Most drinkers will be aware of the way in which a small amount of alcohol makes meeting new people and socialising generally easier, because of the way it acts as a disinhibitor. At low to moderate levels alcohol can also stimulate the appetite. Recent research also indicates that moderate drinking, of about two standard drinks per day (see below), may decrease the risk of cardiovascular disease by increasing levels of high-density lipoproteins (Schuckit 1995:71).

It should be noted that although the notion of a 'standard drink' has wide currency, it is not always realised that the term does not have a standard definition. In Australia, it is usually defined as a drink containing 10 g of absolute alcohol. In New Zealand, for some purposes it has been defined as 10 g of absolute alcohol, but for others as 15 g of pure alcohol (Alcohol Advisory Council of New Zealand 1995; Wyllie, Zhang & Casswell 1993). In Canada, it is 13.6 g (Stockwell & Single 1997:85), although Statistics Canada has used an amount of 1.7 cl (or 17 g) of absolute alcohol (Single, Williams & McKenzie 1994:37).

The long-term effects of excessive alcohol consumption are considerable, including: problems associated with the digestive system (higher rates of ulcers, hepatitis, cirrhosis); increased risks of various cancers; heart disease; hypertension; vitamin deficiencies and anaemia; damage to the nervous system, including permanent brain damage; increased risk of infections; and problems with sexual impotence and menstrual irregularities. Drinking can cause changes in glucose levels, which in turn can elevate blood sugar levels among people with diabetes. Pregnant women who drink more than two standard drinks a day (or even less, in the advice of some) risk delivering babies with Foetal Alcohol Effects or Foetal Alcohol Syndrome, that is, with some mental and/or physical impairment or abnormalities. Accidents and injury, both to oneself and to others, are also closely associated with alcohol consumption, as are a wide variety of mental health concerns such as anxiety, depression and irritability (Moss & Higgins 1986; Schuckit 1995:74–5).

Use and abuse

The alcohol and drug area is a terminological minefield where the unsuspecting player can easily slip. Definitions of use and abuse are not value-free, but compete in a heavily contested domain where health professionals, politicians and private citizens, among many others, advocate terms that have both ideological and practical significance. For instance, in recent years health professionals in many countries have shifted their attention away from prevention of drug use to harm reduction associated with use. This has come about for a number of reasons, including greater difficulties in controlling the availability of alcohol in the light of worldwide declines in consumption, and medical evidence of the beneficial effects of moderate drinking. It also signals a shift away from attempts to reduce consumption among light to moderate drinkers, to a focus on the damage wrought by heavy drinkers (Single 1995:29).

In this context, harm reduction strategies acknowledge the reality of drug use, and attempt to institute measures by which harm associated with use is minimised (Wodak 1994). Some assumptions underlying this approach include: acceptance, but not necessarily approval, of drug use; treating the user as normal and responsible for their own behaviour; and adopting a neutral approach to long-term goals of intervention, focusing instead on immediate and achievable goals (Single 1995:26).

Although initially applied to illicit drug use, harm reduction measures have also been advocated in the case of alcohol. These measures include such practices as the promotion of low alcohol content drinks; restructuring of drinking environments (padding of furniture, reorganisation of space, etc.) in order to reduce injuries from drunken fighting; and training of bar staff in the promotion of moderate drinking, for example by dealing with intoxicated clients in appropriate ways (Single 1995:28).

Contemporary conservative governments in many western countries have instructed their health departments to reject both the harm minimisation/reduction model and some terms which may suggest that drug taking is normal, if not acceptable. They argue instead that prevention of illicit drug use and excessive drinking should be the focus of health promotion. In Australia, this approach is exemplified by the 'Just say no' campaigns directed at young people.

Here we have drawn largely from the literature within the harm minimisation model, as our research and personal experiences have shown the ubiquitousness of drinking and other drug taking among the world's populations. However, as we show later, some indigenous groups share the suspicions of others towards the harm minimisation approach, and within indigenous communities there is vigorous debate about the proper focus of alcohol campaigns.

Contemporary patterns of worldwide alcohol use

Patterns of alcohol use around the world are the result of a complex combination of historically specific social and cultural factors. Alcohol was firmly established in Europe by the time adventurers returned from the New World with previously unknown drugs such as tobacco and mescaline. Perhaps as a result of this situation, at least in part, alcohol remains the drug of preference throughout Europe today. Some drugs are intimately connected to national culture and identity. For instance, in wine-growing regions in France, Spain, Italy and Portugal, wine consumption is part of everyday living for most of the population (Brewers Association of Canada 1993:479).

Some workers have pointed out that the ways in which certain drugs are used have led to the development of particular policies of control which, themselves, have resulted in changes to drug use. For instance, with respect to alcohol, in parts of Europe wine is seen as possessing nutritional value and is a usual accompaniment to meals. Beer may also be drunk with meals but is more importantly connected with social activities outside the home. In Germany, beer drinking is so pervasive that it is thought to contribute to male nutritional levels. Spirits, on the other hand, are not often associated with either of these uses (Sulkunen 1976, in Brewers Association of Canada 1993:479).

Countries with histories of temperance movements have seen a shift away from high alcohol content drinks such as spirits, to lower alcohol content drinks such as beer and wine, and/or reductions in the overall level of consumption. For instance, of pioneering nineteenth-century Canada it has been said:

> Most settlers' accounts emphasize the number of taverns and inns and the drunkenness of the population. Drinking seemed to pervade most festivals, special events, and pioneer bees. Early inns became the focus of social life. Per capita alcohol consumption was probably 25% to 30% higher than it is today. Most people drank whiskey, probably stronger whiskey than we have now (Smart & Ogborne 1986:14).

A vigorous temperance movement in Canada, established in the 1820s, successfully fought for prohibition, and much of Canada was declared dry by the mid-1890s (Smart & Ogborne 1986:63); currently the beverage of choice is beer. In other countries such as Norway and New Zealand, temperance movements also existed but instead of influencing beverage choice, these led to decreases in overall levels of consumption. The opening of borders to both trade and travel after World War II has also had a significant impact on drinking and other drug-taking habits (Brewers Association of Canada 1993:479).

Drinking practices

It has long been recognised that drinking practices vary enormously according to social and cultural context. In what is now a classic article on cross-cultural understandings of alcohol use, Mandelbaum states:

Alcohol is a cultural artifact; the form and meanings of drinking alcoholic beverages are culturally defined, as are the uses of any other major artifact. The form is usually quite explicitly stipulated, including the kind of drink that can be used, the amount and rate of intake, the time and place of drinking, the accompanying ritual, the sex and age of the drinker, the roles involved in drinking, and the role behavior proper to drinking (Mandelbaum 1965:281).

Others have linked these variations in drinking practices to specific alcohol problems, as:

> . . . choices about how much drinking is done, how much intoxication is generated, and how the periods of intoxication are woven into settings and activities that bring drinkers into contact with dangerous parts of the environment seem to be at least as important in creating risks for drinkers as the general level of hazards in their environment (Moore & Gerstein 1981:25).

The anthropological literature contains numerous references to wide variations in drinking patterns in non-western societies, from the very social, convivial beer drinking of the Kafyar of Nigeria in West Africa, to the frequent and heavy drinking in many Central and South American societies, such as the Camba of eastern Bolivia, where:

> Most Camba men participate in recurrent drinking bouts, which may last for a whole weekend. A drinker may pass out several times in the course of a bout and, upon reviving, drink himself quickly into a stupor again (Mandelbaum 1965:282).

The way in which alcohol is consumed has both social and health impacts, and it has been suggested that the type of beverage can influence these. Sulkunen (1976), for instance, has contrasted the 'multidimensional' drinking styles of wine- and beer-drinking countries with the 'one-dimensional' style of countries where spirits are predominantly consumed. Two countries which reflect each stereotype are France and Finland. France is internationally identified with wine growing and drinking, and for the French:

> Drinking is part of our national way of life. The French have a tradition of being 'bon vivants'. They like to drink because it tastes good, it's convivial, it's a sign of friendship. A meal is not a real meal unless there is wine on the table (Fontan 1987, in Brewers Association of Canada 1993:487).

Finland, on the other hand, shares with other spirits-drinking countries, like Sweden, Norway and Poland, the tradition of binge drinking until drunk:

> . . .a typical Finn drinks rarely, usually at the weekend or on holidays, but then he drinks heavily. Most of the total consumption takes place in drinking situations which result in intoxication, and only a small proportion in social situations where the drinkers hardly become intoxicated (in Brewers Association of Canada 1993:487).

Drinking in Canada is much more likely to be part of other social activities, such as at home, at social gatherings such as parties, or while drinking in bars and taverns and eating in restaurants. Canadians are much less likely to drink at lunchtime or while participating in sport and other recreational pursuits, and rarely drink alone (Canada, Health and Welfare 1990a; Single & Wortley 1993). While drinking is moderate on a national scale, these figures disguise much variation including heavy drinking during special occasions such as Christmas and at weddings, and destructive levels of drinking among many indigenous groups and in frontier regions in the north (Smart & Ogborne 1986:187–8).

Many of these anthropological descriptions focus on the patterning of drinking behaviours across cultures. At the extreme, these can become ethnic stereotypes in which particular drinking behaviours are explained merely as culturally appropriate ways of interacting with alcohol. While acknowledging that drinking practices do vary from culture to culture, we are more interested in the social contexts in which particular drinking styles become established and then are challenged by changing social circumstances. That is, we ask the question, what factors contributed to the development of particular drinking practices among this group in the past, and to what extent do these factors continue to influence drinking today?

Worldwide levels of alcohol consumption

Figures on the consumption of alcohol worldwide reflect the predominance of alcohol in the life of most Europeans (see Table 2). Some commentators have also noted the very prominent place Australia and New Zealand have as the greatest consumers of alcohol in the English-speaking world (Australia, Department of Human Services and Health 1994:11). The distinction is somewhat perplexing, but possibly reflects understandings of the ways in which culturally similar countries such as the United States and Canada have experienced more significant declines in consumption.

Some qualifications are necessary before interpreting Table 2. The figures refer to registered consumption only, and the Brewers Association of Canada (1993:481) notes that unrecorded consumption in countries such as Sweden and Norway may add an estimated 29 and 30 per cent to

Table 2   Ranking of countries, per capita consumption of pure alcohol[1], by beverage type, 1991

Rank	Spirits (litres alcohol)	Beer (litres)	Wine (litres)	Total alcohol (litres)
1	Poland 4.5	Germany 142.7	France 66.8	Luxembourg 12.3
2	Hungary 3.4	Czechoslovakia 135.0	Portugal 62.0	France 11.9
3	Cyprus 3.3	Denmark 125.9	Luxembourg 60.3	Portugal 11.6
4	Czechoslovakia 3.3	Austria 123.7	Italy 56.8	Germany 10.9
5	Bulgaria 2.3	Rep. of Ireland 123.0	Argentina 52.4	Switzerland 10.7
6	Germany 2.7	Luxembourg 116.1	Switzerland 48.7	Hungary 10.5
7	Spain 2.7	Belgium 113.3	Spain 34.3	Spain 10.4
8	Greece 2.7	New Zealand 109.5	Austria 33.7	Austria 10.3
9	Finland 2.6	Hungary 107.0	Greece 32.4	Denmark 9.9
10	France 2.5	UK 106.2	Hungary 30.0	Belgium 9.4
11	Canada 2.2[2]	Australia 101.9	Chile 29.5	Czechoslovakia 8.6
12	Iceland 2.1	Netherlands 88.5	Uruguay 25.4	Greece 8.6
13	USA 2.1	USA 87.4	Germany 24.9	Italy 8.4
14	Netherlands 2.0	Finland 85.3	Belgium 23.9	Netherlands 8.2
15	Japan 2.0	Canada 78.3[2]	Yugoslavia 22.1	New Zealand 7.8
16	Cuba 2.0	Spain 70.9	Denmark 22.0	Bulgaria 7.8
17	Soviet Union 2.0[2]	Switzerland 70.1	Bulgaria 20.4	Australia 7.7
18	Romania 2.0	Portugal 67.4	Romania 19.0	Argentina 7.5
19	Switzerland 1.8	Colombia 65.0	Australia 18.6	Cyprus 7.5
20	Rep. of Ireland 1.7	Venezuela 63.8	Netherlands 15.3	Rep. of Ireland 7.4
21	Sweden 1.7	Sweden 59.3	New Zealand 15.1	UK 7.4
22	UK 1.6	Cyprus 54.7	Czechoslovakia 13.9	Finland 7.4
23	Chile 1.6	Japan 53.9	Cyprus 12.6	Poland 7.1
24	Yugoslavia 1.6	Norway 52.8	Sweden 12.3	Canada 7.1[2]
25	New Zealand 1.6	South Africa 52.0	UK 11.5	USA 7.0
26	Uruguay 1.6	Bulgaria 50.3	South Africa 9.0	Yugoslavia 6.6
27	Luxembourg 1.6	Yugoslavia 46.0	Canada 8.9[2]	Romania 6.4
28	Australia 1.5	Mexico 44.2	Finland 7.4	Japan 6.3
29	Denmark 1.3	Brazil 42.4	Poland 7.4	Chile 6.3
30	Brazil 1.3	Romania 42.1	USA 7.2	Uruguay 5.8
31	Belgium 1.2	France 40.5	Soviet Union 6.9[2]	Sweden 5.5

Notes: 1 Calculated by converting the amount of beverage consumed into litres of pure alcohol
2 1990 figures from Brewers Association of Canada (1993:480)

Source: 1993 World Drink Trends, in Australia, Department of Human Services and Health (1994:27)

the total consumption figures for these two countries. On the other hand, because Luxembourg attracts shoppers, tourists and conference visitors, its very high consumption may reflect visitor purchases. Unrecorded consumption includes homemade beer and wine, alcohol brewed in commercial 'u-brew' establishments, illicit production of alcohol, illegal importation, or small amounts legally imported for personal use (Single *et al.* 1995). These qualifications aside, it is clear that Europe remains the largest consumer of alcohol in the world.

The comparative figures for Australia, Canada and New Zealand are important, as it is against these consumption trends that indigenous drinking in each country must be considered. Drinking of spirits is more common in Canada (ranked 11th in the world) than New Zealand (ranked 25th) and Australia (ranked 28th). The position is reversed with respect to beer, however, with New Zealand consuming the most (ranked 8th), followed by Australia (11th) and Canada (15th). The increasing importance of wine in Australia (ranked 19th) and New Zealand (21st) above its use in Canada (ranked 27th) is also apparent. The similarities in consumption patterns between Australia and New Zealand on the one hand, and Canada and the United States on the other, reflect the importance of shared social and cultural factors and histories.

In Australia, since the late 1970s when alcohol consumption was at its highest and close to levels in the early colonial period, there has been a gradual decline in consumption. For persons aged 15 years and older during the period 1988–89 to 1992–93, consumption of beer has declined by 16 per cent, consumption of wine by 5 per cent and overall consumption of pure alcohol has decreased by 14 per cent, from 8.5 litres per head of population to 7.6 litres (1993 World Drink Trends, in Australia, Department of Human Services and Health 1994:27). Although there are no national figures on regional variation in consumption levels, some regions, such as the northwest of Western Australia, record significantly higher levels than the rest of the country (Hunter 1993a).

The trend towards declining alcohol consumption in Canada is reflected in the 1993 General Social Survey, which revealed that the proportion of Canadians aged 15 years or older who:

> . . . reported drinking in the past year was 74.4%, down from 79.0% in 1991. This decline is also indicated in the consumption figures for absolute alcohol, with a 4.4% decrease in per capita consumption from 1990. Canadians drank the equivalent of 7.97 litres of absolute alcohol in 1991. Beer was the most popular beverage (56.4%), followed by spirits (28.4%) and wine (15.2%) (Single *et al.* 1995).

There is much regional variation of alcohol consumption and beverage type throughout Canada, with drinking during 1991–92 highest in the Yukon Territory (14.4 litres per person aged 15 or older), the Northwest Territories (9.6 litres) and British Columbia (9.4 litres). This compares to lower consumption levels in New Brunswick (6.2 litres), Saskatchewan (7.1 litres) and Quebec (7.1 litres). Tourism may play a part in the consumption figures for the Yukon. Beer and wine are important beverages in Quebec, wine in British Columbia and spirits in the Northwest Territories and Saskatchewan (Single *et al.* 1995).

Declines in alcohol consumption have also been recorded in New Zealand. From a high point of 8.82 litres per capita consumption in 1981, the 1990 figure was 7.77 litres. Both beer and spirits consumption have declined in recent years after gradual increases up until the late 1970s. Wine consumption has grown the most significantly, with an eightfold increase between 1960 and 1986. As with beer and spirits, however, wine consumption has also declined, from a high of 16.2 litres per capita in 1986 to 14.7 litres in 1990. More people report consuming alcohol in New Zealand than in both Australia and Canada, with 92 per cent of males and 90 per cent of females reporting that they drink alcohol (Brewers Association of Canada 1993:268–9). However, these figures from 1988 are not as recent as those from Australia and Canada, and it may be that they have also been reduced. Apart from an increase in per capita consumption in 1990–91 (to 7.9 litres), drinking levels have declined consistently from 1991–92 (7.4 litres), through 1992–93 (7.3 litres), to 1993–94 (7.2 litres) (1993 World Drink Trends, in Australia, Department of Human Services and Health 1994:27).

Explaining changes in consumption patterns

Analyses of alcohol consumption in Australia in the second half of this century reveal rapid increases in consumption during the 1950s and early to mid-60s. This is usually attributed to the economic and social recovery after World War II. By the mid-1970s consumption began to level off, and by the 1980s consumption in many countries was declining on a per capita basis. Australia, Canada and New Zealand, for instance, all experienced declines in average annual per capita consumption in the period 1980–90. Much of this decline has been in the area of spirits consumption [although, interestingly, Australia has had the highest in-crease in spirits consumption (more than 2 per cent) over this period] with increases in consumption in lower-alcohol beverages such as beer and wine. Of all countries listed, only Canada and the United States recorded declines in beer, wine and spirits consumption (Brewers Associ-ation of Canada 1993:482–3).

Explaining these types of changes in consumption levels is a complex task as there are obviously many factors at work. To illustrate this, a closer examination of historical trends in alcohol consumption in Australia is helpful. The early European colonists have a deserved reputation as heavy drinkers, but this was not unusual in other parts of the world at that time, where spirits in particular were the drink of choice of the working classes. Comparative analysis of consumption of alcohol in the nineteenth century shows that the New South Wales colonists drank similar amounts to their United Kingdom counterparts in the period 1800–20, slightly more than them in the 1830s, but less than those in the United States, Scotland, France and Sweden. Thus Ward's (1981:35) assertion in regard to the first Australian colonists, that 'no people on the face of the earth ever absorbed more alcohol per head of population', may have made good historical copy, but is not supported by the evidence (Powell 1988:12; Lewis 1992:8).

Consumption of spirits in New South Wales declined by more than half during the depression of the 1840s, but increased temporarily after the 1850s gold rushes. In both New South Wales and Victoria, annual consumption of all alcohol showed a downward trend between 1851 and 1900. Choice of beverage changed somewhat, with rum being replaced by brandy and then whiskey as the preferred spirit by 1900. Wine drinking declined in New South Wales during the nineteenth century, but the growth of viticulture in Victoria saw increased wine consumption there. Beer was being produced in the colonies and was drunk in greater quantities than other alcohol, but average consumption declined in both New South Wales and Victoria during the 1880s and 1890s (Dingle 1980:231–2, in Lewis 1992:8). Twentieth-century consumption patterns continued to reflect the declining importance of spirits, the very significant growth in beer drinking between World War II and the early 1980s, and the increasing place of wine drinking in the 1980s and 1990s (Lewis 1992:8).

Changes in alcohol consumption patterns in Australia have been ascribed to a number of factors. Rapid urbanisation transformed the country from a rural, male-oriented culture where periods of hard physical work were followed by binge drinking, to a more family-oriented, urban-based society where drinking in pubs and also the home became the norm. The growth of the suburbs and increasing emphasis on home ownership and consumer goods meant less available money for alcohol. The provision of public education and the growth of a wide variety of sport and recreational pursuits also had an impact. Increasing numbers of women and children meant not only proportionately fewer drinkers, but also added a moral dimension to attempts to limit drinking, evidenced in the growth of the Temperance Movement particularly in the 1870s and 1880s. While changes in consumption levels are associated in part with changes in income and the price of alcohol, the relationship is more complex than this. Rising incomes were also accompanied in the second half of this century by increasingly cosmopolitan lifestyles, influenced by migration and greater travel and globalisation, and drinking became more firmly entrenched as part of everyday living (Lewis 1992:11–14).

In many countries, tempering these enticements to drink have been concerns about the problems related to alcohol misuse, particularly the relationship between drinking and driving, and consumption by young people. These concerns have resulted in greater regulation of drink-driving, and attempts to encourage the replacement of high alcohol content drinks with lower alcohol content drinks through differential tax rates (Brewers Association of Canada1993:484–5).

Conclusion

This discussion of alcohol use in the wider community demonstrates the significant role alcohol has played and continues to play in the lives of people. Also clear is the way in which context – historical, social and cultural – defines how all drugs, including alcohol, are perceived and used by various groups. The past decades have witnessed the gradual decline of alcohol consumption among the general populations of Australia, Canada and New Zealand, for a number of social and health-related reasons. It is this background of declining consumption that makes contemporary indigenous patterns of alcohol use so stark.

CHAPTER 4

Patterns of indigenous alcohol use

Pre-colonial use of psychoactive substances

The literature on the use of psychoactive substances by indigenous peoples in Australia, New Zealand and Canada is limited, and further research is required before a definitive picture of such use can be drawn. The fermentation process, in which alcohol is produced as the by-product of the chemical interaction between sugars and yeast, occurs naturally. Although knowledge of the process was widespread among indigenous populations throughout the world, there appear to have been some that were either unaware of the process or did not consume alcoholic beverages. Thus, it has been claimed that Canada – unlike what is now the southwest of the United States – was 'bone dry' before the arrival of Europeans, with indigenous Canadians having no knowledge of the fermentation process (Smart & Ogborne 1986:1). Similarly, Cullen claims that 'Alcoholic liquor was unknown to pre-European Maoris' (1984:1)

Claims such as these have been made with regard to indigenous Australians (Millar & Leung 1974; Cleland 1957; Dingle 1980). However, Brady (1991a) cites a number of references that indicate geographically widespread – if not frequent, or copious – use of intoxicating beverages. Tasmanian Aborigines are described as preparing a drink from the sap of the gum tree, *Eucalyptus gunnii*, the imbibing of which made people drunk (Plomley 1966:534). Groups from the Diamantina region of western Queensland prepared a drink from bauhinia blossom and wild honey (Duncan-Kemp 1934:76). Aborigines from south-western Australia soaked the cones of the grass tree *Xanthorrhoea* for a few days until the mixture fermented, and became 'excitable and voluble' after drinking it (McCarthy 1957:71, 154; Carr & Carr 1981:17). In the Northern Territory, Aborigines in the Roper River region produced a 'cider-like' drink from the pounded and soaked cones of the *Pandanus* tree, and on special occasions people would drink more to attain a condition of 'indubitable merriment' (Basedow 1929:154). However, indigenous Australians did not have the technological infrastructure to produce and distribute alcohol on a large scale. As Brady notes:

> ... difficulties of collection and storage (without metal or clay containers) and climatic variation provided natural controls on the production of these drugs (1994:41).

In the case of Australia – though not New Zealand and Canada – significant amounts of alcohol were introduced prior to European colonisation. A hundred years before European settlement in eastern Australia, Macassan fishermen exploiting the resources of the northern coast had introduced *arrack* (palm wine), brandy and gin, which they apparently both bartered and gave to indigenous residents (Thomson 1949; Macknight 1976, in Brady 1991b). According to Warner:

> The gin traded to the natives caused occasional great drunken orgies and much blood was shed in interclan fights that came to a head under this alcoholic stimulation. However, the alcohol seems to have had no effect on the general well-being of the people (1969:449).

Perhaps the most widely used psychoactive substances among indigenous Australians were 'bush' tobaccos. These included various species of *Nicotiana*, and *pituri*, from Central Australia, made from the dried, cured leaves and growing tips of *Duboisia hopwoodii*. These tobaccos were usually chewed, sometimes with the ash of burnt leaves to produce an alkaline reaction which enhanced the release of nicotine (Watson 1991). Along the northern coast of Australia, bush tobaccos were also smoked in pipes, probably of Papuan or Malay origin (Thomson 1939:82).

As well as fermented beverages and tobaccos, there is documentation of use of other plant substances among indigenous Australians. In Tasmania, the use of wattle tree blossoms hung in huts to induce sleep has been described by Robinson (Plomley 1966:302). An 'opium-like' substance made from an intoxicating root was used by the Murray River people (Angus 1874:73), and a 'stupefying' drink made from the root and bark of the bitter quandong, *Santalum murrayanum*, has also been documented (Stone 1911:445; Clarke 1988:71). However, such reports are sketchy and it is not clear what particular psychoactive compounds (if any) are present in these plants and what their effects are.

While alcohol and tobacco were not available to them, it has been reported that the pre-colonial Maori used four substances that had disinhibiting effects. One was a food reserved for chiefs, namely *tawhara*, the over-ripe fleshy bract of the *kiekie* or *Freycinetia banksii*. The others were masticatories:

> The first was a soft pliable exudate of the Kauri tree or the *Agathis australis*. The second of these was the gum of the Tarata or *Pittosporum eugenoides* or lemon wood mixed with the juice of the sow thistle or puwa or *Sonchus oleraceus*. The third of these was a bituminous substance found on beaches (Gluckman 1974:553).

Some indigenous Canadian peoples smoked various substances, but there is little in the literature describing their psychoactive constituents and their effects.

The limited reports available suggest that indigenous peoples made some use of psychoactive substances. This use was regulated by availability, production methods and custom, with resort being made to them on ceremonial or social occasions rather than on an everyday basis. With the possible exception of groups along the northern coast of Australia, none were prepared for the widespread availability of alcohol that occurred with European colonisation.

Alcohol and European colonisation

Initial responses by indigenous peoples to the introduction of alcohol were not positive, and a taste for it had to be encouraged by the colonists. In Australia, an Aboriginal man named Arabanoo, who had been captured by Arthur Phillip, the first governor of New South Wales, refused to drink liquor (Tench 1793, in Langton 1993: 201). A similar response seems to have occurred in New Zealand, where the generic Maori word for alcoholic drinks, *waipiro*, translates as 'foul stinking water' (Cullen 1984:1). In Canada, Smart and Ogborne have written that 'Traders had to work to develop the trade in whisky and teach Indians to drink and become drunk' as initially they did not like the taste (1986:1).

Nevertheless, in all three countries, at least some segments of the indigenous populations soon developed a taste for alcohol. Smart and Ogborne cite tales from Canada in the early days of the fur trade of 'drink-it-all' feasts lasting days or even weeks, where men and women would drink all the available alcohol, neglecting work, families and all other concerns (1986:2); and in New Zealand, nineteenth-century observers wrote of a 'liquor craze' among the Maori (Cullen 1984:4–5).

It should not be thought, however, that in this regard indigenous peoples differed significantly from the colonists. The industrial revolution in Britain – from whence most colonists came – in the eighteenth and nineteenth centuries was accompanied by widespread, high levels of consumption of cheap spirits. In 1788 in Australia, the First English Fleet brought both wine and rum, the latter being used as currency in the early years of the settlement at New South Wales. In New South Wales in 1793, according to one contemporary observer:

> The passion for liquor was so predominant among the people that it operated like a mania, there being nothing that they would not risk to obtain it; and while spirits were to be had, those who did any extra labour refused to be paid in money or any other article than spirits (cited in Lewis 1992:5).

An indication of the importance of alcoholic beverages to the European colonists can be gleaned from the fact that in 1830, within a year of settlement of the Swan River Colony in Western Australia, licences for three hotels and six ale-houses were issued. Six years later Perth, the capital of the colony, had one licensed house for every 75 people (Welborn 1987:17).

Similarly, heavy drinking was also common in colonial New Zealand:

> The historical record shows that brewing constituted an enormous local industry in both Christchurch and Dunedin and that liquor was imported in excessive amounts, considering the size of the population (Cullen 1984:3).

It is reported that in 1847 in Wellington, '. . . there was one conviction for drunkenness for every eight persons' (Cullen 1984:3).

Descriptions of drinking among early Canadian settlers and soldiers are indistinguishable from those among indigenous people there. One trader claimed:

> Of all the people in the world I think the Canadians when drunk, are the most disagreeable; for excessive drinking generally causes them to quarrel and fight, among themselves. Indeed, I had rather have fifty drunken Indians in fort than, five drunken Canadians (in Smart & Ogborne 1986:105).

The soldiers were evidently no better. Jesuit descriptions tell of the soldiers' passionate attachment to gambling and heavy drinking resulting in serious fighting (Smart & Ogborne 1986:105).

Although in some instances there may have been elements of hospitality involved, generally alcohol was not introduced by the colonists for reasons of altruism. While there are reports of colonists providing indigenous people with alcohol in order to selfishly observe their drunken antics, alcohol played a more significant role as a means of exchange, and it was thus in the interests of the colonisers to encourage indigenous drinking and demand for alcohol.

French explorers and traders, followed by missionaries and some settlers, were the first Europeans in Canada (Smart & Ogborne 1986:1). Most of these Europeans sought highly valued furs from the indigenous people, for which they traded blankets, beads, guns and alcohol – brandy, whisky and rum. In Australia, in a colonial society in which alcohol was an accepted medium of exchange (and in which male settlers outnumbered females by more than two to one), alcohol was exchanged by colonists for sexual relations with Aboriginal women, and for Aboriginal labour.

Alcohol was introduced to New Zealand on a large scale early in the nineteenth century in settlements around the Bay of Islands, and here too it became an integral part of the process of colonisation. In the early years of European settlement, without access to free convict labour, there was a demand for Maori labour and agricultural products. Along with other material goods, alcohol was an important element in this trade, and a substantial demand for it soon grew among sections of the Maori population.

In New Zealand, unlike Australia, the British colonial government recognised the prior right of the Maori to land. In 1862 and 1865, in order to facilitate the transfer of land from Maori to settlers, Native Lands Acts were passed, enabling title to land that had previously been communally owned to be vested in individuals. To force Maori to sell their land it became common practice to encourage them to build up considerable debt for alcohol and other goods, and to subsequently force sale of the land to satisfy the debt (Cullen 1984:5–7).

While at first some were willingly seduced by the pleasurable aspects of alcohol consumption, indigenous peoples in Australia, New Zealand and Canada soon became victims of the use of alcohol as a means of escape. With the coming of European colonists, indigenous populations of all three countries were decimated by introduced disease (Saggers & Gray 1991; Kunitz 1994), and as a result of violence, as colonists and indigenous peoples struggled over possession of land and natural resources (Reynolds 1981). Particularly in Australia and Canada, but also in New Zealand, many indigenous people were relegated to the status of dispossessed, poverty-stricken fringe dwellers. In these circumstances, the excessive use of alcohol was fuelled, both as a means of solace and for its own pleasures.

However, just as not all of the colonists drank to excess, neither did all indigenous people. For example, Howay cites a description by Captain George Vancouver, who had entertained three 'Indians' on board his ship:

After dinner they did not make the least scruple of partaking of our repast with such wines and liquors as were offered to them; though they drank very sparingly seeming to be well aware of their powerful effect (Howay 1942, in Smart & Ogborne 1986:102).

On a wider scale, in 1833, groups living in the Columbia River region (in south-western Canada) told of their:

> ... strong aversion to ardent spirits which they regard as poison. They allege that slaves only drink to excess; that drunkenness is degrading to free men (Howay 1942, in Smart & Ogborne 1986:108).

Similarly, the Tlingit people also spoke of the need to resist the power of brandy so as not to succumb to the Russians, who at that time occupied what is now the US state of Alaska (Howay 1942, in Smart & Ogborne 1986). In New Zealand, as early as the mid-1830s, some Maori chiefs were expressing concern about the extent of drunkenness and were calling for control on the availability of alcohol.

Imposed controls on indigenous alcohol use

There is no industrialised state-level society in which government has not sought to exercise some control over the production and distribution of alcoholic beverages, either because the industry is a highly profitable source of revenue or because it has sought to mitigate the harms caused by excessive alcohol use. In Australia, New Zealand and Canada, there have been ebbs and flows in the extent of such control as political lobby groups representing the industry or sections of it, religious and temperance groups, economic rationalists, and concerned citizens have vied for influence. At various times and/or in each country, controls have included: complete prohibition; import restrictions; the imposition of excise duties and licensing fees; restrictions on days or hours of trading; and restrictions on sales to intoxicated persons, minors and – from early colonial times – indigenous people.

While there have been vociferous debates about the desirability of restricting alcohol supplies to non-indigenous people, few questioned the 'need' to control the access of indigenous people to alcohol. Generally, there appear to have been two sets of motives for the introduction of such restrictions. The first and most important of these were the fear of outbreaks of violence, both wide-scale and individual, which might threaten the safety of colonists, and threats to trading relationships or the availability of labour. The second were concerns about the health and well-being of indigenous people.

The earliest of these restrictions was an edict by the French king, Louis XIV, in 1657, which prohibited the sale of alcohol to Canadian 'Indians', although this was very difficult to police. A 1660 attempt by Catholic churchmen to excommunicate traders who sold alcohol to Indians was unsuccessful, in the face of the importance of the trade and arguments that brandy was necessary to retain Indian loyalty in conflicts with the English. Besides which, threats of excommunication held few fears for English and Dutch traders. In 1774, 15 years after the British conquest of Canada, the English repealed early French prohibitions and used their access to rum from the West Indies to gain a virtual monopoly of the fur trade. Any attempts to limit indigenous access to alcohol were countered by the traders' assertions about its inextricability from the fur trade:

> For though we undersell the Canadians (Montreal peddlers) by far in some articles while our goods last, yet when Brandy is out the Indians leave off trading. Last Spring . . . the Indians would not trade their furs because I had no brandy (Rich 1967, in Smart & Ogborne 1986:3).

In other parts of Canada, it was claimed that trade was not so dependent upon alcohol. However, its excessive use was sufficiently problematic for alcohol trade with indigenous people to be banned periodically by trading groups such as the Hudson Bay Company. In 1821 the Hudson Bay Company combined with the North West Company and the joint group more effectively enforced the ban (Oliver 1923, in Smart & Ogborne 1986:3).

One way to get around this ban was to simply give alcohol as 'gifts' prior to any commercial transactions. This was not only done by traders but also by governments, which included alcohol in their presentations to indigenous groups on 'treaty days'. Although this practice was stopped in some areas at the request of indigenous chiefs in the 1820s, it was not until the 1840s that an edict was passed banning the sale, gift, exchange, or barter of alcohol to indigenous peoples in Upper Canada (Smart & Ogborne 1986:3).

The earliest Australian legislation prohibiting the supply or sale of alcohol to Aboriginal people was introduced in New South Wales in 1838. Between then and 1929, in the Australian Capital Territory, various colonial and state governments introduced similar restrictions: Western Australia in 1843, Victoria in 1864, South Australia in 1869, Queensland in 1885, and Tasmania in 1908. These laws and subsequent amendments became increasingly restrictive in their application and, as Brady notes, encompassed Aboriginal people of 'full descent' as well as those of 'mixed descent' and indigenous peoples from the Pacific Islands (Brady 1991b:178–9).

In New Zealand, some Maori chiefs had begun to call for general controls over the availability of alcohol as early as the 1830s. However,

Ordinances of 1845 and 1847 prohibited the sale of alcohol to Maori but imposed no restrictions on colonists (Cullen 1984:2). These laws proved ineffective, and subsequent legislation, including the *Outlying Districts Sale of Liquor Act 1870* and the *Native Licensing Act 1878*, was aimed at encouraging Maori to take an active role in controlling licensed premises, and to declare 'proclaimed areas' where alcohol consumption was prohibited. Under the *Licensing Amendment Act 1910* for those living outside proclaimed areas (almost the whole of the North Island was proclaimed at that time):

> ... Maori males were permitted to buy liquor for immediate consumption on licensed premises, only; Maori women married to Pakeha (non-Maori) men were accorded 'full drinking rights'; all others were forbidden to drink at all (Cullen 1984:13).

Hasluck has written of the situation in Australia that such laws were the first legal refutation of British colonial policy, which stated the equality of Aborigines and Europeans before the law (1970:122–61). This was also true of New Zealand and Canada, and throughout the last half of the nineteenth and first half of the twentieth centuries such discriminatory legislation proliferated. Furthermore, what Cullen wrote with regard to New Zealand is also true for Canada and Australia:

> Of all the discriminatory laws affecting Maoris, strictures on their alcohol use have survived the longest. To this day the state machinery applies differently to Maoris than to any other citizens with regard to drinking (1984:18–19).

In all three countries under consideration, prohibition on the supply of alcohol to, or the consumption of alcohol by, indigenous people proved to be ineffective (Beckett 1964, Cullen 1984). In Australia, as elsewhere, the desire of indigenous people to drink provided the opportunity for non-Aboriginal people to profit from the sale of alcohol to them (Eggleston 1974). Fieldwork by Beckett in 1957 in far west New South Wales revealed that most Aboriginal men (but few women) who had some income were able to procure alcohol. While Europeans were rarely charged for supplying alcohol to Aboriginal people, charges related to drinking were frequently made against Aborigines. The surveillance was oppressive:

> In one centre police trucks patrolled aboriginal (*sic*) settlements as many as six times a day, and police unceremoniously broke into homes where they believed drunken aborigines to be. But often drunken aborigines made no effort to keep out of the way, and certainly they were not deterred by the fines, prison sentences, and beatings inflicted on them (Beckett 1964:40).

Prohibition also influenced both what was drunk and the way in which it was drunk. Aborigines explained to Beckett that the more potent spirits or fortified wines could be more easily concealed than the equivalent alcoholic content in beer. They also argued that fear of detection encouraged hasty, excessive consumption. Notwithstanding the power of that argument, Beckett also claimed that once a taste for stronger alcohol is acquired, drinkers are not satisfied with beer, and that even when drinking in safe locations, people would drink to get drunk (1964:41). Under these circumstances, there were few opportunities for models of restrained drinking behaviour to develop.

As late as 1965, in Western Australia a person could be fined $200 or imprisoned for six months for selling, supplying or simply giving alcohol to a 'native'. The penalty for drinking was a $10 fine or one month's prison. In that same year a sample of convictions in ten Western Australian country towns revealed 155 convictions for 'native receive liquor' and 56 convictions for 'supply liquor to native', in addition to alcohol-related charges laid under the Native Welfare Regulations and under the general law. Apart from the obvious fact that prohibition was not preventing drinking, the figures also demonstrate the inequities in the administration of the law (Eggleston 1974:53–4). This close association between alcohol, indigenous people and the law established during the prohibition period has endured, with most convictions of indigenous people since the 1960s being alcohol-related (Brady 1990a:202).

Cullen (1984) has written that World War II provided a turning point in Maori history. Many Maori served in the armed forces, and others migrated to urban areas to undertake essential work; after the war many never returned to the rural areas from whence they came. In 1948, as a consequence of the changed status of Maori, changes in non-Maori attitudes, and the failure of prohibition, new legislation was introduced which repealed previous restrictions and provided Maori with the same drinking rights as non-Maori.

Similar changes took place in Australia, where – despite lingering paternalism towards Aboriginal people – in the post-war years the policy of assimilation came increasingly into effect, and overtly discriminatory legislation was gradually repealed. In the case of prohibitions on Aboriginal alcohol consumption, this commenced in Victoria in 1957 and was completed in Western Australia in 1968, although some provisions did not take effect until 1971 (Sackett 1977).

In Australia, one of the immediate consequences of the repeal of this discriminatory legislation was a widespread increase in drinking and associated problems. A missionary working in a desert region in South Australia wrote that:

Amounts of money spent on liquor off the reserve are out of all proportion to that spent on food and clothing. General living standards have suffered, more families are being wrecked; and the traditional influence of the older natives has all but gone by the board . . . A strange new situation has developed . . . Many of them regard [the mission] as a haven where they can get away from it all, being content with 'outbursts' when off the reserve (in Rowley 1974:32).

At the time, many commentators saw the increase in drinking and related offences as a response to years of discrimination:

Aborigines whose status had been considerably reduced by legislation, show themselves no more than human by rushing to take advantage of rights and privileges which the rest of the community takes for granted, once legal barriers are removed (Eggleston 1976:222).

Drinking and citizenship in Australia

In Australia during this period, not all Aboriginal people were prohibited from consuming alcohol. As with the New Zealand *Licensing Amendment Act* of 1910, described above, provision was made for the exemption of some indigenous people from the application of such laws.

The various state jurisdictions in Australia each had Aboriginal or 'native affairs' Acts, which defined who was an Aboriginal or 'native' person; and, as indicated previously, over the years such definitions became increasingly inclusive, enabling government control over, and interference in, the lives of increasing numbers of people of indigenous descent. These or other Acts, such as the Western Australian *The Natives [Citizenship] Act 1944*, also provided for those who met non-Aboriginal standards of behaviour, who limited their association with other Aboriginal people, and/or (in some jurisdictions, but not others) had served in the armed forces, to be exempted from the provisions of those Acts. Thus in South Australia the *Aborigines Act 1934* allowed that:

In any case where the Board is of the opinion that any Aborigine by reason of his character and standard of intelligence and development should be exempted from the provisions of this Act, the Board may, by notice in writing, declare that the Aborigine shall cease to be an Aborigine for the purposes of this Act ... (McCorquodale 1987:A474, A505, A511)

Rowley draws the comparison between Australian exemptions from the various Aboriginal Acts and the colonial French and Belgian concept of *évolué* or *assimilé*, which incorporated the notion of the rights of full civic status for 'natives' who could prove they were civilised men (and they were only men). As Rowley points out, the standard of the civilised white man was a very idealised one, probably far from the reality that most indigenous people in rural and remote Australia would have encountered (1974:357).

In the era of prohibition, along with the right to vote in state elections, one of the few obvious benefits accruing to those who were granted 'citizenship' was the right to purchase and consume alcohol. It is clear that many indigenous Australians regarded exemption from these Acts primarily as a permit to drink – as a 'reward' for showing how assimilated to European ways they had become. Such exemptions were not absolute, and could be revoked for, among other things, convictions for 'habitual drunkenness' or supplying alcohol to indigenous people who were not exempt (McCorquodale 1987:A702). Given the links made by policy makers and legislators, in the minds of many Aboriginal people the separate issues of citizenship, voting rights, and the right to drink became inextricably associated.

Many indigenous people found the conditions of these Acts onerous and insulting, and contemptuously referred to the exemptions as 'dog licences' or 'dog tags' (Beckett 1964; Brady 1991b). They felt that they should be treated with equality, and chafed at having to apply for such exemption. As one man angrily told Beckett:

> Those darkies have got no right to go fighting for the whites that stole their country. Now they won't let 'em into the hotel. They've got to gulp down plonk in the piss-house (Beckett 1964:40).

In the period from the late 1950s through the 1960s a number of important legislative changes took place. These included: repeal of state legislation prohibiting alcohol consumption by indigenous people; passage of the *Commonwealth Electoral Act 1962*, which enabled but did not require indigenous people to vote in federal elections (McCorquodale 1987:A49); and the passage of a 1967 referendum which enabled amendment of the constitution to enable the Commonwealth government to make special laws with regard to Aboriginal people and to count them in the census (McCorquodale 1987:A57). For many indigenous people, these changes, either separately or together, constituted or have come to constitute the granting of 'citizenship'.

Around Australia anthropologists and others have recorded Aboriginal responses to these changes. In the Northern Territory, for instance, where the right to drink was not granted until 1964, a significant increase in alcohol-related convictions in the years 1962–3 was explained by one official as the result of confusion among indigenous people, who believed that previously granted rights to vote conferred drinking rights (Sansom 1980:75). Working with indigenous fringe-dwelling people around

Darwin in the Northern Territory, Sansom found that people commonly associated citizenship and grog:

> The point is that 'citizen' is usually uttered thus (tapping a beer can) in camp: it is a word to be said with an obligatory nod to grog (Sansom 1980:50).

In Central Australia, too, the word was the same: 'Citizens we are now. We can drink liquor' (Myers 1986:40).

For some, drinking alcohol made them like white people. One Aboriginal fringe dweller in the Northern Territory told Collmann, 'When I drink, I'm a whitefellow, not a blackfellow. We . . . are two whitefellows' (1979:217). Here, as in other countries where indigenous peoples were subject to discriminatory prohibitions against drinking, the right to drink came to be seen as symbolic of equality (Brady 1991b; Heath 1987); and for some that equality and citizenship conferred almost an obligation to drink.

Consumption, drinking environments and drinking populations

Consumption

Determining how much alcohol people drink is an exercise fraught with difficulty. The most general measure involves calculating the amount of pure alcohol contained in beverages produced for sale within a particular country in a given year (i.e. excluding export sales) plus imports, and calculating the amount per head of population. Although a relatively simple calculation, it is based on estimates of the amount of alcohol in various beverages and is thus an approximation rather than an absolute measure. The generality of the method is also one of its major limitations. Not all people within a population drink or drink to the same extent, and it sheds little light on intra-population variations in consumption based on factors such as age, gender, region and ethnicity.

Based on such data, in 1991, at 7.8 and 7.7 litres of pure alcohol per person per year, there was little difference in per capita consumption between New Zealand and Australia, which rank 15th and 17th respectively in terms of national consumption. At 7.1 litres per person, on average Canadians consume about 8 per cent less than Australians, and rank 24th overall (1993 World Drink Trends, in Australia, Department of Human Services and Health 1994:27). In all three countries there has been a significant decline in per capita consumption since the 1970s.

The second approach to measuring consumption, which enables description of variation and the factors associated with it, is to survey people and ask them how much they consume. As well as the technical problems associated with sampling and the wording of questions, this approach is beset by the problem of determining the relationship between what people say they do and what they actually do; and surveys are notorious for underestimating consumption. In New Zealand, a 1988 national survey 'accounted for approximately 64% of the alcohol that was available for consumption' (Wyllie, Zhang & Casswell 1993:12). Similarly:

> ... the number of drinks per week reported in the (Canadian) National Alcohol and Drug Survey of 1989, was 3.7 compared with 11.2 drinks per week indicated by sales data (Single, Williams & McKenzie 1994:18).

This problem was illustrated in an innovative archaeological project conducted in Tucson, Arizona, in the 1970s, in which a household survey of people's consumption habits was complemented by analysis of their discarded rubbish. Twenty-seven per cent of the sample grossly under-estimated the amount of beer consumed by the household, with the greatest discrepancy between self-reported use and actual material discards of beer containers occurring in very low income Mexican–American neighbourhoods. As Rathje notes, it should surprise no-one that people under-report how much they drink, and this is more likely among those groups whose drinking already receives unfavourable press (1978:61–3).

An important issue when attempting to compare the results of studies in different populations has to do with questions about the number of 'drinks' consumed. (See the discussion of the 'standard' drink concept in Chapter 2.) When making comparisons, differences in definition among health professionals or researchers need to be identified and corrections made for them. However, it is not always clear that survey respondents are using the same definitions as researchers, and this introduces another element of uncertainty.

Further difficulties arise when attempting to compare patterns of consumption between indigenous and non-indigenous peoples, both within and between studies. The first of these has to do with definitions of indigenous persons. As indicated previously, different countries use different definitions with different levels of inclusivity, and there are both similarities and differences in culture and lifestyle between people who are encompassed by these various national definitions. It is likely, though not always definitely known, that these differences also include differences in patterns of alcohol consumption; and that selection of survey participants based on the varying definitions of aboriginality will yield different results. The problem associated with the definition of indigenous people is further compounded because of: the sampling error that arises when indigenous people comprise a small proportion of the sample of a larger population surveyed; difficulties in locating potential

Table 3   Alcohol use among urban-dwelling Aboriginal and Torres Strait Islanders and the general urban population

Levels of alcohol use	Proportion of all urban Aboriginal and Torres Strait Islanders (1994 survey)	Proportion of urban general population (1993 survey)
Current regular drinker (at least once a week)	33%	45%
Current occasional drinker (less than once a week)	29%	27%
No longer drink	22%	9%
Never had more than one glass of alcohol	15%	13%
Don't know	1%	6%

Source: Australia, Department of Health & Family Services (1995:27)

Table 4   Frequency of drinking among urban-dwelling Aboriginal and Torres Strait Islanders and the general urban population

Frequency of drinking	Proportion of Aboriginal and Torres Strait Islander peoples who have had a drink in the last 12 months (1994)	Proportion of the urban general population who have had a drink in the last 12 months (1993)
Every day	8%	11%
At least once a week	41%	50%
At least once a month	29%	22%
At least once a year	14%	15%
Less often/no longer drink	8%	2%

Source: Australia, Department of Health & Family Services 1995

indigenous participants; the unwillingness of some indigenous people to participate; and the heterogeneity within indigenous populations, which is disguised when people are lumped together.

All of these issues must be borne in mind when considering comparative data from Australia, New Zealand and Canada, and the results of surveys should be treated with caution. Nevertheless, they do provide a broad indication of consumption patterns.

As part of the Australian National Drug Strategy, the Commonwealth Department of Health and Family Services (previously known as the Department of Health, Housing, Local Government and Community Services, and the Department of Human Services and Health) has commissioned a series of household surveys among people aged over 14 years to measure levels of drug use, knowledge and attitudes to drugs, law

Table 5 Amount usually drunk when alcohol is consumed among urban-dwelling Aboriginal and Torres Strait Islanders and the general urban population

Amount usually drunk when alcohol consumed	Proportion of urban Aboriginal and Torres Strait Islanders who currently drink (1994 survey)		Proportion of urban general population who currently drink (1993 survey)	
Number of drinks	Males	Females	Males	Females
1–2	9%	16%	44%	68%
3–4	9%	17%	31%	20%
5–6	11%	18%	14%	7%
7–8	10%	11%	5%	3%
9–12	18%	17%	2%	1%
13 or more	42%	21%	3%	0%

Source: Australia, Department of Health & Family Services (1995:29)

enforcement indicators, and awareness about, and impact of, the drug strategy (Australia, Department of Health and Family Services 1996). These surveys were conducted in 1985, 1988, 1991, 1993 and 1995.

The sample size in each of these surveys is about 3,500 people, and as indigenous people comprise such a small proportion of the Australian population, the numbers included in the sample have been insufficient to estimate levels of consumption among the indigenous population. For this reason the Department of Health and Family Services commissioned a survey of urban-dwelling indigenous people in 1994, which sought to obtain data comparable to that gathered on urban dwellers in the 1993 survey of the general population. Comparative results of these surveys are presented in Tables 3 to 5.

The data in Table 3 indicate that among indigenous Australians, approximately 62 per cent are either regular (33 per cent) or occasional drinkers (29 per cent), defined respectively as those drinking on at least one occasion per week, and those drinking less than once per week. Of the remainder, 22 per cent had been drinkers but no longer drink, and 15 per cent had never been drinkers. When compared to the results of the survey of non-indigenous urban dwellers, this indicates that there is a significantly lower proportion of regular drinkers among indigenous people (12 per cent) and a significantly higher proportion of people who have given up drinking (13 per cent).

Tables 3 and 4 show that among indigenous urban dwellers there were fewer drinkers, and that those who did drink did so less frequently than non-indigenous people. However, Table 5 shows that, when they do drink, indigenous people usually consume greater amounts than do non-indigenous people. Thus 68 per cent of indigenous people reported that, when they did drink, they usually consumed alcohol at what are considered harmful levels – defined by the Australian National Health & Medical Research Council as ≥41 g of alcohol per day for women and ≥61g per day for men (Pols & Hawks 1987) – whereas only 11 per cent of non-indigenous people reported drinking at those levels. The report states:

> When analysis is restricted only to regular drinkers (i.e. those drinking at least weekly), the health risk of alcohol among the indigenous community is more noticeable with 79% of regular drinkers consuming at harmful levels, compared with only 12% of regular drinkers among the general community (Department of Health and Family Services 1995:30).

As indicated, the 1994 survey undertaken as a supplement to the regular National Drug Strategy Household Surveys was confined to indigenous people living in urban areas. However, in the same year, in response to the paucity of statistical information on indigenous people identified by the Royal Commission into Aboriginal Deaths in Custody, the Australian Bureau of Statistics (1995) conducted a national survey among over 15,700 Aboriginal and Torres Strait Islander people aged 13 years or over. Among the health-related questions asked was one on the period of time since respondents had last consumed alcohol. It was found that 69 per cent of males and 55 per cent of females had consumed alcohol in the previous 12 months. This suggests that the proportion of indigenous drinkers nationally is similar to that found in urban areas – not surprising since, at the 1991 census, about 68 per cent of the indigenous population lived in such areas. However, as a subsequent publication shows, this masks considerable regional variation in the proportions of people who had never consumed alcohol (McLennan and Madden 1997:30).

Prior to these two surveys, no national studies of alcohol consumption among indigenous Australians had been undertaken. The knowledge that was available came from either local or regional studies. The earliest of these was conducted by Kamien in Bourke, New South Wales, in 1971–72. He reported 'heavy drinking' – that is, 81 g or more of absolute alcohol per day – by 53 per cent of Aboriginal males aged 15 years and over, but among only 3 per cent of Aboriginal females. Problem drinkers – those who drank to such an extent that it interfered with work, family and social life – comprised 31 per cent of the adult male population but only 4 per cent of the female population (Kamien 1975). (It should be noted that Kamien's figures overestimate the consumption of absolute alcohol because he took a 7 ounce glass of beer as being equivalent to 10 g of alcohol, whereas more general usage in Australia equates a 10 ounce (285 ml) glass of beer to 10 g of alcohol.)

A follow-up study was undertaken in Bourke ten years later. Although not all of the results are directly comparable, it was found that more men (31 per cent as against 10 per cent in Kamien's study) and fewer women (55 per cent versus 71 per cent in the earlier study) were abstaining. While the proportion of heavy drinkers in the male population had decreased from 55 per cent to 25 per cent, there had been an increase in the number of teenage drinkers in the town (Harris *et al.* 1987).

In 1986–87 a quantitative and qualitative survey of drug use (alcohol, tobacco, kava, analgesics) was conducted among non-urban Aboriginal communities in the Northern Territory. One of the most surprising findings at that time was the significant number of people who were either lifetime abstainers or ex-drinkers. More people abstained than drank (59 per cent), with women more likely to abstain than men (80 per cent as against 35 per cent). Although less than half of the population drank alcohol, two-thirds of both men and women who drank did so at 'harmful' levels. When drinking at 'hazardous levels' (between 21–40 g for women, and 41–60 g for men) is included, most women (81 per cent) and men (81 per cent) who drank did so excessively (Watson, Fleming & Alexander 1988:10–17).

A survey of 516 adult Aboriginal people conducted in the Kimberley region of Western Australia produced findings similar to those from the Northern Territory. Extrapolating to the population from a stratified random sample, it was found that there were more lifetime abstainers and ex-drinkers (54 per cent of women and 22 per cent of men) than among non-Aboriginal people (25 per cent of women and 13 per cent of men). However, those Aboriginal people who did drink were much more likely to do so at 'harmful levels' than were non-Aboriginal people. More than half of the Aboriginal men (53 per cent) and a smaller number of Aboriginal women (19 per cent) drank nine or more standard drinks (that is, 90 g of absolute alcohol) on each drinking occasion. In the general population, many fewer men (4 per cent) and women (0.5 per cent) report drinking at this level (Hunter, Hall & Spargo 1992).

Comparisons of these patterns of consumption among indigenous people in rural and remote areas with those among people in urban situations are of interest. A recent study of Aboriginal drug use in two New South Wales towns demonstrated that, as in rural and remote communities, there are more abstainers among urban Aboriginal people (35 per cent of males and 50 per cent of females) than there are among non-Aboriginal people. However, as in the country studies, a large proportion of those who drank (60 per cent of males and 43 per cent of females) did so at harmful levels. This is significantly higher than that reported among the non-indigenous population. Much of the drinking reported during the seven days preceding the survey was 'binge drinking' (75 per cent of

Table 6   Indigenous Australian alcohol use indicators from selected regional studies

Study	Indicator	Males %	Females %	Total %
Kamien (1975)	Abstainers	10	71	41
	≥ 81 g per day	53	3	27
Harris et al. (1987)	Abstainers	31	55	46
Harris 1989	≥ 81 g per day	28	5	22
Watson, Fleming &	Abstainers	35	80	59
Alexander (1988)	Harmful	69	68	69
Hunter, Hall & Spargo (1992)	Abstainers	22	54	39
	Harmful	66	38	52
Perkins et al. (1994)	Abstainers	35	50	57
	Harmful	60	43	51

males and 86 per cent of females), defined as consuming 100 g or more for males, and 60 g or more for females, on one or more occasions during the previous week (Perkins et al. 1994).

Taken in conjunction, the national and regional surveys reveal a similar pattern of consumption among indigenous Australians when compared with the non-indigenous population. That is, among indigenous people: there is a larger proportion of people, particularly women, who have never drunk or who have given up drinking; there are fewer current regular drinkers; and more of those who drink do so at harmful levels. However, as Table 6 illustrates, within this pattern there is significant local and regional variation, again particularly among women. The studies show that between 10 and 35 per cent of males and 50 and 80 per cent of females were abstainers and that, while there was little variation in the proportion of men drinking at harmful levels (60 to 69 per cent), the proportion of women drinking at this level ranged from 43 to 68 per cent.

The published statistical data from New Zealand are not directly comparable to those from Australia. However, they reveal broadly similar patterns of alcohol consumption among Maori and indigenous Australians:

Results from the 1978 national survey of alcohol consumption among the New Zealand population indicated that a smaller proportion of Maoris were regular drinkers than among the Pakeha population. The Maori drinkers also reported drinking less frequently on average than did the Pakeha drinkers. However, the amount consumed during a drinking session was considerably

Table 7   Alcohol consumed in the previous seven days
by Maori and non-Maori

Alcohol consumed in the previous 7 days	Maori %	Non-Maori %
Light use: 1–60 g	34	47
Moderate use: 61–199 g	37	34
Heavy use: ≥ 200 g	21	18

Source: New Zealand, Te Puni Kokiri & AACNZ 1995

greater than that consumed by non-Maori respondents, making the estimated daily intake greater among Maori than non-Maoris. This difference was apparent even when socio-economic status was taken into account (Casswell, Cullen & Gilmore 1984:30).

Similar results have been found in more recent New Zealand surveys. As in Australia, a greater proportion of indigenous people report abstaining from alcohol: 13 per cent of Maori males compared to 6 per cent of non-Maori males, and 28 per cent of Maori females compared to 12 per cent of non-Maori females (New Zealand, Te Puni Kokiri & AACNZ 1995:16). The data presented in Table 7 show that slightly larger proportions of Maori are moderate or heavy users of alcohol than non-Maori. However, although the average amount consumed by Maori and non-Maori in the week prior to being interviewed was not significantly different, there was an important difference in the way in which it was consumed:

The median quantity of absolute alcohol consumed on the last drinking occasion was 60 ml for Maori males compared with 30 ml for non-Maori males, and 36 ml for Maori females compared with 21 ml for their non-Maori counterparts (New Zealand, Te Puni Kokiri & AACNZ 1995:16).

Canadian government agencies gather survey data similar to those collected in the Australian National Drug Strategy Household Surveys. These include the 1989 Alcohol and Other Drugs Survey, the Health Promotion Survey of 1990, and the General Social Survey of 1991 (Single, Williams & McKenzie 1994). With regard to the proportion of drinkers and levels of consumption, these have produced similar results, with only small variations in percentages (Single *et al.* 1994:27). In addition, in 1991 Statistics Canada conducted the Aboriginal Peoples Survey, which collected some data on alcohol consumption. However, the latter survey has major limitations. As Single *et al.* note, there was not a high non-response rate (23 per cent), 78 native communities were excluded from

Table 8   Alcohol use among indigenous and non-indigenous Canadians*

Levels of alcohol use	Proportion of Aboriginal population[1]	Proportion of general Canadian population[2]
Current drinker	67%	78%
No longer drink	14%	15%
Never drank	15%	7%

*Errors due to rounding
Sources: 1 Statistics Canada 1993, cited in Single *et al.* (1994:182)
             2 Canada, Health and Welfare (1990a:4)

the survey and, as Statistics Canada also notes, the consumption estimates may be particularly low (1994:163–4). Furthermore, apart from data on the proportions of drinkers and non-drinkers, the data from the Aboriginal Peoples Survey was not gathered in a manner which enables direct comparison with the National Health Promotion Survey. This makes both intra- and inter-national comparison difficult.

According to the Aboriginal Peoples Survey, significant numbers claimed to be lifetime abstainers (14.8 per cent) or former drinkers (14.4 per cent), with about two-thirds (67 per cent) claiming they were currently drinking. As in Australia, regional differences were apparent, with the proportion of drinkers being highest in Newfoundland (71 per cent), and lowest in Prince Edward Island (54.8 per cent) and Nova Scotia (56.9 per cent) (Single, Williams & McKenzie 1994:164). When compared with the results of the National Alcohol and Other Drugs Survey, these data suggest that, as in Australia and New Zealand, among indigenous people current drinkers comprise a smaller proportion of the population than they do among the general Canadian population.

For the reasons cited above, the data on frequency of alcohol consumption presented in Table 8 need to be interpreted cautiously. Nevertheless, they suggest that, like their counterparts in Australia and New Zealand, indigenous Canadians consume alcohol less frequently than their non-indigenous counterparts. In reviewing these surveys, Single *et al.* report that:

> No information is available about how much alcohol native people drink per occasion or under what circumstances drinking occurs (1994:164).

However, regional reports cited in the *Report* of the Royal Commission on Aboriginal Peoples (1996) suggest that, as in Australia and New Zealand, among those indigenous people who do drink, 'heavy drinking is more common than moderate consumption'.

Table 9 Frequency of alcohol use among current indigenous and non-indigenous Canadian drinkers*

Frequency of alcohol use	Proportion of Aboriginal population[1]	Proportion of general Canadian population[2]
Four or more times per week	5%	11%
Two to three times per week	11%	
One to three times per week		38%
Once a week or less	50%	
Less than once per week		25%
Less than once per month	29%	26%

*Errors due to rounding
Sources: 1 Statistics Canada 1993, cited in Single *et al.* (1994:182)
         2 Canada, Health and Welfare (1990a:3)

Drinking environments

Recent research has shown the ways in which alcohol drinking patterns are influenced by such factors as context of, and expectations about, drinking. The contexts in which drinking takes place: influence the availability of alcohol; carry within them particular norms about the appropriateness of particular drinks (champagne for picnic brunch, beer for after-sports functions, etc.); and influence the amount that can reasonably be consumed (a Parents & Citizens quiz night at your child's local school is less likely to be accompanied by heavy drinking than an adults-only party to celebrate a sporting victory or other such event) (Single & Wortley 1993). Similar work by Holyfield, Ducharme & Martin found unambiguous evidence that drinking contexts (at home, out, socialising) can predict the frequency of alcohol consumption, drunkenness, and binge drinking (1995).

In Western Australia, researchers found that the drinking environment, in this case licensed premises, was associated with higher frequencies of alcohol-related harm such as violence and drink-driving offences (Stockwell, Lang & Rydon 1993). Another Australian study in Sydney concluded that a combination of factors produced violence after drinking. These included the cheapness of the alcohol, poor quality of live entertainment, crowding and the presence of mostly young, single men (Homel, Tomsen & Thommeny 1992).

This link between the drinking environment, consumption patterns, and alcohol-related harm is particularly pertinent to questions of indigenous drinking, where a variety of legal, social and cultural norms dictate where drinking will take place. Recognition of the link is evident in post-prohibition attempts by some non-indigenous people, such as missionaries, to control indigenous drinking in remote Australian communities, moves which Brady (1990a) suggests were probably influenced by similar attempts in the US to encourage 'civilised' drinking practices among indigenous people. In one remote community, the Lutheran Church was granted a licence to sell beer and stout to the local Aboriginal community in 1968. A church spokesman said the canteen represented 'the lesser of two evils, and we believe controlled drinking to be the lesser' (*The Australian*, 7 December 1968:12, in Brady & Palmer 1984:15). However, in this community, these attempts at encouraging moderation were thwarted by the bartering of beer for both cash and artifacts, and its incorporation into gambling as currency, thus enabling some members of the community to consume large amounts. In the 1980s and 1990s, some indigenous Australian communities themselves have attempted to control both the drinking environment and the availability of alcohol by establishing or proposing to establish social clubs in which alcohol is provided along with meals and entertainment. Attempts by some non-indigenous Australians to oppose these clubs on the grounds that they are discriminatory ignore the history of the exclusion of Aboriginal people from many of the drinking places available to other Australians.

Until the mid to late 1960s, most indigenous Australians were excluded from licensed premises. However, since the repeal of the legislation that sanctioned this, in many places such exclusion has continued. This exclusion has been achieved by various means, including overt discrim-ination, such as 'barring' them; and more covert strategies, such as failure to provide adequate levels of amenity, and the imposition of dress requirements which many indigenous people are not able to meet (Brady 1988; Brady 1990a). Particularly in rural and remote areas, these formal and informal policies of exclusion have contributed to high levels of public drinking among indigenous people. In such environments, drinking tends to be both less constrained and subject to closer scrutiny by the law.

A number of Australian studies have clearly demonstrated that the range of drinking environments for indigenous Australians is more restric-ted than that for the general population (Brady & Palmer 1984; Brady 1988; d'Abbs 1991). In Tennant Creek in the Northern Territory, non-indigenous people who complied with dress requirements could drink at any one of two hotels, two taverns, five clubs and two restaurants. Aboriginal people, on the other hand, were largely restricted to the front bar of one hotel, described as:

> . . . a tight area, containing determined drinkers who are inevitably of a variety of language groups, visitors and residents, the slightest push or wrong word is potentially volatile. The door of the front bar opened directly onto the main street, with no entrance hall or doorway drinkers and arguers spill out onto the main street . . . where they are in full view of vigilant citizens or cruising police . . . (Brady 1988:43).

Apart from the exclusionary policies of non-Aboriginal licensed premises, however, it is clear that many indigenous Australians prefer open, public drinking environments, and attempts to encourage them to drink in canteens or other more easily supervised settings have proved largely unsuccessful. Ethnographic reports of indigenous drinking provide rich accounts of the very different environments in which drinking takes place. For example, people living in fringe camps in Darwin, Northern Territory, are described as recognising distinctive sites (called camps or pitches) where drinking may take place. According to Sansom:

> Their distinctiveness is crucial to patterns of drinking for satellite pitches are occupied by sets of people who now wish to be exclusive. To take drink to the king pitch is to invite one's fellow countrymen to try and wrest it from one. To select fellows and then arrange them round a flagon or a carton of beer on a satellite pitch is . . . to declare that the drink belongs exclusively to the current pitch-occupiers. However, maintaining a boundary about any exclusive drinking set is required activity and pitch-occupiers who possess drink are in no way immune to pressing demands from any countrymen who may approach them. The pressure to share is a function of supply and demand and its general measure is the distance between today and the last pension day. Use of a king pitch and its satellites is managed by the dominant home camp people in association with those 'close up' countrymen who are currently in town (1980:56).

Sansom goes on to describe the 'dangers' associated with grogging in the public domain with countrymen, compared with the relative safety of grogging in pubs. His comments are interesting, not least because of the contrast with research on non-indigenous drinking environments, which shows licensed premises to be the most 'risky' in terms of alcohol-related harm (Stockwell, Lang & Rydon 1993). For the indigenous Australians described by Sansom, pub drinking, which involves the anonymous dispensing of alcohol in individual glasses, reduced the risk of 'mystical contagion', which can occur if strangers are using communal glasses or flagons. Outside the pub, safety from this risk could be assured only by private drinking in a small, commensal group around a single hearth (1980:58).

Brady and Palmer (1984) describe how, rather than drinking in a purpose-built canteen, indigenous people in one remote settlement collected their ration of beer and consumed it either in their camps, or in the open during gambling sessions. When people acquired the more potent port, it was hurriedly purchased from the hotel and then transported to a safe drinking camp in order for 'serious drinking' to take place (1984:19–20).

The most detailed studies of indigenous drinking environments are from remote and rural areas, not the least reason for which being the

ease of observation in the more open and communal living arrangements in such places. Despite the fact that indigenous peoples are
becoming increasingly urbanised, there are no detailed descriptions of
the drinking environments of such populations. Anecdotal evidence and
data we have collected on indigenous drinking in two Western Australian
towns suggest that in these areas, while there is some increase in indigenous drinking on licensed premises, most drinking continues to be
communal but takes place in people's homes or yards. Clearly this is an
area which requires further research.

Understanding of the establishment and maintenance of separate drinking environments for contemporary indigenous and non-indigenous
drinking must take account of a number of factors, including the historical
contexts in which different groups first experienced drinking, and the
effects of both prohibition and subsequent covert exclusion. However,
these factors alone are not sufficient to explain differences in drinking
patterns. Indigenous drinking places are also highly symbolic social and
cultural domains, which show both great diversity and also some cultural
continuities, and these also must be understood.

Drinking populations

As with drinking environments, in understanding drinking populations
there are both anthropological concerns with social and cultural order
and construction, and more practical health concerns about the ways in
which various populations are associated with particular types of drinking
and associated harm. As we have seen, the epidemiological literature tells
us that indigenous drinking populations around the world are most likely
to be male and younger than non-drinkers, and that a high proportion of
them will drink excessively. This is an important start but more information is required both to understand the nature of this drinking and to
reduce some of the harm associated with it.

Anthropological descriptions of indigenous Australian drinking populations collectively describe a way of life in which drinking is central and
where codes of conduct have been constructed around grog (Brady
1988; Brady & Palmer 1984; Collmann 1979; O'Connor 1984; Sansom
1980). Sansom's identification of different drinking regimes, where town
is associated with drinking and the hinterland with limitations on that
drinking, was one of the earliest cultural accounts. On cattle stations,
missions or government settlements, grogging regimes are imposed by
non-indigenous overlords. In these situations drinkers are rationed their
grog, whereas the Wallaby Cross fringe camp outside Darwin is a place of
'free grogging':

> . . . a collectivity in which the ordinary man can be frankly and unapologet-ically a drinker . . . a place that has no edicts that ration or prohibit the supply of alcohol but has, instead, conventions that govern its use (Sansom 1980:51).

In these grogging communities the non-drinkers, not the drinkers, are set apart and known collectively as 'missionaries'. Sansom describes two different rule-bound drinking situations. The first is one in which all drinkers are equal, and communal drinking is ordered by rules of sharing and avoidance of contagion. The second is supervised by a 'Masterful Man', who takes responsibility for both the pace of drinking and the accompanying etiquette. In addition there are many different drinking styles attached to this population. Sometimes drinking has to be slow; at other times, for example, after a hard time on the cattle station, a man might want to really 'hit the piss' (Sansom 1980:60–71).

The collective nature of much indigenous Australian drinking comes through in other work. Town camps in Alice Springs in the Northern Territory have also become identified as heavy drinking communities, in which this drinking style has become a form of 'group dependence'. As among the Darwin fringe dwellers, members are included in, or excluded from, the collectivity on the basis of their drinking status:

> To belong to the group and to live in the fringe camp is to drink with the group. If one does not drink with the group one may have a physical presence there, but one does not belong. The choice is simple: drink and belong, or abstain and remain outside (O'Connor 1984:181).

It has been suggested that alcohol plays a central role in exchange in this type of drinking community. Collmann (1979) argues that the pattern of binge drinking that is typical of these drinking populations provides a way in which drinkers can establish credit among a 'genera-lised collectivity'. That is, alcohol is shared among a man's drinking companions, thereby ensuring reciprocal gifts of both alcohol and other goods and services. In this way his ability to provide alcohol secures his reputation as an affluent and productive person. Collmann extends this analysis by suggesting that the women in his study population had begun to drink in order to develop the same type of credit facilities enjoyed by the men, particularly in an environment of declining female employ-ment. In this sense, Collmann suggests, alcohol has become what Bourdieu terms 'symbolic capital':

> . . . a sort of advance which the group alone can grant those who give it the best material and symbolic *guarantees* . . . (Bourdieu 1977, in Collman 1979:181).

Complementary research has shown the ways in which young people are introduced to drinking, and how expectations of reciprocal sharing exert enormous pressures – particularly on young men – to join and remain with drinking groups (Watson *et al.* 1988:62).

It is important to recognise, however, that the role alcohol plays in social exchange in these communities is not necessarily unique, and shows striking similarities to that in other populations. For example, Mars has described differences between two categories of longshoremen in Newfoundland – regular men who drink at the taverns, and outside men who never drink in the taverns. The latter:

> . . . use drink to repay obligations and to balance reciprocities. Instead of passing beers between themselves as regulars do, they all drink from a single bottle of wine or cheap rum . . . which they pass among themselves (1987:96).

Drinking does more than confer opportunities to accrue social credit. It may also be central to the identity of drinking populations. For all of the indigenous Australian drinking groups we have discussed – and for the longshoremen described by Mars – drinking acts '. . . as markers of personal identity and of boundaries of inclusion and exclusion' (Douglas 1987:8). From this perspective, drinking endows individuals with style, but more importantly 'endows the collectivity with a style of life' (Sansom 1980:9)

Problem deflation and characterisations of indigenous drinking

As anthropologists, we are concerned with, and acknowledge the importance of, the cultural richness of accounts of indigenous drinking environments and populations provided by people such as Sansom and Collman. However, the emphasis in such accounts should not be allowed to obscure two important aspects of indigenous drinking – the harm caused by it and the fact that not all indigenous people are heavy drinkers.

First we must be careful to avoid what Room (1984b) has termed 'problem deflation'. Although he records long lists of alcohol-related convictions, including murders, assaults, and a raft of drink-driving offences, Sansom's attention is clearly focused upon drinking as 'sedulously controlled behaviour' (1980:44). In this emphasis, Sansom is not alone. However, as Room and some indigenous observers point out (Langton 1992), studies in this vein often obscure the harmful consequences of indigenous drinking, which are well documented in the epidemiological literature (Unwin, Thomson & Gracey 1994).

Not all anthropological accounts of indigenous drinking suffer from this shortcoming, however. Sackett (1977; 1988) and Brady and Palmer (1984) also record the ways in which drinking is bound by rules. They note, however, that these rules are not able to prevent transgressions against traditional Aboriginal 'Law' (a matter of great concern to the tradition carriers) and European laws relating to alcohol, or to minimise the sometimes horrific illness and death associated with heavy drinking. Indigenous people in a community studied by Brady and Palmer (1984) recognised 'good' and 'bad' drinkers. A good drinker was someone who could get drunk without inflicting harm on others. A bad drinker was not so fortunate, attacking others or causing damage. Problematically, however, bad drinkers could only be avoided, and the damage associated with their drinking minimised, by rules related to the witnessing of conflict and intervention if things got out of hand. Drinkers and others saw alcohol-related harm, not as a necessary consequence of heavy drinking, but as a breakdown in the rules associated with that (Brady & Palmer 1984:25–30).

Accounts of Australian indigenous drinking largely focus on men. However, it is important to note that women are increasingly becoming part of drinking communities. A number of researchers have noted that among them, starting to drink was often associated with personal trauma, such as the loss of a close family member. Others did so to keep up with their menfolk, but tried to remain only 'half drunk' rather than 'full drunk' to avoid some of the dangers associated with heavy drinking (Kamien 1975; Bell & Ditton 1980; Brady 1994).

While indigenous communities are often characterised as 'heavy drinking', it is important to reiterate that they contain significant proportions of abstainers, many of whom are women. The ability of the abstainers to exert moral authority over drinkers and the harm they cause is circumscribed because of Aboriginal insistence on individual autonomy (being 'bosses for themselves'; Bell 1993) but can make a difference. Brady and Palmer (1984) describe the sobering effect of a fundamentalist Christian revival at Diamond Well, which was accompanied by a decline in the number of heavy drinkers and reductions in social and health problems. Although the sobriety was not permanent, the fact that it did occur indicates the often 'contingent' nature of much Aboriginal drinking (O'Connor 1984). In the Northern Territory survey conducted by Watson, Fleming and Alexander (1987), nearly a third of those sampled had given up alcohol. Brady's (1995a) latest book, *Giving Away the Grog*, also provides important insights into the processes by which people who were firmly entrenched in drinking groups leave them.

The material we have discussed in this chapter indicates that while there may be similarities with some sections of the wider societies in which they are located, in aggregate there are marked differences in patterns of alcohol consumption among indigenous peoples in Australia, New Zealand and Canada. The proportions of non-drinkers in those populations are generally higher than those found in the non-indigenous populations, although it should be noted that many current non-drinkers are ex-drinkers, many of whom have given up drinking because of the harm it caused. Among those who do drink, young males comprise a large proportion and a greater proportion than in non-indigenous populations consume alcohol at harmful levels. In addition to differences in the amount of alcohol consumed, there are also differences in the pattern of consumption, with binge drinking being more common. At least in rural and remote areas, the drinking environments also differ, with more indigenous drinking occurring in public places where there are fewer constraints on drinkers, and which thus contribute to higher levels of consumption and associated harm. Also, at least among some segments of the indigenous populations, despite the harms associated with it, the patterns of consumption we have described are positively valued. In Chapter 2 we noted that many indigenous people have expressed concern at the harm caused by excessive alcohol consumption. We will examine this harm and what is being done to alleviate it in more detail in Chapters 7 and 8. Before doing so, however, we wish to examine the ways in which differences in patterns of consumption between indigenous and non-indigenous peoples have been explained.

CHAPTER 5

Explanations of indigenous alcohol use

The data we reviewed in the previous chapter clearly demonstrate that stereotypes such as those of the 'drunken Aborigine' or the 'drunken Indian' – stereotypes that have been described as 'firewater myths' (Leland 1976; MacAndrew & Edgerton 1969) – are simply not tenable. As we saw, not all indigenous people are heavy drinkers, and significant proportions either do not drink or do so moderately, although at the aggregate level, larger proportions of indigenous populations consume alcohol in a harmful fashion.

In this chapter, we will examine some of the various, and sometimes contradictory, perspectives on indigenous alcohol consumption. In doing so, we – unlike some of those whose views we discuss – are not trying to explain why indigenous people drink. Like people in many societies, indigenous people drink for a variety of reasons: to become intoxicated to some degree or other, as part of social interaction, to relieve stress. What we are trying to explain is *why there are higher rates of harmful alcohol consumption and related harm among indigenous peoples than among non-indigenous people in the societies of which they are both a part.*

Some have seen this as a fruitless task. For example one commentator has written:

> Sorting out cause and effect within this complex of social problems is difficult and may not be worthwhile (Storm, in McKenzie 1993:61).

We strongly disagree with this position. The problem of explanation should not be shied away from simply because it is complex; and, more importantly, to do so means that we are ill-equipped to find adequate solutions to the misuse of alcohol and its consequences.

68

Biology

In the sixteenth century, Western European powers began a series of conquests aimed at the colonisation of the far corners of the globe. The conquerors came in search of luxury goods and wealth, and later for raw materials and markets for the products of their industrial revolutions. The conquered peoples were regarded variously as savages, barbarians, heathens, and even as less than human; and the conquests were rationalised in terms of civilising or Christianising these 'inferior' peoples. The notion of European 'superiority' was characterised initially in terms of morality, but in the latter half of the nineteenth century this became wedded to a bowdlerised version of Darwinian evolutionary theory which attributed it to biological fitness.

The notion that indigenous peoples were biologically inferior struck a chord with European notions of ethnocentrism and gained widespread popularity. It also complemented 'upper'-class notions of superiority and was used to 'explain' and justify inequalities within European societies. It gave rise to the eugenics movement and, in its most extreme form, was a pillar of the ideology of Nazism. Among significant segments of popular opinion this biological reductionism is still used to 'explain' differences between ethnic groups, including different patterns of alcohol use and their consequences.

In the 1970s a number of attempts were made to examine whether or not there were genetic differences which affected the response to alcohol. Attention in these studies focused on differences in the rate at which alcohol is metabolised. Underlying these studies was the notion that if they consumed an equivalent amount of alcohol – when controlling for other factors such as body size and body composition – groups which metabolise alcohol more slowly should maintain and/or build up higher levels of blood alcohol, thus becoming and remaining intoxicated for longer, than those who metabolise it more quickly.

Among the first of these studies was one undertaken by Fenna *et al.* (1971). They administered similar doses of alcohol to Whites, Eskimos and 'Indians' and calculated that the amount of alcohol in grams metabolised per kilogram of body weight per hour in each group respectively was 0.1449, 0.1098, and 0.1013. However, a similar study of alcohol metabolism in Whites, Chinese and Ojibwa 'Indians' by Reed *et al.* (1976) produced contradictory results. They found that the 'Indian' group metabolised alcohol at significantly greater rates than both Chinese and Whites: 182.7 mg/kg/hour versus 136.6 and 103.6. In a study conducted in Hawaii among Whites, Chinese and Japanese, Hanna (1978) found that both Chinese and Japanese subjects (who are genetically more closely related to indigenous Americans than to Whites) metabolised alcohol more rapidly than Whites, thus lending some support to the finding of Reed and his colleagues.

A similar study was conducted in Australia among a small group of Aboriginal and non-Aboriginal prisoners by Marinovich, Larsson and Barber (1976). They found that, although there were wide differences in the rates of alcohol metabolism between individuals, there was no significant difference in the mean rates in each group, which were 17.7 mg/100 ml blood/hour for whites and 18.1 for Aborigines. They wrote that:

> Considering these factors we must conclude that there appears to be no genetically determined difference in blood alcohol degradation between Aboriginals and whites (1976:46).

In recent years attention to the biological basis of 'alcoholism' (alcohol dependence) has shifted from rates of alcohol metabolism to the role of genetically determined variation in dopamine D_2 receptors in the brain (Blum *et al.* 1990; Noble 1992). Dopamine is a neurotransmitter, the release of which is stimulated by alcohol (among other chemical compounds). It has various effects, one of which is to induce feelings of pleasure when it attaches to D_2 receptors in certain brain cells. The number of these receptors is determined by one of two alleles (variants of a gene). In brain samples from deceased persons, Noble and his colleagues found that the allele which genetically codes for fewer receptors was more common in deceased 'alcoholics' than in non-alcoholics, and that there was no difference between Caucasian and Black subjects (Noble 1992). They hypothesised that people with a lower number of receptors '. . . *may* need a very strong stimulation of their fewer receptors' (emphasis added, Noble 1992:27) and thus seek the stimulation provided by alcohol.

As Karp has pointed out, while some research groups have conducted similar studies which appear to confirm this result, others have failed to find an association (1992:786). Setting aside the major issue of what constitutes 'alcoholism', as Saunders and Phillips (1993) point out, the relationship between 'alcoholism' and the presence of the D_2 receptor remains simply an association, that is, no causal relationship has been demonstrated.

It is important to emphasise here that we are not denying that there are biochemical and physiological factors which influence individual responses to alcohol and its metabolites. Clearly there are (Mathews 1984). However, popular prejudice to the contrary, there is no firm evidence that these differences cause the misuse of alcohol or that they explain differences between populations in either patterns of alcohol consumption or its consequences.

Alcohol dependence as 'disease' or dysfunction

The rise of industrial capitalism in Western Europe and the United States was accompanied by the growth of the values and ideology of liberalism. As we have written elsewhere, liberalism emphasises the 'right' of individuals to pursue their interests (particularly economic interests) unfettered by the intrusion of the state (Saggers & Gray 1998). It is now the dominant – though not uncontested – ideology in Anglo-western societies.

For John Stuart Mill (1859), perhaps the most articulate proponent of liberalism, the use of alcohol and other drugs was simply the act of independent people rationally exercising their 'tastes and pursuits'. This view was congruent with an older one in which the excessive use of alcohol was perceived as being a moral problem. That is, individuals who used alcohol excessively were seen as doing so by choice, and were held to be morally culpable for that choice.

In the early decades of this century, a change occurred in the way excessive alcohol use was viewed. On the one hand, there were novel elements in this view. Individuals with alcohol problems came to be viewed as 'sick' rather than 'immoral'. On the other hand, observations that the problem of alcohol misuse is not evenly distributed across all segments of populations – as it would be if the problem was an individual phenomenon – were disregarded. In accord with the underlying liberal ideology, the problem remained located at the individual level.

This sickness or disorder was characterised by a craving for alcohol and loss of the ability to control the level consumed. Two explanations of this approach emerged. The first saw this loss of control primarily as the manifestation of a physical disease, 'alcoholism'. While there are some variations in definition, generally those who view it as a disease characterise it as occurring among individuals who, among other things: are genetically predisposed; are physiologically dependent upon alcohol (that is they are so accustomed to its intake that they suffer withdrawal symptoms on cessation of drinking); and suffer alcohol-related brain damage which further impairs their ability to control their level of consumption (Jurd 1996:2–4). The second approach viewed the excessive consumption of alcohol as a psychological disorder characterised in terms of an uncontrolled craving for alcohol, which was often a manifestation of underlying psychopathology. It should be noted, however, that these were primarily differences in emphasis, for proponents of both views usually acknowledged elements of the other approach.

These concepts of alcohol misuse are not uncontested. In the 1970s, the term 'alcoholism' was removed from the International Classification of Diseases because no agreement could be reached on its definition. It was replaced by 'alcohol dependence syndrome', defined in terms of observable physical aspects and separating these from behaviour and affective factors whose ætiology is more controversial.

As indicated previously, the evidence for a genetic predisposition to alcohol abuse is equivocal. Some genetic markers have been identified which are *associated* with 'alcoholism' but a causal link remains to be clearly demonstrated. The issue of establishing such a causal relationship is further complicated by the lack of agreement on what constitutes 'alcoholism'.

Except where they are linked specifically to notions of population-based genetic differences, the concepts of 'alcoholism' and 'alcohol dependence' are rarely invoked to explain differences in the frequency of excessive alcohol consumption between population groups. This is because, as indicated previously, they are explanations which focus on the causes of excessive drinking in individuals, and in these approaches broader social differences in the patterning of excessive alcohol consumption are largely ignored. Nevertheless, as we will discuss later, these approaches have been particularly influential in indigenous treatment programs.

In a widely cited paper, O'Connor has argued that excessive alcohol consumption by indigenous Australians cannot be explained by the same theories used to explain alcohol dependence in the non-indigenous population. He reports that, depending on the social environment in which they are located, individuals who might be classified as heavy drinkers demonstrate an ability to abstain from or control their drinking in ways that are inconsistent with the behaviours of persons who are alcohol-dependent in terms of the criteria discussed above (O'Connor 1984). This is consistent with our own observations in a town in the northwest of Australia, where individuals who were referred to as 'alcoholics' by medical and nursing staff were able to completely abstain from drinking for periods of weeks, and sometimes months, when they went to work on pastoral stations. It is also consistent with Levy and Kunitz's findings among the Navajo people that:

> ... most of the individuals in this study who did become aware that alcohol consumption is more costly than it is worth were apparently able to stop drinking with little difficulty, regardless of whether they were in a treatment program and whether intensive follow-up treatment was provided. This indicates to us that excessive drinking amongst most Navajos does not originate in the same pathological motives as it does among Anglo alcoholics. The behaviors are labelled the same because they look the same, and often produce the similar end results (1974:193).

The application of the disease model to indigenous societies has also been criticised on the basis of its ethnocentrism, a point made above in terms of the liberal ideology which underlies it. In this regard Heath has written:

> . . . although drinking – and even heavy drinking – is widespread among North American Indians, with episodic drinking being both commonplace and condoned in many groups, the concept of alcoholism, or even problem drinking is relatively rare. . . . it is not banal to underscore the crucial – and often ignored – fact that problems are in the eye of the beholder (Heath 1983:384).

While we strongly contest the view that excessive alcohol use is a 'disease', we do not deny that among some indigenous people problem drinking is a manifestation of psychopathology or a response to psychological trauma. However, to view the observed patterns of excessive alcohol consumption among indigenous peoples as simply the sum of individual differences is to tear them from the social contexts in which they occur. Much of the psychological trauma among indigenous people is a consequence of the continuing legacy of colonialism, and while the trauma requires treatment the underlying causes must also be addressed.

Loss of culture and culture change

As we saw in Chapter 1, by the early years of this century the indigenous populations of Australia, New Zealand and Canada were again increasing in size after the devastation wrought by early colonisation. No longer could they be regarded as remnants of dying populations, to which the only responsibility of governments was to 'smooth the dying pillow'. As in the United States, the response of governments in all three countries was to seek to assimilate indigenous peoples.

But assimilate them to what? All three countries had been British colonies, most migrants to each had come from the British Isles, and each was dominated by a political and economic elite that was British or of British descent. The culture of this group was held up as the ideal which all members of society should seek to attain in a process leading to homogeneous societies. Of course, this ideal did not reflect reality. In Canada there was a sizeable French population, and in all three countries migrants also came from other parts of Europe. These groups were variously integrated into the political and economic lives of the three countries and maintained important cultural differences. Nevertheless, the ideology of homogeneity prevailed.

This ideology was reflected in the functionalist anthropological and sociological theory of the day. Societies were conceived as organic wholes, in which institutions and values functioned to preserve the integrity of society. Those groups that did not behave like, or subscribe to the beliefs and values of, members of the wider society presented an anomaly, and various studies were undertaken to explain these 'deviant' subcultures (Levy and Kunitz 1974:9–24).

Inevitably, similar perspectives were applied to the study of indigenous peoples. Central to this development was the notion that, with few exceptions, indigenous peoples had 'lost' their cultures. According to this perspective there were two aspects to this loss: indigenous people were in a state of 'anomie' (or normlessness), or were in a state of stress as a consequence of difficulties acculturating (or assimilating) to the supposedly homogeneous wider society.

The concept of anomie was first developed by the French sociologist Emile Durkheim (1952). Durkheim used it to describe a 'pathological' state of society in which consensus on social norms had broken down as a consequence of industrialisation and modernisation, and increasing individuation. As Merton noted, later writers extended the term to include the state of mind of individuals living in such a society (1968:215–17). Subsequent writers applied the concept and related theory in analyses of the state of indigenous peoples. As a result of colonisation, indigenous cultures were regarded as having irretrievably broken down and been lost. As a consequence, indigenous people were seen as having lost traditional roles, and as having no social rules to guide their behaviour, nor institutions that could exercise effective social control over behaviour. It was argued that this supposed breakdown of culture was manifested psychologically in loss of individual autonomy, identity and self-esteem, and in alienation from both traditional and colonial cultures.

Related to the notion of anomie is that of acculturative stress. In this conceptualisation, indigenous peoples were seen as accepting the goals and values of the wider societies and attempting to assimilate into them. However, their attempts were restricted by a variety of factors including discrimination, poverty and lack of skills. As McKenzie has written:

> Only about two generations of Aboriginal Canadians have made contact with the mainstream population. To some extent, their integration with the population has met with great frustrations because Aboriginal Canadians need to acquire certain skills to adapt to the patterns of the larger society. This situation placed certain stressors on Aboriginal communities (1993:48–9).

Various writers have argued that high levels of alcohol consumption among indigenous peoples are a means of dealing with the psychological distress caused by either anomie or the frustrations arising from not being able to achieve the goals they have adopted from the wider societies (Albrecht 1974; Eckermann 1977; Kamien 1978; Graves 1967).

This explanation of higher levels of alcohol consumption among indigenous peoples has been criticised from two perspectives. First, extensive field research undertaken among Navajo people in the United States by

Levy and Kunitz found that the explanation was not supported by the pattern of consumption among subgroups of the population. In contradiction to the theory:

> . . . the highest intensity of involvement with drinking and the greatest use of alcohol was found among the most traditional and least acculturated group, while the lowest use and involvement was found in the most acculturated off-reservation group (1971:109)

Second, research that has documented the life of contemporary indigenous peoples – as opposed to attempting to reconstruct 'traditional' patterns of culture – has demonstrated that they do not live in a cultural vacuum. The cultures of indigenous peoples, like all cultures, change through time in response to the broader social, political and economic environment. In the course of such change, older patterns are discarded – sometimes by choice, sometimes by force. Nevertheless, the people maintain living cultures, which are both distinct from, and share characteristics with, 'traditional' indigenous cultures and the cultures of the colonising societies.

This is not to deny that some indigenous people feel considerable pain and a sense of great loss as a consequence of not being acquainted with the cultures of their forebears. The report by the Aboriginal Legal Service of Western Australia on the experiences of indigenous Australians who were removed from their families as children makes this poignantly clear (1995). Again, however, this alone cannot explain patterns of indigenous alcohol consumption.

Cultural explanations

For much of the first half of this century – in the face of the changes wrought by the spread of industrial capitalism, modernisation, and attempts to assimilate minority populations – a great deal of anthropological effort was expended in trying to document the ways of life of 'other' peoples before they disappeared. Much of this effort involved trying to reconstruct 'traditional' ways of life (disregarding the fact that all of them had been affected one way or another by colonial expansion for long periods of time), and little attention was focused on contemporary indigenous cultures, which were often implicitly, and sometimes explicitly, devalued. It was assumed that indigenous cultures were rapidly disappearing and that policies of assimilation were succeeding. As two prominent Australian anthropologists wrote in the early 1960s:

> Generally . . . the majority of these people (Aborigines in remote areas) are becoming more and more like those in the south – who are already, both in

appearance and in manner of living, European in all but physical characteristics, and often very largely so in that respect as well (Berndt & Berndt 1964:443).

However, such views were not based on extensive first-hand experience among 'non-traditional' peoples, and from about the 1960s, a number of ethnographic studies appeared that highlighted the fact that, while they were not 'traditional', indigenous peoples had distinct cultures which demonstrated continuities with the past, had adapted to present circumstances, and had incorporated for their own purposes elements of the culture of the colonialists. This realisation was accompanied by a turning away from explaining indigenous drinking as a consequence of cultural breakdown to attempts to explain it in terms of indigenous cultures themselves. In this approach, three strands of explanation can be identified: those that focus on the characteristics of 'traditional' cultures; those that focus on aspects of contemporary indigenous cultures; and those that emphasise the adoption and incorporation of drinking styles learned from non-indigenous peoples.

Characteristics of traditional indigenous cultures

A commonly cited explanation for excessive alcohol consumption among indigenous peoples has centred on its absence in pre-contact societies. According to this line of argument, because they did not have access to alcohol (or other psychoactive substances), no social rules or conventions were developed to control its use. Thus when it was introduced, consumption was largely unregulated and people drank, and continue to drink, excessively.

This position has been refuted on two grounds. First, as we saw in the previous chapter, there is clear evidence that at least some groups did have access to psychoactive substances, including naturally fermented alcoholic drinks; and there is no evidence to indicate that the response to the introduction of large quantities of alcoholic beverages was any different between those who did and those who did not have prior access to such substances. Second, it sees culture as relatively unchanging, a view clearly contradicted by archaeological studies of traditional indigenous cultures, and by studies of contemporary indigenous cultures, both of which demonstrate a long history of successfully incorporating a range of ideas and material goods (Flood 1995; Rowley 1974). Furthermore, various recent studies demonstrate that indigenous peoples have incorporated the use of alcohol into their societies in regulated ways (Collman 1979; Sansom 1980), if not the ways that some non-indigenous people would prefer.

Some indigenous cultures, such as those of the north American plains, particularly valued and actively sought 'altered states of consciousness', often as a means of obtaining personal power from the supernatural. This has led some commentators to claim that alcohol was consumed as a means of achieving such states (Carpenter 1959; Jilekaal 1974, both in Smart & Ogborne 1986:104–5). While there might have been some truth in this in an early contact situation, it has been suggested that people soon learned that any such gain was illusory. More importantly, however, there are no ethnographic records of indigenous people drinking alcohol to achieve religious ends – as the Native American Church did with peyote (La Barre 1969) – on a scale that would explain contemporary patterns of consumption.

Another attempt to explain indigenous patterns of drinking in terms of continuities with traditional cultures sought to link it with the nature and consequences of the social organisation among some peoples. It has been argued that the small-scale nature of indigenous communities required members to suppress their emotions and personal feelings in the interest of social harmony to an extent not required in larger-scale societies, and that excessive drinking provided an opportunity to escape from such restrictions (Hallowell 1955). In a similar vein, Rubel and Kupferer (1968) attributed patterns of alcohol consumption among the Inuit of northern Canada to traditional patterns of social relations. These approaches grew out of the 'culture and personality' school of anthropology, which was prominent from the 1940s to the 1960s and which sought to link 'modal personality' types to particular cultural forms. However, as Harris (1968) has written, this approach has largely been discredited because it failed to adequately account for the wide range of personality types occurring in any particular society.

An alternative approach, which linked contemporary patterns of alcohol consumption and 'traditional' society, was taken by Levy and Kunitz (1974). They viewed drinking less as a consequence of the pathological aspects of indigenous culture and more as a reflection of positively valued forms of expression. They have written that:

> We maintain that drinking behavior is mainly a reflection of traditional forms of social organisation and cultural values instead of a reflection of social disorganisation (1974:24).

and

> . . . it is important to make the distinction between people who drink excessively because they are normal young men in Navajo terms and people who drink because of pathological processes, whether these processes derive from the stresses of acculturation or from more personal difficulties. Our findings indicate that the former group – normal young men – is the vast majority and accounts for what is regarded as Navajo problem drinking (1974: 193).

While it is not seen as a factor that explains drinking patterns *per se*, the emphasis placed on the value of personal autonomy in indigenous Australian societies has been the subject of some attention. In some circumstances this is seen as facilitating excessive consumption, because individuals are loath to impose on the personal autonomy of others, and thus the excesses of individual drinkers are not curbed (Brady 1995b; Rowse 1993).

Learned behaviour

In a well researched and widely cited book, MacAndrew and Edgerton (1969) point out that there are two aspects to the ways in which people respond to alcohol. The first of these is the impairment that alcohol causes to sensorimotor skills. This is fairly uniform and is clearly attributable to the toxic effects of alcohol itself. The second is the manner in which people behave, or 'comport' themselves, after consuming alcohol. They cite numerous examples – many from indigenous American societies – demonstrating that such behaviour is so varied that it cannot be attributed to the effects of alcohol itself. They go on to show that such behaviour is learned and is culturally determined.

This is a theme that has been taken up by a number of observers in Australia, Canada and the United States to explain indigenous drinking patterns (Honigmann 1979; Smart & Ogborne 1986; Brady 1991a). It has been argued that indigenous people in each of these countries learned their drinking behaviour from the Europeans with whom they first came into contact on the 'frontier'. These people were variously convicts, traders, soldiers or itinerant farm and pastoral station workers, who drank excessively and in binges and responded to it in a relatively uncontrolled manner. It is argued that this pattern has been incorporated into the cultures of indigenous peoples and continues to be the way in which they drink and respond to alcohol.

In a similar approach, it has been argued by some that the way in which indigenous people drink is based on patterns that were established during the years in which they were prohibited from drinking liquor (Beckett 1964; Hawthorne *et al.* in Smart & Ogborne 1986). Under these circumstances people would have to obtain alcohol illegally and consume it rapidly to avoid detection by the police and confiscation of their drink. Again, it is maintained that this pattern of drinking has become part of indigenous cultures and remains so.

While there is certainly an element of truth in such explanations, alone they imply a rather static view of indigenous cultures, in which, once they have been adopted, patterns of behaviour remain unchanged. Such explanations do not stand alone, and they need to be linked to others that show how and why such patterns have been maintained.

Alcohol in contemporary indigenous cultures

Particularly in Australia, in the last 20 years there have been a number of studies which examine the role alcohol plays in contemporary indigenous communities. These studies emphasise the valued nature of drinking within those communities, which is seen by the drinkers themselves as an opportunity for socialising and enjoyment and as a means of relieving boredom (Beckett 1964; Brady 1992a; Watson, Fleming & Alexander 1988). Some observers have suggested that activities focused on drinking serve as a substitute for traditional ceremonial and ritual life (Bain 1974), an observation that has also been made with regard to Maori drinking (Awatere *et al.* 1984).

The detailed accounts of indigenous Australian drinking by Sansom (1980) and Collman (1979), which we have cited in Chapter 4, also highlight the elaborate but unwritten rules surrounding alcohol consumption. In doing so, they act as a refutation of the view that indigenous people misuse alcohol because they had, or developed, no mechanisms to control its use. The examples provided by these researchers clearly demonstrate that indigenous people have developed their own sets of rules governing consumption. As we remarked earlier, it is simply that these rules do not accord with non-indigenous, middle-class notions of appropriate behaviour.

These accounts, which stress the normative nature of indigenous drinking, have been subjected to some criticism by both indigenous and non-indigenous observers. Following Room (1984b), it is argued that such accounts 'deflate' the problems associated with excessive alcohol consumption. To some extent, such criticism is not warranted. For example, Sansom (1980) lists the problems associated with alcohol misuse, including acts of violence and traffic accidents. However, this was not the objective of his study. Nevertheless, it is important to note that while some indigenous people might claim that 'being Aboriginal is being a drinker', this is certainly not the case for a large proportion of the indigenous population; Gilbert (cited in Brady 1991a) and Langton (1991), among other indigenous people, have spoken out against this notion.

Political and economic factors

As well as the psychosocial and cultural explanations discussed above, various political and economic explanations of indigenous drinking patterns have also been invoked. The most common of these is the dispossession and consequent political and economic marginalisation of indigenous peoples. As Kahn *et al.* have written:

> . . . the majority of attempted explanations implicate factors connected in some way with the subordinate position of Aborigines in Australian society over the last 200 years (1990:361).

The role of dispossession in explaining indigenous alcohol misuse and related harm has been most cogently argued by Hunter (1993a). In a well researched book, he situates the position of indigenous peoples in the Kimberley region of Western Australia in a historical context. He shows how the process of dispossession and subsequent eviction of indigenous peoples from their land has left them in a relatively powerless position, and he convincingly demonstrates how alcohol misuse, suicide and other forms of violence are a consequence of that powerlessness. This is a theme echoed in a review by Moore, who has argued that, to reduce the incidence of alcohol-related problems:

> Aboriginal people need to be supported in their struggle for self-determination, the shaping of contemporary Aboriginal identities and in the attainment of power to make decisions affecting their lives (1992:187).

It is not surprising that indigenous people are generally more likely to invoke dispossession and its consequences as an explanation than are non-indigenous people, especially in a climate in Australia where the Liberal–National Party coalition government is unwilling to acknowledge past injustices to indigenous Australians. The Australian National Aboriginal Health Strategy Working Party reported that:

> . . . there is a consensus in the Aboriginal community which understands the 'alcohol' problem . . . as a symptom (ultimately a symptom of dispossession) of alienation which leads to loss of self-esteem (1989:194).

In Auckland, New Zealand, Maori themselves cited '. . . the stress of unemployment, unsatisfactory jobs, poverty and the experience of racial discrimination' among the reasons for heavy alcohol consumption (New Zealand, Te Puni Kokiri & AACNZ 1995:15). Similarly, Health and Welfare Canada notes that among indigenous peoples, high rates of alcohol use and abuse are correlated with low income, education and occupational status (Canada, Health and Welfare 1989:21–2).

In Australia:

> In general terms, poverty, the economic disparity between Aborigines and whites, lack of education and job skills are mentioned by many writers (Kahn *et al.* 1990:359).

Despite this recognition, there are few studies that directly link patterns of alcohol use to specific social and economic indicators. However, our own research and that of our colleagues has clearly linked such inequalities to alcohol and other drug use among young indigenous people in Albany, Western Australia. There we found that among 15- to 17-year-olds, those who were unemployed were 13.5 times more likely to be frequent users of some combination of alcohol, tobacco, cannabis, or other drugs than those who were employed, in training, or still at school (Gray *et al.* 1996:71).

The role of broader socioeconomic factors has been taken up in Canada by Brody (1977), who has argued that Inuit and Dene communities are subject to the same negative impacts of industrial expansion as non-indigenous people, with similar results, including high rates of alcohol misuse. Going further, Graves (1970) claimed that patterns of alcohol misuse among Navajo people in Denver, in the United States, were similar to those among whites of similar social class, and were a consequence of the same social structural factors acting on both, rather than being a consequence of their identity as Navajo.

While we do not agree that drinking among indigenous peoples can be explained without any reference to their histories and cultures, we do believe that the similarities between indigenous drinking patterns and those in some segments of non-indigenous populations require further investigation. In Canada, for example, Smart and Ogborne note that heavy drinking is not confined to indigenous people in the north, and suggest similarities with drinking patterns among sections of the non-indigenous population (1986:108). However, as we highlighted in Chapter 3 – where we had to compare studies of alcohol use in indigenous communities with data from aggregated non-indigenous populations – there is a paucity of studies on comparable non-indigenous communities. In the words of McKenzie:

> We don't know if non-Aboriginal populations and poor people show the same level of problems as Aboriginal populations (1993:48).

How do dispossession, political and economic marginalisation, and discrimination 'cause' alcohol misuse? Here, a variety of mechanisms have been suggested. Perhaps the most prominent of these is the use of alcohol to ease the psychological pain caused by a barrage of assaults including rejection, the break-up of families, institutionalisation, and consequent loss of self-esteem. Excessive alcohol use is also seen as making bearable the impoverished conditions in which people are forced to live, and in communities that lack access to other recreational activities it is one of the few means of 'having fun'.

It should not be thought that indigenous people have been helpless pawns in the process of colonisation, and that excessive alcohol consumption has simply been a passive response to it. There are various well documented accounts of indigenous resistance and protest. In Australia, for example, this has included armed resistance (Reynolds 1981), strikes against working conditions and the appropriation of land (Hardy 1968), the establishment of a 'tent embassy' to draw attention to the condition of indigenous peoples, and legal actions to reclaim land (Rowse 1994). Alcohol has also been used by indigenous people to make statements of protest. Indeed, Lurie has described the drinking patterns of indigenous peoples in North America as 'the world's oldest on-going protest demonstration' (1979). Writing about a desert fringe community in Western Australia, Sackett has said that indigenous people drink to '. . . express their antipathy to the idea and practice of others administering their lives' (1988:76). Similarly in Australia, others have described excessive indigenous drinking as an alternative to compliance with the existing power structure (Brady & Palmer 1984), and as a way of 'kicking back' at non-indigenous administrators and institutions (Albrecht 1974). As Brady notes, however, such a mode of protest takes a toll on indigenous people themselves.

As well as protest, drinking has also been used to make other political statements. It has been employed as a means of asserting indigenous identities opposed to those of non-indigenous peoples (Braroe 1975; Lurie 1979; Heath 1983). It has also been used as a statement of equality with non-indigenous people, as noted in the discussion of drinking and citizenship in Australia (in Chapter 2).

Despite acknowledging its historical role, some writers have expressed ambivalence about invoking colonialism and its economic consequences to explain contemporary patterns of alcohol consumption. For example, Brady has written:

> In the circumstances surrounding Aboriginal uses of alcohol in Australia, these causes are most commonly attributed to Aborigines' history of colonisation and oppression and contemporary socioeconomic deprivation, unemployment and marginalisation. These somewhat global postulated causes for the misuse of alcohol (among those Aboriginal people – apparently in a minority – who drink) (Watson, Fleming and Alexander 1988) mean that public health models stressing prevention and personal responsibility are left, somewhat uneasily, unresolved (Brady 1992a:700).

The implication of this statement is that if all indigenous people have experienced the effects of colonisation, then the misuse of alcohol should be more widespread among them and not confined to a minority. However, we believe that this is a simplistic way in which to view the effects of the political and economic forces of colonialism. These forces provide the overall framework for the interaction between indigenous and non-indigenous societies, but they have differential impacts on indigenous societies and/or sections within them, and individuals and communities have responded to those forces in different ways. For example, it is likely that fewer indigenous women than men drink excessively, because their roles in domestic economies have been far less disrupted than those of men. They have obligations to family and children, which entail considerable responsibility and leave them with both less inclination and less time to become involved in heavy drinking groups.

In Canada also, some observers who favour culturally based explanations of indigenous drinking patterns have sought to minimise the role of political and economic factors. Smart and Ogborne do so based on their assertion that, before traditional cultures were undermined, 'Indians' still had problems with alcohol (1986:104). We suggest that this view is untenable, for while some of the more obvious trappings of traditional cultures remained in place, the economic bases of traditional cultures had already been undermined by the involvement of indigenous people in the fur trade. Storm discounts the role of broader political and economic factors by arguing that, contrary to his expectations, problems of alcohol and substance use continue despite increasing political awareness among indigenous organisations (Storm 1993, in McKenzie 1993:62). However, as various Australian studies demonstrate, political awareness is necessary but not sufficient to bring about change in the absence of an economic base (Howard 1978; Tonkinson & Howard 1990).

Eclectic approaches to the explanation of indigenous alcohol use

Most of the categories of explanation that we have discussed are not mutually exclusive, and many writers have invoked some combination of them in their work. For example, most observers have cited the role of colonialism and dispossession, at least as a background to their explanations. In Australia, writers such as Larsen (1979) and Ward (1978) have attempted to situate psychosocial approaches within the context of a broader socioeconomic framework. Others, such as Albrecht (1974) in Australia and Smart and Ogborne (1986) in Canada, attribute indigenous drinking patterns to an eclectic assortment of historical and cultural factors. This eclectic approach is also evident in several review papers on indigenous drinking (Alexander 1990; Heath 1983; Kahn et al. 1990), in which various approaches are canvassed, some rejected, most accepted as containing some element of explanatory value, but not presented in any consistently coherent framework.

Some observers have not seen this as problematic. For example, Heath, writing about indigenous North Americans, has said that:

> ... it should be obvious that ... no single theory can reliably and parsimoniously explain such cross cultural diversity (in 'Indian' alcohol related beliefs and behaviour) (1983:375).

Like Heath, Brady eschews 'the search for unified "causes" for drug and alcohol abuse' (1995b:10). Unlike him, however, she has attempted to place explanations for indigenous alcohol misuse in an inclusive framework which gives priority to none. To do this, she has employed the model elaborated by Zinberg (1984) – discussed in the previous chapter – who has argued that to understand any drug use it is necessary to consider the interaction between drug, set, and setting – that is, the physiological effects of the drug itself, the state of mind of the person using the drug, and the environment in which the drug is used.

From our perspective, while this model usefully draws attention to the broader context of alcohol and other drug use, it suffers from the same weakness as the systems theory on which it is based. That is, like the more particularistic approach of Heath, it provides no theoretical basis for establishing the priority of the explanatory factors included in the model. In failing to do so, it ignores the vast empirical literature that shows that political and economic structures impose a constraining influence on human behaviour (Harris 1968, 1979; Roseberry 1988), and it thus provides no guide to an optimal strategy of intervention.

The political economy of indigenous alcohol use

Most of the approaches to the explanation of patterns of indigenous alcohol consumption that we have reviewed appear to shed some light on the phenomenon. However, each has its limitations, as do most attempts at combining some or all of them. As we said at the beginning of this chapter, we do not believe that this should lead us to abandon the search for a comprehensive explanation.

In our previous work on the health of indigenous Australians, we have employed a 'political economy' approach (Saggers & Gray 1991; Gray & Saggers 1994). Although this approach is not popular – largely because of its materialist emphasis – we believe that it is best able to explain the difference in health status of indigenous and non-indigenous peoples, and is best able to help in the identification of strategies that will bring about a reduction in that inequality. Similarly, like Singer (1986), we believe that it is the approach best able to explain differences in patterns of alcohol consumption and related harm between indigenous and non-indigenous peoples, and that it directs our attention to the ways best able to reduce that harm.

What is a 'political economy' approach? It is an approach to the explanation of human social behaviour that takes as its starting point the complex web of political and economic relations that constitute the environment in which individuals and social groups exist (Roseberry 1988). These relations, and the ways in which they allocate resources and the fruits of economic production, set greater or lesser constraints upon the life chances of individuals and groups, and the power they have to choose the ways in which their lives are lived. These relationships are not 'determinative' in any absolute sense; they and their effects are shaped by history and by the ability of individuals and groups to change them. We do not claim that this approach can explain all human social behaviour. However, it does provide a basic framework for understanding the context in which social behaviour takes place and the constraints upon it.

The political economy approach is similar in some respects to others that emphasise the role of political and economic factors. However, it differs from such approaches in that it does not treat those factors as discrete variables; and it treats current political and economic systems not as givens, but as shaped by history and differential power relationships. Thus, for example, differences in the distribution of wealth between indigenous and non-indigenous peoples are not viewed as the outcome of abstract 'market forces', but as the outcome of differential power relations between those peoples.

Within anthropology and comparative sociology, there has always been a tension between those approaches that have emphasised the unique character of particular societies and those aimed at developing theoretical frameworks that identify the commonalities of human experience. Many of the studies we have reviewed in this chapter clearly fall into the former category. That is, they have sought to explain patterns of indigenous alcohol consumption in terms of the characteristics, cultures, or histories of particular individuals, groups, or indigenous populations. However, a review such as this highlights a number of interrelated problems with such approaches. The first of these is the commonality of drinking patterns and the broad similarity of experiences that become evident when they are compared.

A second problem arising from seeking an explanation for drinking patterns within the culture of particular groups is that it ignores the fact that such groups do not exist in a vacuum. Indigenous societies are not social isolates. Most have been in contact with Europeans for at least 150 years (and often longer), and even where direct contact has been more recent (as late as the 1950s in parts of the Australian desert), they have been indirectly affected by colonisation. The environments in which they live and the social organisations and cultures of indigenous peoples in Australia, New Zealand and Canada have all been shaped in response to colonial societies, and they cannot be adequately understood apart from that.

A third consequence of particularistic approaches to the study of indigenous alcohol consumption is a focus on demand. That is, by looking inward, such studies usually seek to explain why there is an inordinate demand for alcohol by some segments of indigenous populations. However, levels of consumption are a function of supply as well as demand, and – as we discuss in Chapter 6 – an increase in supply can increase consumption. While, at a practical level, several indigenous Australian community groups have sought to limit the supply of alcohol, few studies address this issue in any detail.

As we have indicated, the material we presented in Chapter 3 – although there are gaps in it – reveals a remarkably similar pattern of alcohol consumption among indigenous peoples in the countries under consideration. Given this similarity, it is unlikely that it has arisen from unique circumstances within indigenous societies. In our view, explanation of this phenomenon requires consideration of what is common to them all. That is, the experience of colonialism, the destruction of traditional economies, exploitation and marginalisation, the loss of power entailed in these processes, and the responses of indigenous peoples to them. A model of indigenous drinking must take this as the starting point, and other factors need to be considered in the context of these political and economic relationships.

Colonisation was a disaster of catastrophic proportions for indigenous societies in Australia, New Zealand and Canada. Although there were differences in pattern and timing between and within countries, the results were essentially the same. The combination of the appropriation of the most valuable land and resources and the decimation of populations due to violence and introduced diseases undermined the economic bases of traditional societies. With the influx of significant numbers of non-indigenous migrants, indigenous people became largely irrelevant to the labour market. The remnants of indigenous populations were herded onto reserves or reservations, or left to congregate on the fringes of European towns and cities. They were provided with only meagre education, or denied access to it altogether, and their access to vocational training was similarly restricted. Non-indigenous people regarded them as inferior, took their impoverishment as evidence of that supposed inferiority, and actively discriminated against them. Indigenous people were regarded as a 'problem'; and when that 'problem' did not disappear as anticipated, an attempt to solve it was made through policies of assimilation. In the attempt to assimilate indigenous people, children of mixed descent were taken from their indigenous parents and placed in institutions and foster care, causing untold psychological trauma for both parents and children.

Indigenous people have not been helpless victims in this process of colonisation. They have struggled and resisted, and it is not to detract from that continuing struggle to acknowledge that European victory has generally rendered them dependent and relatively powerless. This is so even in those remote areas where cultural continuities with traditional societies – in the form of language and religion, for example – are more evident, and sometimes obscure the political and economic realities. The effects of colonisation have been particularly devastating for men. Women's social roles in the domestic economy have largely remained intact. However, for men, their exclusion from the labour market has meant that there has been little to replace their traditional economic roles. This has heightened their sense of dependence upon the wider societies – and, often, on their own women – and their sense of power-lessness.

Alcohol has always played a role in the process of colonisation. In the pre-contact indigenous populations with which we are concerned, there was little or, more commonly, no demand for alcohol. As we saw in Chapter 3, such demand had to be created. Once it had been, alcohol was used as an item of trade, as a means of intoxicating indigenous people in order to obtain more favourable terms of trade or to enter into sexual relations, as a means of securing indebtedness which could be redeemed for land, and in exchange for labour (in some times and locations). In periods when the sale of alcohol to indigenous people was legally prohibited, there were always non-indigenous people prepared to break the law to reap the profits of illicit sales. As Kahn and his colleagues note with regard to indigenous Australians:

> . . . the exploitation of Aborigines as an economic resource through alcohol certainly continues, via sale and taxation, via 'grog-running' to remote communities, and perhaps the growth of bureaucratic structures set up to service alcohol-affected Aborigines (1990:359).

In the context of colonisation and its continuing consequences, excessive alcohol consumption plays many roles. In the absence of other meaningful employment and recreational activities it is simply a means of 'having fun'. For many young men, it is one of the few ways open to them to express their masculinity. As we have seen, for some indigenous people it is a symbolic statement, a protest against their powerlessness. Many people have been psychologically scarred, and for some of them it is a means of coping with that trauma. Being drunk also helps to make deplorable living conditions bearable. Because it serves so many purposes, it is little wonder that the excessive use has become institutionalised among some segments of indigenous societies and has become a self-perpetuating activity.

It is at this level that excessive alcohol consumption may be seen as having many 'causes' and, clearly, at this level various interventions may be required by indigenous groups that wish to address the problem. Nevertheless, these reasons for drinking are themselves a function of relationships between indigenous and non-indigenous societies within the broader web of political and economic relationships. That is, they are symptoms of underlying inequalities. However, interventions aimed solely at these symptoms – while alleviating some of the pain – will not address the underlying cause, and the symptoms will continue to re-emerge.

CHAPTER 6

Supply and promotion of alcohol to indigenous Australian communities

'Behind every blackfella gettin' drunk, there's a whitefella gettin' rich.'

Anonymous

In Chapter 5 we discussed the ways in which indigenous alcohol use has been theorised, and indicated our interest in theories of political economy, which direct attention to the ways in which global economic interests in alcohol can affect alcohol use at the level of the local community. In this chapter we examine the issue of the supply and promotion of alcohol to local indigenous communities in Australia, drawing upon our own research in Western Australia, and the work of others across Australia. In the first half, we outline the general debates surrounding alcohol control policies, and then show how they can be applied to the indigenous Australian situation. In the second half, using material we have presented elsewhere (Saggers & Gray 1997), we demonstrate how these general issues apply at the local level by presenting a case study of the supply and promotion of alcohol in two Australian communities. Our concern about the supply and promotion of alcohol is strengthened by research that demonstrates how the availability of alcohol affects levels of consumption and consequent harm.

Reviews of the general literature by Room (1984a), Single (1988), and Holder (1994) demonstrate that with increases in the availability of alcohol, *per capita* consumption within populations increases, and that with increases in consumption, there is an increase in alcohol-related health and social problems. Factors that affect the overall availability of alcohol include types of control systems, restrictions on distribution (for example, trading hours/days, age limits, advertising), density of outlets, pricing and taxation; and these have been shown to have an impact on consumption not only by 'social' but also by 'heavy' drinkers (Single 1988). Furthermore, density of outlets is not simply a response to demand but also acts to stimulate it (Gruenewald, Millar & Treno 1993). These arguments are important to our focus on the supply and promotion of alcohol, so it is worth examining them in some detail. A very helpful discussion, which has guided what follows, has been that provided by Stockwell (1995:119–38) who attempts to answer the question 'Do controls on the availability of alcohol reduce alcohol problems?'

Alcohol control policies

The availability hypothesis

In an attempt to introduce some rigour into the proposition that there is a relationship between the availability of alcohol, levels of consumption, and alcohol-related harm, Lederman (1956) posited a mathematically quantifiable relationship between levels of drinking and the number of drinkers consuming excessive amounts in every society. Although subsequent work has cast doubt on the precision of Lederman's estimates (Duffy & Cohen 1978; Skog 1985), his basic hypothesis has not been refuted. The relationship depends upon three connected propositions; first, increases in the availability of alcohol result in higher average consumption; second, with higher average consumption, the number of people drinking excessively will increase; and, finally, that it is this increase in the number of excessive drinkers which leads to the increase in alcohol-related problems (Single 1988; Stockwell 1995:123).

As Stockwell points out, the second and third of these propositions are unproblematic; what is in dispute is the first. Explaining why requires some understanding of the ways in which alcohol problems have been conceptualised since the 'disease model' of 'alcoholism' has given way to more sophisticated classifications that distinguish between:

(i)   problems of regular consumption (for example, liver cirrhosis, cognitive impairment);
(ii) problems of dependence (for example, withdrawal symptoms, impairment of control); and
(iii) problems of intoxication (for example, alcohol-related violence, road trauma, falls) (Stockwell 1995:124–5).

Because each of these problem areas is associated with different types of excessive drinking, controlling the availability of alcohol may differentially affect each area. For example, allowing more licensed premises – thus increasing availability – may result in an increase in deaths from liver cirrhosis; however, it may reduce the number of alcohol-related road accidents and associated trauma, as drink-drivers have shorter distances to travel (Smith 1989a, in Stockwell 1995:125). Stockwell goes on to point out that much of the research on alcohol availability has focused on regular consumption and dependence, rather than problems of intoxication. Consequently, it has tended to measure drinking in aggregate amounts over specified periods, for instance, the last week or month. This means that occasional binge drinking, which may lead to a number of health and social problems, is unlikely to be detected.

The preventive paradox

'The preventive paradox' is a term used by Kreitman (1986b) to describe the apparently contradictory finding that most alcohol-related harm occurs among those who drink moderately. Kreitman found when classifying drinkers on the basis of their average weekly consumption, that in aggregate moderate drinkers were responsible for many more alcohol-related problems than heavy drinkers because, while individually they were at less risk than heavy drinkers, there are many more of them. It was research of this kind that led health professionals to advocate alcohol policies and health promotion campaigns that attempt to reduce levels of consumption among *all* drinkers, rather than focusing only on heavy drinkers (Stockwell 1995:126).

Subsequent research, both in Australia and overseas, has revealed that occasional binge drinking, rather than average weekly consumption, is a better predictor of alcohol-related harm (Hawks 1992; Crawford 1993). These findings are important, for both the general population and indigenous groups, because they direct attention to the need to reduce the frequency of occasions when people drink excessively. Among the non-indigenous population this is most likely among the young, those aged between 16 and 29 (Lang *et al.* 1991). As we have indicated elsewhere in this book, although there are more indigenous than non-indigenous abstainers, those indigenous people who do drink are much more likely to drink excessively. Researchers such as Stockwell (1995:127) see this research as providing the justification for refocusing control policies and health promotion on binge drinkers, especially given the growing research linking moderate alcohol consumption with reductions in cardiovascular disease (Addiction Research Foundation 1993).

Alcohol control, consumption levels and alcohol-related harm

Although research has shown that there is a relationship between the availability of alcohol, levels of consumption, and alcohol-related harm, as indicated above, the relationship is not straightforward. It is necessary, therefore, to try to specify those control measures that have consistently been linked with reduced consumption levels. The price of alcohol, outlet density, hours of trading, and the legal drinking age have all been investigated.

Although there is some evidence that methodological and situational factors affect the observed relationship between the price of alcohol and sales (Gruenewald 1993), all available research shows that as the price of alcohol increases, sales will decrease (Lloyd 1985, in Stockwell 1995:132). Although 'commonsense' ideas about heavy drinkers would suggest otherwise, there is good evidence that these people are as likely to modify their drinking patterns in response to price changes in alcohol as light and moderate drinkers (Kendell, de Roumaine & Ritson 1983; Babor *et al.* 1978).

Various forms of taxation on the production, importation and sale of alcohol have long been an important contributor to government revenue; and the levels of such taxes significantly affect the price paid by consumers, and hence levels of consumption. Micro-level changes in the price of alcohol, such as the discounting of drinks during 'happy hours', also affect the consumption levels of both light and heavy drinkers (Babor *et al.* 1978). Although there is little evidence to link this type of promotion to increased levels of alcohol-related harm (probably because of the short duration of the promotions), such discounting has been shown to contribute to violence on licensed premises (Smart & Adlaf 1986; Homel *et al.* 1992).

Controls in many liquor licensing jurisdictions on the number of licensed outlets may have more to do with concerns about the economic viability of such outlets than levels of consumption. Although research has shown a link between the density of liquor outlets and levels of alcohol-related harm, most workers have been unable to demonstrate whether increases in the number of outlets stimulate demand for alcohol or simply reflect stronger demand from customers (Stockwell 1995:133–4). However, one cross-sectional time-series study of outlet densities in the United States has shown that increases in the number of liquor outlets *preceded* increases in the level of consumption of wine and spirits (sales data for beer were not available) (Gruenewald *et al.* 1993). As we will show later, this type of research accords with local communities' understandings, and supports their efforts to limit the number of liquor outlets.

Much less ambiguous than data on outlet density is the evidence from Australia and elsewhere showing a strong relationship between the minimum legal drinking age and alcohol-related morbidity and mortality (Smith 1989b; Wagenaar 1993; Smith & Burvill 1986). In all places where the legal drinking age has been lowered – thus increasing the size of the market and levels of consumption – studies have shown it to be followed by dramatic increases in alcohol-related harm. For example, in Western Australia in 1970, when the legal drinking age was lowered from 21 to 18 years, rates for serious assaults by juveniles increased by 231 per cent when compared with the state of Queensland (Dull & Giacopassi 1988, in Stockwell 1995:134–5). Although there is clear evidence that raising the legal drinking age prevents alcohol-related harm, such a move is seen by many young people and their advocates as an affront to their civil liberties. Attempts to raise the legal drinking age are therefore politically fraught. At issue too is the extent to which the legal drinking age affects indigenous populations, among which young people comprise significantly higher proportions.

A number of liquor licensing authorities have restricted the trading hours of licensed premises in order to satisfy community demands (d'Abbs, Togni & Crundall 1996). However, the evidence linking restricted trading hours with reduced consumption is at best equivocal. For instance, a Western Australian study of the effect of extended trading hours in the city of Fremantle – introduced for the 1987 America's Cup yacht racing series – did not show any significant increases in either consumption or alcohol-related harm (McLaughlin & Harrison-Stewart 1992). In this study, it appeared that local residents were least likely to take advantage of the extended trading hours, except heavier drinkers, who welcomed the opportunity to drink in hotels after midnight.

Results such as these have led influential researchers to claim that in most contemporary western societies, where alcohol has become much more available, small-scale restrictions on trading hours of licensed outlets are unlikely to have much effect (Nieuwenhuysen 1986), and therefore place an unnecessary restriction on the drinking habits of the general population. As we show in our chapter on alcohol interventions, however, the relevance of this research for indigenous drinking needs to be considered carefully.

To some extent attempts by indigenous communities in Australia to restrict the supply and promotion of alcohol have taken place outside the debates in the non-indigenous population about the proper role of alcohol control policies and their effects. Instead, most attempts at control have come from local-level 'gut feelings': the need to stem the flow of alcohol in as many ways as are acceptable to local people. Some, however, have linked these grass-roots actions with broader understandings of the ways in which the alcohol industry has operated against the best interests of indigenous peoples.

Profit seeking by the alcohol industry

Marcia Langton sees the focus on the misuse of alcohol by indigenous people in Australia as part of a colonial construct of the 'drunken Aborigine', which:

> . . . glosses over the economic facts of the distribution of alcohol. The icon also deprives the set of problems involved in the misuse of alcohol by indigenous people of the contradictions, ambiguities and subtleties to do with

the social use of alcohol in indigenous and non-indigenous societies. The 'drunken Abo' does not require that the economic and political factors which lead to and perpetuate the misuse of alcohol be understood or that any theoretical approach which might include such questions as 'Who benefits from the distribution of alcohol to indigenous people? Who profits?' be developed. Such questions are quite simply unnecessary to the discourse of racial superiority (Langton 1993:199).

Clearly, although they are not the only ones to do so, those who profit most directly from the sale of alcohol to indigenous people are those who produce and those who sell alcohol, and increases in their profits are primarily dependent upon increases in consumption.

It is in the interest of national and multinational producers of alcoholic beverages to increase consumption of their products in all segments of the market. However, as indigenous people comprise only a small segment of the national market, they are not directly targeted in alcohol promotions. Rather, it is at regional and local levels, where indigenous people represent a larger market segment, that direct promotion, by retailers, takes place.

A study of the use of sex shows to sell alcohol to indigenous people in Tennant Creek in the Northern Territory provides some answers to the questions raised by Langton (Boffa, George & Tsey 1994). A decline in the town's economic fortunes following the closure of the meatworks and downturns in mining in the mid-1980s led to increased promotion by local licensees to attract a share of the reduced market. The Tennant Creek Hotel, historically a place for indigenous drinkers, was bought in 1987 by Australian Frontier Holidays, which had previously used sex shows to promote alcohol sales elsewhere in Australia. Sex shows in the Tennant Creek Hotel included live sex acts and audience participation, and the presence of many under-age patrons.

An anti-sex show coalition – including local politicians, members of the indigenous community and public health practitioners – was pitted against miners, cattlemen, hotel owners and others who wanted the shows to continue. The hotel owners bowed to public opinion only after adverse publicity seriously affected their national image and led to local boycotts of the hotel. Subsequent changes to the Northern Territory *Liquor Act 1979*

> . . . made it compulsory for licensees to warn the public that the shows were on, to conduct them behind closed doors, not to allow audience participation and to keep a specific distance between the strippers and audience (Boffa *et al.* 1994:363).

The importance of the action, for our purpose, is the clear connection made by indigenous and other participants between the availability of alcohol and alcohol-related problems, and the perceived need to identify those instances where the profit motives of the liquor industry are opposed to the public interests of indigenous individuals and groups. Subsequent to this action, an inter-agency group formed a 'Beat the Grog' campaign, and resolved to: oppose new liquor licences and alcohol sales promotion; demand strict enforcement of laws on under-age drinking and sale of alcohol to intoxicated people; and support grog-free concerts, further reduction in trading hours, and the declaration of more alcohol-free living areas in communities. Another significant outcome of the action was the adoption by the Northern Territory Legislative Assembly of a special liquor tax – recommended in 1989 by the Sessional Committee on the Use and Abuse of Alcohol by the Community – raising $10 million annually for alcohol prevention, rehabilitation and treatment programs. Indigenous and other community groups have subsequently benefited from these funds (Boffa *et al.* 1994:364).

Research by one of us (DG) in Western Australia, with indigenous community-controlled agencies, identified a number of other strategies used by local suppliers of alcohol to increase their market share among indigenous patrons. These included sales to minors and intoxicated persons, credit sales, promotion of low-cost, high-alcohol beverages, early trading, and reduction of costs by not providing appropriate levels of amenity on their premises (Gray *et al.* 1995). These practices were not investigated in detail, and we realised that what was needed were local-level analyses of the ways in which alcohol is sold and promoted, details of which are discussed below. What this research also highlights is the important role of the state in the control of alcohol supply to indigenous communities.

The role of the state

The role of the state (that is the legislative, judicial and administrative arms of the federal and state/territory governments) with regard to the consumption of alcohol among indigenous people cannot be considered apart from its broader roles. From colonial times the Australian state has 'mobilised public resources for private gain' (Davis *et al.* 1988:15). That is, the state has acted to promote the interests and development of the private sector. Despite the rhetoric of aggrieved or extreme advocates of private enterprise, no government has acted in a contrary manner. However, this action has not occurred in an untrammelled way. In order to maintain its legitimacy, the state must be seen to be responsive to the concerns and welfare of a broader constituency.

Since the establishment of the first British colony in Australia, the state has provided encouragement and support to the alcohol industry (or sections of it). It has done so in the interests of the industry itself and because of the revenue the state obtains through various forms of taxation, licensing fees, and excise duties. Nevertheless, the state has had to balance competing interests, and at various times has acted to curb levels of alcohol consumption. Such restrictions have been put in place when levels of consumption and its consequences have been perceived by sections of the private sector as threatening the productivity of workers, as being a disproportionate cost to government and/or tax-payers, or as being disruptive of social life. When such threats have receded, restrictions have been relaxed (Lewis 1992).

At times such as the present, when the service industries are increasingly dominating the economy, the support by the state for the liquor industry has been particularly explicit. For example, the stated objectives of the Western Australian *Liquor Licensing Act 1988* include:

- to regulate and contribute to the proper development of the liquor, hospitality and related industries in the state;
- to cater for the requirements of the tourism industry; (and)
- to facilitate the use and development of licensed facilities ...

Such legislation provides a framework that facilitates efforts by various segments of the alcohol industry to vigorously promote and sell their products. The thrust of this legislation is to regulate the industry *per se* (rather than the impact of alcohol on the community) and to ensure its economic viability. Furthermore, various provisions of the Western Australian legislation, purportedly designed to facilitate community input, actually serve to hinder community attempts to restrict the availability of alcohol (Gray *et al.* 1995). Such provisions include culturally inappropriate measures for the advertising of licence applications and cumbersome procedures for the lodging of complaints.

Currently we are examining liquor licensing legislation in all states and territories of Australia to determine the extent to which they meet indigenous community demands for harm minimisation and community participation objectives. Although the research is incomplete, there appears to be considerable variation across Australia with respect to the way in which state and territory legislators acknowledge community, particularly indigenous, interests in the granting of liquor licences.

Aboriginal affairs policy

As well as evaluating its policies with regard to the promotion of the private sector in general and the alcohol industry in particular, when examining the role of the state with regard to indigenous alcohol consumption, it is also necessary to consider specific policy towards indigenous alcohol consumption and broader indigenous affairs policy. In the past 200 years the state has had, and continues to have, a significant role in the lives of indigenous people, even to the extent of attempting to define who is and who is not indigenous and the degree of Aboriginality. While not completely successful in its aims, for most of this period the state has sought to impose limitations on the availability of alcohol to indigenous peoples.

In the nineteenth century, it was the official policy of the British colonial governments that the interests of indigenous people should be 'protected' (although the meaning of this was limited). Part of this protection included prohibition of the supply of alcohol to indigenous people, and various pieces of legislation were passed giving effect to this (Brady 1990a; Eggleston 1974; Lewis 1992). Such prohibition was not all altruistic; in part it was a response to the colonists' fears and sensibilities about the behaviour of intoxicated indigenous people. However, Langton has argued that despite official policy, alcohol was used

> ... unconsciously or consciously as a device for seducing indigenous people to engage economically, politically and socially with the colony (1993:201).

Brady also cites accounts of early colonial life where Europeans enticed indigenous people with alcohol so that they would fight or provide sex (Brady 1990a). Furthermore, again in the interests of the private sector, in Western Australia early prohibition on the supply of alcohol to indigenous people specifically excluded employers, who were permitted to pay indigenous employees with alcohol rather than wages (McCorquodale 1987).

From the 1920s through to the 1960s, access to alcohol was a potent symbol in the attempt by various governments to assimilate indigenous people. As we have discussed in Chapter 4, among the benefits of citizenship granted to those who limited their contact with other indigenous people and who adopted a European lifestyle was the 'right' to purchase and consume alcohol. Conversely, withdrawal of citizenship was a sanction imposed on those who were frequently inebriated or who used their right of citizenship to purchase alcohol for others (Biskup 1973; Brady 1990a).

In the 1960s, as a consequence of indigenous resistance to assimilation, increased international scrutiny and the dominance of liberal ideology, Australian governments began the repeal of legislation that restricted the rights of indigenous people, and adopted the policies first of integration and then self-determination/self-management. These legislative and policy changes included the provision of the right to vote in 1962, constitutional amendment to count indigenous people as Australian citizens in 1967, and relaxation of restrictions on the availability of alcohol to indigenous people. It should be noted, however, that at least in Western Australia there remain in force legal provisions against street and park drinking, which impact disproportionately against indigenous people (Gray *et al.* 1995).

Elsewhere we have argued that, despite attempts at amelioration, the ill health of indigenous people is a direct consequence of indigenous affairs policy and practice (Saggers & Gray 1991; Gray & Saggers 1994). Similarly, the excessive consumption of alcohol and resultant harm among indigenous people are consequences of the same policies. These policies have created the groups and the conditions that have had the indirect consequence of promoting consumption through the stimulation of excessive demand for alcohol.

As we have shown, the excessive demand for alcohol among sections of the indigenous population is recognised by both indigenous and non-indigenous people as being linked to colonial relations of dependence, experiences shared by indigenous peoples elsewhere:

> Tangentyere (Council) recognises that alcohol abuse is only a symptom of an even more profound distress in contemporary indigenous life which flows directly from people's experiences of colonisation, their brutal dispossession and removal from traditional lands and from continuing assaults on their culture and community (Lyon 1990:14).

Apart from the dispossession of indigenous people and their marginalisation from the dominant economy, colonialism in Australia created different levels of indigenous sociality, and these creations have exacerbated the consumption of alcohol and its control. For example, indigenous people from different language and clan groups were herded into government settlements run by welfare authorities or missionaries, and subsequently came to be known as 'communities' (Brady 1990a). Most of these settlements were marginalised economically, socially and politically from mainstream society. Indigenous people from these so-called communities in Western Australia, South Australia and the Northern Territory subsequently formed the nuclei of heavy drinking camps, with associated high levels of alcohol-related harm (Brady 1988; Brady & Palmer 1984; Collmann 1979; Sackett 1988).

Control of availability in indigenous Australian communities

While indigenous affairs policy has had the effect of promoting alcohol consumption and, over the past three decades, legislative change has had the effect of increasing the availability of alcohol to indigenous people, some sections of indigenous communities have sought to reduce excessive consumption through controls on the availability of alcohol. These attempts highlight ideological differences within both indigenous communities and the wider society, and the ambiguous role of the state.

The issue of the rights and responsibilities associated with alcohol and citizenship have been thoughtfully addressed by Rowse. Using a Foucauldian perspective, he illustrates how:

> ... the content of 'citizenship' is not only variable historically (through time) and culturally, but is also subject, in any one time/jurisdiction, to disjoint logics (or 'rationalities') of government (1993:394).

He shows that the 'progressive liberalism' which, in the 1960s, sought to improve the conditions of indigenous peoples by arguing for an end to legal inequalities between indigenous and non-indigenous Australians, 'constitutes a new conservatism', which opposes indigenous attempts to control the availability of alcohol and reduce its harm on the same grounds (Rowse 1993:394).

Counter to this, political progressives have proposed an alternative construction of rights based on notions of the rights of cultural groups. This would allow indigenous community groups to control the availability of alcohol, on the grounds that non-indigenous drinking patterns are:

> ... neither culturally suitable nor sufficiently accessible to be put into practice by most Central Australian Aborigines (Rowse 1993:395).

The Race Discrimination Commissioner has taken the matter of the collective rights of groups further in the *Alcohol Report* (Australia, Race Discrimination Commissioner 1995) and recommends changes to the *Racial Discrimination Act 1975* to ensure that collective rights in areas such as alcohol distribution have legal status (1995:154). This would enable community interest to be defined more narrowly in terms of the health and social consequences for people living in specific areas. However, such a definition is problematic. This approach challenges a widely asserted view of the autonomy of the individual in indigenous communities (based on both traditional values of being one's own 'boss' and the historical link between citizenship and the right to drink), and the consequent difficulties in controlling drunken behaviour (Brady 1990a).

This ideological conflict is reflected also in the non-indigenous community. As Lyon (1990) notes, in the Northern Territory there has been a fluctuation between an economically 'wet' approach, supporting increases in government control over the availability of alcohol and, to a lesser extent, spending on programs; and a 'dry' approach, favouring individual responsibility, free enterprise and small government. In Lyon's (1990) view, the extent of alcohol-related problems in the Territory warranted the former approach. It is a view shared by many indigenous people. In the words of Iamampa:

> The Liquor Commission is not interested in us and is not listening to us. . . . We have been talking for too many years and too many people are dying, and still nobody wants to make the hard decisions to help our people (in Lyon 1991:13).

At the same time as these philosophical and political debates are occurring, indigenous and non-indigenous groups have been pragmatically attempting to limit the sale and consumption of alcohol by legislative means. d'Abbs (1990) has identified three approaches aimed at restricting the consumption of alcohol within certain areas:

• The community control model, embodied in Western Australia's *Aboriginal Communities Act 1979*, enables some indigenous communities to establish their own by-laws to regulate alcohol consumption (among other things), but provides little support for enforcement of those by-laws.

• The statutory control model, exemplified by provisions of the South Australian *Liquor Licensing Act 1985*, which enables local councils to apply to have certain areas declared 'dry', and by provisions of the Northern Territory *Summary Offences Act* introduced in 1983 (the 'Two Kilometre Law'), which make it an offence to consume alcohol in a public place within two kilometres of a licensed premises.

• The complementary control model, which combines both community and statutory control. It is exemplified by provisions of the Northern Territory *Liquor Act 1979*, which enable indigenous communities to apply for various restrictions on availability and provide for enforcement of those provisions.

Important philosophical differences underlie these models. While the community and complementary control models aim to give varying degrees of control to indigenous people, most commentators see the 'Two Kilometre Law' as a transparent attempt to clear the streets of indigenous drinkers while doing nothing to address the underlying problems. Designated alcohol-free zones in NSW have apparently served a similar purpose (Mark & Hennessy 1991).

In reviewing the success of these models of control, d'Abbs (1990) stresses the need to separate concerns about public drunkenness from those of prevention of alcohol abuse. Policies to deter public drunkenness should not impede individuals or groups from acting against alcohol-related harm. d'Abbs claims that restricted area policies will be successful only if they promote the capacity of indigenous individuals and groups to control the use of alcohol, and that they require support to enforce restrictions, given the vested interests in the sale and promotion of alcohol and the widespread desire for drinking. For these reasons, d'Abbs (1990:132) supports the complementary control model, particularly the restricted area provisions of the Northern Territory *Liquor Act.*

There are a number of studies describing attempts at restricting alcohol consumption under these legislative arrangements (d'Abbs 1990; Larkins & McDonald 1984; Mark & Hennessy 1991; Langton 1992; Lyon 1990, 1991). The general consensus appears to be that they have been a qualified success. Reviewing Northern Territory initiatives in the early 1980s, Larkins & McDonald (1984) cite the improved standards of licensed premises, easier public access to the licensing and review process, restricted areas designation, and restrictions on trading hours for take-away sales as being well received by indigenous people and health and welfare agencies, if not the liquor industry.

Research we are doing on liquor licensing legislation throughout Australia suggests that indigenous control over alcohol in the Northern Territory may be under threat. The Northern Territory *Liquor Act* is currently being rewritten, and discussions we have held with key stakeholders revealed widespread dissatisfaction, among police in particular, with restricted area provisions. Citing problems with indigenous people from remote areas visiting Darwin and other centres to obtain alcohol, and high rates of alcohol-related accidents on roads between 'wet' and 'dry' communities, some police stated that all communities should make provision for their drinking populations. This suggestion has alarmed some indigenous groups, which want to maintain restricted areas as a respite for women, children and non-drinkers.

Attempts to restrict the availability of alcohol under various liquor licensing Acts have been pushed even further by community groups. In November 1992, as a result of petitioning by the Halls Creek Alcohol Action Advisory Committee in Western Australia, the Director of Liquor Licensing placed restrictions on the sale of packaged alcohol in the town. Under the new regulations, the sale of packaged alcohol was prohibited prior to midday on any day, and cask wine could only be sold between 4:00 pm and 6:00 pm, with a limit of one cask or flagon per person (Holmes 1994).

A 13-week trial of 'grog free days', prohibiting trading in hotel front bars and bottle shops on Thursdays was introduced in Tennant Creek in 1995. This was the first time bans were imposed on non-indigenous as well as indigenous people in an Australian town with a majority of non-indigenous residents – 3,000 total population with indigenous people comprising about 35 per cent – and they resulted from an appeal to the Northern Territory Liquor Commission by women from the local Julalikari Association. The bans were opposed by alcohol retailers in the town, one of whom estimated that the ban had cost her $5,000, or half her week's earnings in the first week of operation. Local indigenous women, however, had no reservations:

> We are pretty happy with it and the old people too. It's the first time they have had decent sleep (Valda Shannon, of the Julalikari Association, *The West Australian*, August 19, 1995:38).

Attempts by indigenous people to restrict alcohol sale and consumption demonstrate an understanding of the link between availability and excessive consumption, and the need

> . . . to remove alcohol from an everyday item and return it to its position as a special substance, a drug which must be treated with caution (Langton 1992:23).

These comments by indigenous people, and the various actions taken by communities to restrict the availability of alcohol, suggested to us the need for more rigorous research on the ways in which the alcohol industry operates in the local community. Many people desiring controls over availability assume that unfettered competition between liquor outlets and demands for greater profitability prompt hotels and liquor stores to promote and sell alcohol as aggressively as they can. However, apart from a few studies, such as that by Boffa *et al.* (1994), very little is known of the strategies used by the alcohol industry to sell and promote their products. This makes it difficult to plan effective interventions, and provided the impetus for our own research on the supply and promotion of alcohol.

Supply and promotion of alcohol in two Western Australian towns

Recently, with the support and assistance of local indigenous community organisations, we examined the supply and promotion of alcohol to indigenous people in two rural Western Australian towns. The objectives of the project were to: document the extent of alcohol consumption and related harm in both locations; describe alcohol promotion activities used by licensees; examine the extent to which these factors influence drinking patterns of indigenous people; and identify factors that may be amenable to acceptable and appropriate intervention by local communities. To do this, as well as collecting various documentary data, we and our colleagues interviewed a range of people – including indigenous community members, the licensees or managers of liquor outlets, and representatives of various government agencies – and made direct observations in each of the liquor outlets.

The towns and the local indigenous people differ in significant ways. Needup (pseudonyms are used for both towns) is located in the south of the state and has a total population of around 19,000 people. It is the centre of a rich agricultural industry and has a thriving tourist trade. Indigenous people comprise a little over 2 per cent of the population, and come from a number of small, outlying localities where their ancestors had been dispossessed of their land soon after initial European settlement in Western Australia.

Mitchell, located in the northwest of WA, has a population of about 7,000. Its economy is diverse, being centred on pastoral, mining, fishing and tourist industries. About 15 per cent of Mitchell's population are indigenous people. Indigenous cultures in the town are diverse, with many people being urbanised but a significant proportion maintaining contacts with 'country', where outstations are maintained.

Alcohol sales and consumption

Needup had a total of 35 licensed premises. These included nine hotels or taverns. The difference between hotels and taverns is that the former provide accommodation in addition to sales of alcohol. Colloquially both are called 'pubs', and for convenience we will simply refer to them as hotels in what follows. In addition to the nine hotels in Needup, there were four take-away liquor stores, and 22 other outlets (mainly clubs and restaurants). This gives a figure of 1.85 licensed premises per 1,000 people. Mitchell had 15 licensed premises, five hotels or taverns, three take-away liquor stores, and seven other types of outlet: 2.1 outlets per 1,000 people.

As no routinely collected data are available on alcohol consumption, we used data on the amount of alcoholic beverages purchased by licensees for sale in 1995–96 as a proxy measure. In 1995–96, these purchases totalled 2,908,148 litres in Needup and 1,777,674 litres in Mitchell. At least some of the purchases made by these licensees were sold for consumption outside the towns. However, it is likely that this percentage was relatively small, and was similar for both towns. On a *per capita* basis, consumption of alcoholic beverages in Needup was approximately 154 litres per person per year. For Mitchell the rate was approximately 258 litres per person per year, 1.7 times the rate of consumption in Needup.

In Table 10, we present each beverage type by the type of outlet from which they were sold as a percentage of total alcohol purchases in each town in 1995–96. In both towns the most commonly consumed beverage was high-alcohol beer (47 per cent in Needup and 48 per cent in

Table 10   Alcoholic beverage consumption (litres) by licence type by town, 1995–96*

Town	Licence type	High beer %	High wine %	Spirits %	Low beer %	Low wine %	Total %
Needup	Hotel/tavern	23	4	3	8	1	39
N = 2,908,148	Liquor store	20	11	3	19	0	53
	Other	4	1	0	2	0	7
		47	16	6	30	1	100
Mitchell	Hotel/tavern	19	1	2	7	0	30
N = 1,777,674	Liquor store	28	9	2	26	1	65
	Other	1	0	0	3	0	4
		48	11	4	36	1	100

*Errors due to rounding
Source: Western Australia Office of Racing, Gaming and Liquor

Mitchell), followed by low-alcohol beer (30 and 36 per cent of total purchases). In Needup, as a proportion of total purchases, purchases of high-alcohol wine were 1.45 times greater than in Mitchell.

Although we do not have statistical data, observation and interviews indicate that there was a significant difference in the type of high-alcohol wine purchased in each town. In Needup, a large proportion of high-alcohol wine was premium bottled wine, whereas in Mitchell, most high-alcohol wine is purchased in relatively inexpensive four-litre casks.

In Needup 53 per cent, and in Mitchell 65 per cent, of all alcoholic beverages were purchased from take-away liquor stores; and in both towns nationally based liquor stores made sales greatly in excess of both their off-licence and on-licence competitors. In addition to sales from liquor stores, an unknown proportion of sales from hotels were for consumption off premises.

In both towns, the number of hotels was about twice the number of liquor stores, and their individual shares of the market were generally lower than those of liquor stores. However, again in both towns, those hotels that made the greatest proportion of sales were those that had large take-away bottle shops. These were also the hotels that sold the largest proportion of high-alcohol wine. While the number of other licence types – mainly licensed restaurants and clubs – was greater than, or almost equal to, the number of hotel/tavern and liquor store licences, their combined proportion of sales in each town was relatively small (7 and 4 per cent).

Table 11   Estimated percentages of alcohol-caused hospital discharges by sex by Aboriginality by town, 1995*

Town	Alcohol-related condition	Indigenous		Non-indigenous		Total
		Male	Female	Male	Female	
Needup	Alcoholic psychosis	1	0	1	1	3
$N = 161$	Alcohol dependence	0	3	4	1	7
	Alcohol abuse	0	0	4	4	7
	Alcoholic gastritis	1	0	2	0	2
	Alcoholic liver cirrhosis	0	1	1	0	1
	Chronic pancreatitis	2	0	1	2	6
	Road injuries	0	0	9	1	11
	Fall injuries	1	1	13	19	33
	Assault	1	1	8	1	12
	Other alcohol-related conditions	0	1	9	7	17
		5	7	52	36	100
Mitchell	Alcoholic psychosis	1	1	1	0	3
$N = 379$	Alcohol dependence	2	3	12	1	17
	Alcohol abuse	2	3	0	0	4
	Alcoholic gastritis	3	0	4	0	8
	Alcoholic liver cirrhosis	0	2	2	0	3
	Chronic pancreatitis	5	0	5	0	10
	Road injuries	0	1	3	1	4
	Fall injuries	4	2	6	5	17
	Assault	12	11	3	3	28
	Other alcohol-related conditions	2	1	3	2	7
		30	22	38	11	100

*Errors due to rounding
Source: Western Australia Health Department

Alcohol-related harm

In Needup in 1995, it was estimated that there were 161 hospital discharges for conditions that were caused by alcohol, a rate of 8.54 per thousand person–years. In Mitchell, there were 379 alcohol-related discharges, yielding a rate of 54.9 per thousand person–years, a rate more than six times that in Needup. In Table 11 the percentages of these discharges, by condition, by Aboriginality and by sex, are presented for each town. The figures on which the table is based are too small to permit meaningful comment about individual conditions. However, in Needup indigenous people comprised 2 per cent of the population but accounted for 12 per cent of hospital discharges; and in Mitchell they

Table 12 Percentage of arrests by selected offences by Aboriginality by sex by town, 1995*

| Town | Offence | Indigenous | | Non-indigenous | | |
		Male	Female	Male	Female	Total
Needup	Assaults	9	3	16	2	30
N = 318	Property damage	3	1	13	0	17
	Liquor licensing	2	1	11	1	15
	Trespassing & vagrancy	0	0	2	0	3
	Other offences against good order	8	4	22	2	35
		21	9	64	5	100
Mitchell	Assaults	16	6	3	1	26
N = 419	Property damage	7	1	2	0	10
	Liquor licensing	11	2	2	0	14
	Trespassing & vagrancy	4	0	1	0	5
	Other offences against good order	26	7	9	1	43
		63	16	17	3	99

*Errors due to rounding and missing data
Source: Crime Research Centre, University of Western Australia

comprised 15 per cent of the population but 54 per cent of alcohol-related hospital discharges. That is, their representation was 5.5 and 3.4 times greater in the Needup and Mitchell hospital discharge data than their proportion of the populations of each town, respectively.

Table 12 provides the percentage of arrests for offences usually associated with alcohol, by Aboriginality and sex, for each town in 1995. In Needup there was a total of 318 arrests, a rate of 16.7 per thousand person–years. In Mitchell, the number of arrests for these offences was 419, a rate of 59.9 per thousand person–years. As with hospital discharges, indigenous people were disproportionately represented in the arrest data. In Needup, indigenous people comprised 30 per cent of those arrested, or 13.6 times their proportion of the total population; and in Mitchell they made up 79 per cent of those arrested for these offences, or 5.1 times their proportion of the population.

As would be expected, perceptions of indigenous drinking varied according to the perspectives of those being interviewed. In general, because of the small proportion of indigenous people in the town, and because of the locations in which it took place – despite the statistical data presented above – indigenous drinking in Needup was not viewed by most people as a major problem. As one of the licensees said:

> When I think of Aboriginal drinking I think of places like Halls Creek and the Northern Territory. I've been here two and a half years and it seems to me that the local Aboriginal people are more responsible.

Those most likely to view it with concern were workers with welfare or community organisations, several of whom cited mental health problems and crime associated with heavy drinking as playing a major role in their daily work. They indicated that the problems were concentrated in particular families. For the young, drinking was also seen as an important rite of passage. One indigenous informant said that young people are 'in charge of their life if they get drunk and still stand up. Getting a charge is being in charge'.

In contrast, in Mitchell the problematic nature of some indigenous drinking was more widely acknowledged. Much of the behaviour that was regarded as antisocial was attributed by non-indigenous people, and many indigenous people, to those residing in an indigenous housing estate on the outskirts of town. The term 'Aboriginal drinking' was used by many only to describe the behaviour of people from the estate or those whose behaviour was problematic.

Government and community workers in Mitchell were unanimous in their views that drinking by indigenous people was a significant contributor to poor health and social conditions in the town. The police estimated that 95 per cent of their work was involved with alcohol-related crime and public order issues, citing recent public concern with young indigenous people, and law and order issues. Welfare authorities spoke of the negative impact on children of their parents' drinking – including poor school attendance, and adolescents and younger children roaming the streets and sometimes becoming involved in criminal activity.

Supply and promotion strategies

Potential patrons did not form a homogeneous market with similar demands for alcohol and other services. Thus licensees sought to cater for particular niches within the broader market. The market segment they attracted was a consequence of both the strategies they employed (and the resources available to implement a set of strategies) and local demand factors. Determining the extent to which Aboriginality influences supply, promotion and demand of alcohol is a complex matter. Although we collected data on many promotional strategies, we report here only on those we found to have some impact on indigenous people in these particular towns; thus we exclude, for example, material on so-called 'happy hours', sex promotions, and the provision of food.

Off-licence premises and on-licence premises

In both Needup and Mitchell the most obvious division in the market was between those who purchase alcohol for off-licence consumption and those who drink on licensed premises. The former were catered for both by liquor stores and, to a lesser extent, by the bottle shops of hotels. The major strategies used by liquor stores were price and location, and each aimed to attract (within the constraints imposed by location) a broad range of those who drink off-licence. Reliance on these strategies was reflected in the uniform amenity of those premises, most of which were either owned by or affiliated with large discount liquor chains, which have certain minimum standards for their outlets.

In both towns, anecdotal evidence suggested, and our observations confirmed, that most indigenous drinking occurred off licensed premises. Liquor stores captured a significant proportion of indigenous drinkers. For example, in Needup, licensees estimated that indigenous people ranged from 10 to 40 per cent of their clients, and in Mitchell, the proportion was even higher. The managers of two liquor stores estimated indigenous patronage at about 60 per cent, while the third licensee suggested that around 50 per cent of his clientele were Aboriginal.

The market advantage enjoyed by off-licence premises caused resentment on the part of some hotel/tavern owners in both towns, but particularly in Mitchell, and some licensees attributed indigenous drinking problems to the cheaper alcohol available through them. However, in both towns the bottle shops of some hotels also had proportions of indigenous patrons at least twice those of their proportion in the population in each town. Indigenous people tended to use those outlets primarily for convenience of access by motor vehicle, or during late evenings when liquor stores were closed – although in Needup, one hotel/tavern sold four-litre casks of wine more cheaply than any of the liquor stores.

Drive-through service offered customers a higher level of security, as others were not harassing them for alcohol or money, a situation seen by both indigenous and non-indigenous people as problematic in Mitchell, and people were prepared to pay slightly higher prices for this service:

> Our policy here is safe and secure service, and we make sure that in our bottle shop we actually advertise that publicly. Directing straight at . . . (a discount liquor store) again, which I can dirt [*sic*], because it's very unsafe sometimes to be walking around through the back doors, every second person who goes there gets hassled. Yeah they'll get a cheap price but no one wants to pay an extra $5 and get hassled . . . Here, they drive in the bottle shop, they get what they want, if there's anybody lurking around here they get shunted real quick (Licensee, hotel bottle shop, Mitchell).

The high levels of taxi use by indigenous people also made drive-through purchase more financially viable, rather than have a taxi wait while they made an in-store purchase. Once alcohol was purchased, drinking could take place at a number of locations. In Needup, there was little public drinking – the exception being by young people on Friday and Saturday nights in a park on the main street. In Mitchell, by contrast, public drinking was more visible, and included a wide age group, with people congregating at a number of well known locations. While this visibility was partly a consequence of the larger proportion of indigenous people in the town, other factors included a larger transient indigenous population and a climate that is more congenial to drinking outdoors throughout the year.

In contrast to the liquor stores, hotels each aimed to attract a particular sub-segment of that segment of the market which drank on licensed premises. In Needup, most catered for either predominantly blue-collar patrons, or for a predominantly white-collar or white-collar and family or tourist clientele; while a small number provided separate bars for both types of patrons, or, particularly on weekends, aimed at a largely undifferentiated youth market. This kind of distinction was more blurred in Mitchell, where the white-collar market was considerably smaller.

A typical blue-collar establishment in both towns was clean and relatively well maintained (much less so in Mitchell), had practical but inexpensive furnishings, durable and usually quite old floor coverings, bar-snack or counter-meal type food, and a range of games. Drinking mostly took place at the bar or in the immediate vicinity of pool tables and darts boards, despite there being a number of tables and chairs available throughout the area.

The white-collar or family-oriented hotels had a higher grade of furnishings and floor coverings, and a range of quality foods. They tended to have more restrictive dress standards, and had a more genteel atmosphere than the blue-collar premises. Clerical workers, public servants and business people, and women in particular, frequented this type of premises. While these class-based distinctions were fairly obvious in Needup, they were much less so in Mitchell. There the distinction was between the two almost exclusively blue-collar pubs, and the others, which catered to both blue- and white-collar workers in particular bars, and for particular events.

In addition to these two broad types of drinking environment, Needup, with its larger resident and more affluent tourist populations, also supported a five-star hotel and two 'boutique' hotel/taverns. These had more expensive furnishings, collectibles or artwork, open fireplaces, and stylish fittings. They provided food of four- to five-star quality, a range of premium alcohol (boutique beers, bottled wines and spirits), and a very high standard of service.

While no licensee spoke of attempting to discourage indigenous take-away custom, some hotel/tavern licensees admitted to attempting to deter indigenous people or 'problem' indigenous drinkers from their premises. One Mitchell licensee said:

> We actually discourage them from drinking here. We do this by not opening until 12 o'clock on any day. In no way do we encourage them from drinking at our premises. I'm not racist but they can't handle alcohol and they become a complete and utter nuisance to my premises because of my good, regular clientele.

Although a small number sought to discourage all indigenous people, it was more common for licensees to speak about the ways they tried to discourage 'problem' indigenous drinkers, particularly by means of the application of strict dress standards and by complying with laws against the serving of intoxicated patrons. This itself might have had the effect of incidentally encouraging what they considered to be a 'better' indigenous clientele. For instance, one licensee in Mitchell said that the use of such strategies encouraged some young indigenous women to use his bar.

Price and active discouragement by licensees were not the only reasons that some indigenous people did not drink on licensed premises. Some preferred to drink elsewhere to avoid overtly racially motivated conflict, or because in the controlled environment of licensed premises they were unable to respond to racial taunts from non-indigenous patrons. Others, especially in Needup, were discouraged (as are some working-class non-indigenous people) by the 'up-market' surroundings and 'higher' social status of patrons in some hotels.

While none of the licensees or managers of hotels claimed to encourage indigenous patronage, and some actively discouraged it, there were in both towns hotels that were known as 'Aboriginal pubs' or that had proportions of indigenous patrons significantly in excess of their proportion in the population. In Needup, there were four hotels whose licensees or managers each reckoned indigenous people to comprise about 10 per cent of their clientele, although the attendance of these patrons was sporadic, often occurring on or after 'pension day'. In addition, a nightclub in Needup was also frequented by young indigenous people. In Mitchell, one hotel in particular was known as '*the* Aboriginal pub', with the manager estimating that 60 to 70 per cent of the clientele were Aboriginal. Two other hotels regularly attracted around 30 per cent indigenous patronage. When asked why these places were popular, licensees suggested a variety of reasons including location (proximity to residences), in-house TAB, pool tables, popularity with young people, and price with respect to take-aways. Some mentioned all of these.

In addition to the strategies employed by licensees, another important factor that contributed to the greater availability of alcohol in Mitchell was the role of taxi drivers. During our first visit to the town, the comparatively high number of taxis was obvious, and a number of government workers recounted anecdotes involving taxi drivers obtaining alcohol for indigenous people, including minors. One worker had previously driven for one of the taxi operators, and on the basis of his first-hand experiences, made allegations of drug dealing and bank keycard and bankbook abuse in the taxi business. According to this informant the interest rate charged was $5 for every $20 advanced by the drivers. Children were allegedly permitted to book up taxi fares against their parent's keycard, and drugs and alcohol were alleged to have been provided in the same way. Both indigenous and non-indigenous informants in the town supported these allegations. This situation is complicated by the fact that taxi drivers often provide valuable services to indigenous people who do not have cars or bank accounts, or who dislike going to banks. These informal, beneficial arrangements should not be included in the same category as exploitative relationships that encourage harmful drinking.

Trading hours

In Needup, all of the liquor stores opened between 8:00 am and 8:30 am and closed between 5:00 and 7:30 pm. The hotels opened between 10:00 and 11:00 am and were licensed to close at midnight. During our periods of fieldwork many of the hotels closed before this, sometimes several hours before midnight. In Mitchell, under the terms of a local 'Accord' between licensees and the community, none of the outlets opened until 10:00 am. Both indigenous and non-indigenous people, including licensees, cited attempts to limit indigenous drinking as the reason for the later opening hours. The liquor stores there closed between 5:30 and 8:00 pm, and the hotels between midnight and 2:00 am. All hotels in Mitchell remained open as long as they were licensed to do so.

Regulation of trading hours was seen by most licensees as an effective means of either attracting or discouraging patrons, particularly indigenous patrons; and its impact on drinking patterns varied according to the type and style of outlet. Licensees of comparably priced stores also saw control of trading hours as the means to secure a greater proportion of the same market. Mitchell's regulated trading hours meant that off-licences could not open until 10:00 am, but licensees agreed that the later opening time had not affected their total liquor sales; and for some, it has had the benefit of saving wages. Hotels also found that they mostly sold take-away liquor after the discount liquor stores had closed, especially those with drive-through bottle shops.

Table 13   Average price for selected drinks by licence type by town

Town	Licence type	Bar sale middy beer Std drink	Take-away beer		Take-away wine		Jim Beam Bourbon	
			24-can carton	Std drink	4-litre cask	Std drink	700 ml bottle	Std drink
Needup	Hotel/tavern	2.20	28.60	0.79	10.80	0.27	31.64	1.59
	Liquor store		27.11	0.75	9.96	0.25	27.15	1.36
Mitchell	Hotel/tavern	2.20	28.50	0.79	12.33	0.31	32.62	1.63
	Liquor store		28.95	0.80	9.45	0.24	26.98	1.35

Trading hours for on-licence premises appeared to be dictated more by consumer demand than licensing regulations. Many hotels shut before their official closing time because they had insufficient patrons, but one blue-collar hotel in Needup always remained open late because it serviced shift-workers.

Extended trading hours for hotels were slightly more contentious in the towns, as many premises in both towns wished to have them. Most linked extended hours to discos and live music, which in turn attracted young people and bigger crowds. This had proved to be the case for two hotels in Mitchell, which traded until 2:00 am. Requests for extended trading by two hotels in Needup were rejected, and there was a blanket ban on hotel trading after midnight in the town. Only a licensed supper club and the one nightclub were permitted to trade after that time.

Price

In both towns, the bulk of alcoholic beverages were sold by liquor stores and, to a lesser extent, hotels for off-premises consumption. The major reason for this is evident in Table 13, which presents the mean cost per 'container' and per standard drink for over-the-bar 'middy' (285 ml glass of beer) sales and for take-away beer, cask wine and Jim Beam bourbon at the time the study was conducted. These mean costs hide some variation – for example, in Needup one of the liquor stores sold cartons of beer for between $4.00 and $5.00 less than any of the hotels, and in Mitchell one of the liquor stores sold four-litre casks of wine for almost $4.00 per cask less than any of the hotels. Overall, however, the price per standard drink of take-away beer, cask wine and Jim Beam bourbon purchased from a hotel/ tavern was approximately 35, 87 and 17 per cent less than the price of a middy at the bar of one of those premises. When compared to the average price per standard drink for cask wine and bourbon from liquor stores, the difference in price was even more marked. For indigenous people, this price differential of take-away alcohol provided a powerful incentive.

While there was a marked price difference between beverages purchased for on- and off-premises consumption, there was no inter-
premises variation in over-the-bar middy prices in Mitchell, and a $0.15
variation in Needup.

As well as the standard items for which we recorded prices, the liquor
stores also provide discounts on various 'specials'. In both towns, large discount liquor stores were selling damaged four-litre wine casks at heavily
discounted prices. One store in Needup, where the normal price for a
particular wine was $12.95, was selling the 'bladders' (internal plastic sacs)
for $5.00 each and damaged boxes for $7.50 each. Similarly, in Mitchell,
bladders were being sold for $5.00 each, at a limit of one per customer.
These discounts were justified by the store managers as being more
economical than paying for freight back to the wine distributor. At these
prices, the cost per standard drink was reduced to about $0.13. Given this,
the ubiquity of bladders among many indigenous drinkers, particularly
among public drinkers in Mitchell, came as no surprise.

Location

In both towns the liquor stores and hotels with the greatest volumes of
liquor sales were centrally located. This was an important factor in attracting clients, especially tourists, for both on- and off-licence premises.
Centrality allowed people to choose where they would drink and gave
them the opportunity to move between premises if they were unsatisfied
with their current location. Those premises that were not centrally located
tended to rely upon the inconvenience of travelling to the centre of town
or particular marketing strategies, such as the provision of entertainment,
to attract patrons.

Location was one factor acknowledged by licensees to be important for
indigenous patrons. Those hotels and liquor stores close to the centre of
town, where indigenous drinkers went to collect money, shop and conduct other business, were certain to attract significant numbers of indigenous people, particularly on days when social security payments were
made.

Apart from centrality, proximity to areas of high indigenous housing or
public drinking areas guaranteed regular indigenous custom. In Mitchell,
one off-licence premises located very close to the indigenous housing
estate was popular because people from the estate could go there on foot,
or preferably, hire a taxi to go there for much less than the fare to town.

Dress standards and security

The standards of dress required by licensees of hotels varied according to
the market segments at which they were aimed, and they served to both

attract and deter potential patrons, particularly indigenous people. Those premises with a predominantly blue-collar clientele generally required only a shirt and footwear, at least before 7:00 pm. Other premises required a minimum of 'neat, casual dress' – a standard which, several licensees explicitly stated, was to exclude certain types of patrons. During peak periods, one of the tasks of security personnel was to enforce dress standards. Although most stated that they did not intentionally discriminate against indigenous people because of their dress, they were aware of the consequences of the imposition of dress standards on many indigenous people:

> (T)he easiest way to not let them come in is that they don't like to wear shoes and the . . . (two other hotels) are pretty strict about their dress standards. (Licensee, liquor store, Mitchell)

Security is used by both off-licence and on-licence premises in Mitchell and Needup. For the former, security measures are directed mainly at theft, while for the latter, the control of violence and patron safety is the focus. All off-licences in both towns cited theft by indigenous people as their main problem:

> It's all Aboriginals, but it's worse among the young ones. They try to steal scotches and bourbons. They come into the store in groups of four wearing big overcoats, two of them will stand in one section and the other two will go and stand somewhere else. (Licensee, liquor store, Needup)

Indeed, a manager of a discount liquor store with minimal security measures believed that the absence of security could also encourage indigenous people to frequent a premises. Measures employed by the stores in direct response to the high levels of alleged theft by indigenous people, and others, included: security grilles on windows; gates at drive-through bottle shops to prevent ram-raids; security buzzers at entrances; video surveillance cameras; store security guards; and store policies for calling additional staff to attend the bottle shop.

In Needup, only one hotel out of nine and the nightclub used security personnel, while in Mitchell, three out of five hotels used them. Licensees with security claimed that many incidents requiring intervention involved indigenous people, and that the presence of security could discourage indigenous people from drinking at a premise because both dress and behaviour standards were more stringently enforced:

> If it's Friday night and it's 11 o'clock and you get a group of say 5–10 Aboriginal people walk into your front bar, I would immediately be on edge. You

would expect to have a problem. In fact they would direct the security people to just keep their eye out because invariably there'll be a fight. There's no bias, there's no non-serving, same rules apply to one as the other, but because of vast experiences, be aware. But then again if a bunch of bikies walked in, we would take the same stance. (Licensee, hotel, Needup)

In both towns, licensees and police agreed that they had an excellent working relationship with each other, and in Mitchell, an Aboriginal community patrol was utilised as a way of diffusing potentially volatile situations by removing troublesome and intoxicated people from the premises and taking them home.

Entertainment, gambling and games

There was widespread acknowledgement by licensees in both towns of the importance of music and dancing venues as a promotional strategy, particularly for young people. This is the case for indigenous, as well as non-indigenous, young people. Licensees in the towns have tried to create a market niche by providing certain types of music, ranging from rock to blues to country. One licensee in Mitchell said he had tried every kind of music before settling on disco, which attracted all age groups. One Needup hotel popular with young people was known as the place for rock-n-roll music. The success of music as a strategy varies from place to place, and is sometimes restricted by liquor licensing conditions regarding noise limits or extended trading permits. The more diverse markets in Needup are reflected in the music provided, with one smaller 'boutique' hotel targeting an older crowd with traditional and acoustic music.

Gambling or gambling-related activities on licensed premises took many forms in the two towns: PubTAB (a state government operated betting shop housed on licensed premises), gaming machines, and Sky-Channel (a Murdoch-owned satellite television channel on which horse races and other sporting events are broadcast), which was a popular draw card for indigenous and non-indigenous people. Licensees identified access to TAB facilities as a particularly important factor in attracting indigenous people. In Needup, people mentioned that many indigenous people went to the hotel with PubTAB to bet, not to drink. When asked where indigenous people drink, one licensee said:

The Public Bar because the TAB is the only one in town. That's the reason they come here, because they gamble . . . and lose. (Licensee, hotel, Needup)

Mitchell has only one hotel with PubTAB, but four of the five hotels are located within easy walking distance of a TAB and all but one hotel has SkyChannel. In Needup, there is a PubTAB in one hotel, a TAB situated directly opposite another hotel, and most hotels have SkyChannel. Additionally, there are many in-house competitions, such as the lottery-style happy hours mentioned earlier, and video gaming machines are on most premises in both towns. These gaming machines are of some interest. Supposedly labelled 'for amusement only' (although we had difficulty seeing the labelling on some machines), in Western Australia players are unable to win money on the machines. It would seem to us that these machines are conditioning hotel patrons for the introduction of poker machines, a quite controversial subject in Western Australia at present.

Games such as pool and darts were ubiquitous in all but one establishment in the towns. They were popular among indigenous patrons, according to licensees and our own observations. Pool competitions at one hotel in Mitchell ensured healthy patronage at least one night of the week. Sports sponsorship occurred in most premises, but licensee opinions as to whether this attracted more customers varied somewhat. Some cited their sponsorship as simply part of a publican's civic responsibility in a small rural town.

Advertising and other strategies

Alcohol advertising focused on a combination of products, price and other promotional activities. In general, advertising in Needup and Mitchell was fairly standard across premises, with particular brands of beer and spirit most likely to be featured. Liquor stores undertook the heaviest advertising. Weekly specials at those stores were statewide discounts issued either in Perth or Sydney by the stores' parent companies, and advertised in local newspapers. It was common practice for liquor stores to advertise the price of beer on large signs outside the stores, and to advertise other major weekly specials on blackboards both outside and inside the stores. Other specials, such as 750 ml bottles of wine, tended to be advertised on small placards directly above the discounted line inside the store.

Apart from large signs at their drive-through bottle shops, advertising displays in hotels were less overt than in the liquor stores in both towns. While advertising in Needup was somewhat more obvious than in Mitchell, there were some hotels in Needup that had minimal advertising. Spirits were more likely to be advertised in Mitchell hotels and beer in Needup hotels, with no single brand predominating.

During our research in both towns, indigenous people and those working with them gave anecdotal accounts of hotels and liquor stores selling alcohol to minors and intoxicated persons. This was particularly the case in Mitchell, where these stories often implicated taxi drivers in the transportation of under-age drinkers to hotels, and also in the supply of alcohol to minors. But these occasions are usually rare events, and are difficult to record unless in a clandestine manner. The small size of the hotels and liquor stores meant that unobtrusive observations were not possible.

Existing control strategies

In both towns, concerns about excessive drinking had resulted in agreements or 'Accords' between licensees to certain restrictions relating to the sale and promotion of alcohol. These 'gentlemen's agreements' between licensees, city councils and police are now widespread in Australia (Rydon & Stockwell 1997). In Needup this simply meant a more rigorous enforcement of liquor licensing legislation and special conditions for the town imposed by the Director of Liquor Licensing, which stipulated, for instance, no sex promotion of alcohol. The agreement halted both the advertising of 'happy hours' and the staggering of them, which enabled customers to move from one hotel to the next for several hours of discounted drinks. Mitchell's agreement was somewhat stronger, restricting trading hours from 10:00 am instead of 8:00 am, and banning the sale of large brown beer bottles ('King Browns') in the town.

Licensees in Needup were generally lukewarm in their support for the agreement, either apathetic or more openly contemptuous of what one described as 'just a warm fuzzy thing', simply the 'Licensing Act revisited'. Some licensees in both towns were incensed by what they perceived to be an infringement of individual liberties, reflecting broader suspicion of government regulation of subject populations (Burchell 1996). Referring to the restriction on beer bottles, one in Mitchell said:

> . . . you try putting wine in a cask and give it to a Frenchman, it would be really hopeless. Try give them wine in aluminium cans. They've been doing it for thousands of years, why can't we do it here? They (Aborigines) should try a little bit of discipline, that's the problem, that's the whole problem.

More generally, while most licensees and others in Mitchell agreed that the Accord was effective in delaying drinking during the day (while not apparently reducing consumption) and reducing the amounts of broken glass around the town, most believed that it did not deal with the perceived problems of discounting by the liquor stores, and the general availability of alcohol.

Police operations in both towns incorporated alcohol-related patrols. This was much more apparent in Mitchell, with a 30-person police force largely employed to deal with law and order issues directly related to drinking. Community policing in the form of an action group in Needup provided a Friday night patrol for under-aged children, warning offenders and chauffeuring children to their homes if necessary. In Mitchell, an indigenous community patrol operated three nights a week, concentrating mostly on young people, sweeping the areas outside licensed premises and known public drinking places to pick them up and deliver them safely home, if possible.

Models for intervention

Mitchell has more liquor outlets per head of population, and a higher rate of consumption of alcohol among the general population, than Needup. Alcohol-related harm, measured in terms of hospital discharges and arrests, was much higher among indigenous people than among non-indigenous people in both towns. However, again against our predictions, this excess was proportionately higher in Needup. We believe that this can largely be explained by the significantly greater indigenous population in Mitchell, where drinking and alcohol-related harm are consequently much more visible.

Surprisingly to us, given the social and cultural differences between the two towns, there were few apparent differences with respect to the type of alcohol sold. Our prediction that low-alcohol beer sales would be higher in Needup was not supported. This indicates its growing popularity among non-indigenous people, as neither our observations nor interviews revealed any preference by indigenous people for this beverage.

Promotional strategies in both towns were similar, with competitive pricing of alcohol the paramount approach. In these two towns, we found little evidence of promotional activities targeted specifically at indigenous people, but there were a range of strategies used to promote alcohol generally; and, because of the nature of alcohol problems among some sectors of the indigenous population, these strategies affected indigenous people disproportionately.

Contrary to what we had anticipated, in neither town did we find licensees attempting to attract indigenous people to licensed premises. In fact, many hotel licensees – particularly those in Mitchell – actively discouraged indigenous patrons from drinking on their premises, through their use of measures such as dress standards, levels of security and trading hours. Researchers, such as Stockwell (1997), who have shown the links between drinking alcohol on licensed premises late at night and increases in threats to law and order, and a wide range of alcohol-related problems among the general population, may see this as a positive phenomenon. However, given the very different nature of indigenous drinking and its consequences, we believe that this is not necessarily the case. For many indigenous drinkers, hotels provide a regulated environment for drinking, where dangers potentially present in unrestrained public drinking are constrained. This is an under-researched issue in indigenous communities.

Given existing control policies, and the continuing problems of excessive consumption among some people in both towns, we wanted to know what other policies or strategies might reduce consumption, or at least some alcohol-related harm. As we indicated earlier, research has highlighted four factors that may affect consumption, namely price, density of outlets, the legal drinking age, and restricted trading hours, in order of their demonstrated effectiveness (Lang *et al.* 1991).

While the bar prices of the same drinks in both towns varied only a little across hotels, alcohol from liquor stores was sometimes heavily discounted. In Mitchell, for example, cask wine could be purchased $4.00 cheaper, and beer cartons $3.00 cheaper at discount liquor stores. Licensees of hotels were angry about their inability to match the prices of the liquor stores, and some people in Mitchell suggested that such discounting should be prohibited. We believe that, in both towns, consideration should be given to the banning of the sale of damaged wine casks.

The relationship between outlet density, consumption and alcohol-related harm is complex. For instance, increasing outlet density may reduce road crashes (reducing the driving distances between licensed premises and the home) while increasing liver cirrhosis (Smith 1989a). There are also studies that suggest that the increased availability of alcohol is more likely to increase demand, than the converse case, and that the physical availability of alcohol directly contributes to increased consumption (Gruenewald, Ponicki & Holder 1993; Edwards *et al.* 1995; Stockwell 1997). In spite of this evidence, reducing the number of licensed outlets has not been politically popular. However, the economic downturn in rural Australia has contributed to intense competition for declining patronage. This is perhaps more apparent in Mitchell, where several people mentioned the desirability of removing the licence of one of the hotels. This may increase the number of patrons in the remaining premises and reduce some of the pressures to promote the sale of higher amounts of alcohol to fewer patrons.

There is evidence that increasing the legal drinking age can significantly reduce consumption, but unlike the situation elsewhere, there does not appear to be strong community support for such a move in Australia (Stockwell 1997). Certainly no-one we spoke to mentioned this as a viable option. People were concerned, however, about under-age drinking, and anecdotal evidence from both towns supported research from elsewhere that demonstrates that being under age or obviously intoxicated is no barrier to being served alcohol (Lang *et al.* 1991; Rydon *et al.* 1996).

Added to this is the part that taxis play in the supply and promotion of alcohol to indigenous people, both minors and adults. Given our observations of the ubiquitous presence of taxis ferrying indigenous people to and from alcohol providers, and the very wide concern expressed to us about the nature of the relationship between certain drivers and their indigenous clients, a review of the role of taxis does seem appropriate.

Although the general literature indicates that varying the hours of trading tends to have a limited effect on consumption, restricted trading in indigenous communities in parts of Australia has received quite strong support (Brady 1990a; d'Abbs 1990). This relates to the distinctive purchasing practices of problem indigenous drinkers (and problem non-indigenous drinkers, for that matter), which see increased sales on days when social security payments are available. Restricting or banning sales of particular drinks on those days has apparently reduced alcohol-related harm in some towns, although the evidence is equivocal because of the complex set of factors at work (d'Abbs *et al.* 1996). This type of restriction, for instance the banning of bulk liquor purchases on pension days, is less problematic when indigenous people comprise a significant proportion of the population, and would probably be supported by many indigenous people, and some non-indigenous people, in Mitchell. It is unlikely to receive strong support in Needup because of the much smaller indigenous population.

Indigenous people in both towns regard excessive alcohol consumption as a dangerous threat to their health and well-being. They, like other indigenous people throughout Australia, are looking for practical ways in which this problem can be tackled. They know that the strong demand for alcohol among many indigenous people has to be faced on both an individual and a community level. But they also recognise the factors outside their communities that contribute to the increased supply and promotion of alcohol, and are demanding a greater role in the regulation of these factors.

The focus on supply also spreads the responsibility for alcohol-related harm more equitably within the Australian community. Indigenous people and health and welfare advocates are insisting that the state and its agencies, such as Liquor Licensing Commissions, accept the responsibilities they have with respect to the supply and promotion of alcohol to indigenous people. Measures such as the increase of licensing fees for full-strength alcohol and corresponding reductions for low-strength drinks; decriminalisation of street and park drinking; the provision of minimum standards for amenities on licensed premises; stronger laws to facilitate prosecution of licensees serving juveniles and intoxicated persons, and those transporting liquor onto 'dry' communities; simplification and development of more appropriate complaint procedures;

appointment of local inspectors to ensure that licensed premises comply with the law, and to negotiate local resolution of disputes, have all been suggested by indigenous community organisations such as the Aboriginal Justice Council in Western Australia (Gray *et al.* 1994:16).

Much of the effort to control the availability of alcohol in indigenous communities has focused on the need to reduce the demand for the substance. This necessarily means that attention is directed to indigenous drinkers, rather than the alcohol producers and promoters, who aggressively seek to increase their market share when health authorities the world over are arguing for moderation, and agencies of the state, which have the legislative authority to limit market expansion but which, for ideological reasons, may prefer the excesses of the free market. These are the kinds of relationships a political economy of alcohol in indigenous Australia needs to explore.

CHAPTER 7

The consequences of misuse

Films such as *State of Shock* (Ronin Films, Australian Film Commission & Australian Broadcasting Corporation 1989) and *Once Were Warriors* (Communicado Film *et al.* 1994), which graphically depict the often apparently anarchic and violent consequences stemming from indigenous drinking in Australia and New Zealand, have polarised views in both indigenous and non-indigenous communities. An important question arises here as to how the drinking environments that cause such havoc to people's health and well-being can be realistically portrayed without contributing to popular racist assumptions about indigenous use of alcohol. While some people are very uncomfortable about the public airing of what they regard as being private indigenous matters, others reject the notion that confrontation by indigenous people of issues such as alcohol abuse and its violent consequences reinforces negative stereotypes (Brady 1995b:11). Not talking about this issue will not remove it from the public domain. As this is being written, a news report is being broadcast of a drunken riot in the Western Australian town of Halls Creek, which involved a number of injuries, resulted in thousands of dollars worth of damage, and required police reinforcements to quell it. The consequences of alcohol abuse are impossible to avoid, and as this chapter will illustrate, the very serious nature of those consequences means that it is imperative that they not be ignored.

Death and illness

Any analysis of the health effects of alcohol needs to be contextualised by an understanding of indigenous health generally. Life expectancy can be a very dramatic indicator of the relative health status of any population. Given the similarities of the colonisation experience, consequent dispossession, and health and social aftermath, one might expect that the indigenous peoples of Australia, Canada and New Zealand would have very similar life expectancies. This proves not to be the case. At birth, indigenous Australians can expect to live 18 to 20 years less than non-indigenous Australians (Australian Institute of Health and Welfare 1994:26). For indigenous Australians in their forties and fifties death rates are about ten times higher than among the non-indigenous population of the same age (Veroni, Gracey & Rouse 1994). The discrepancies between the life expectancies of indigenous and non-indigenous populations in New Zealand and Canada are not nearly so dramatic; nevertheless, the differences are significant. In New Zealand the gap between Maori and non-Maori life expectancy has been declining consistently, and currently Maori men can expect to live 7 years less than non-Maori men, while Maori women live 8.5 years less than non-Maori women (Durie 1994). Indigenous Canadians live an average of 10 years less than the general population (McKenzie 1993).

The main causes of death among indigenous Australians are similar to those among the non-indigenous population. They are cardiovascular diseases, external causes (such as accidents, poisoning and violence), respiratory disorders, various forms of cancer, and diseases of the digestive system. However, while the causes of death are similar, indigenous people die from them at rates between 2.3 and 4.6 times higher than do non-indigenous people. In addition, indigenous Australians die from endocrine, nutritional and metabolic diseases (particularly diabetes) at rates up to 12 times higher than non-indigenous people. Furthermore, indigenous Australians suffer higher levels of morbidity associated with these diseases, as well as others including preventable communicable diseases (Veroni, Gracey & Rouse 1994; Bhatia & Anderson 1995).

The pattern of ill health is similar among indigenous peoples in New Zealand and Canada. Maori have higher death rates from cardiovascular diseases, cancers and diseases of the digestive system (particularly alcohol-related cirrhosis of the liver) than do non-indigenous people; and they have twice as many post-neonatal deaths. They have higher rates of diabetes, violent accidents and respiratory diseases, and are institutionalised in psychiatric hospitals in disproportionate numbers. Maori children are more likely to suffer rheumatic fever, asthma, ear infections and subsequent hearing loss (Durie 1994).

A Health and Welfare Canada report on the health of indigenous peoples indicated that the leading causes of death among these groups were injury and poisoning (including suicide), circulatory diseases, neoplasm and respiratory system disease (Canada, Health and Welfare 1986, in Scott 1993). The only regions where this order was different were the Atlantic, Quebec and Ontario regions, where circulatory system diseases accounted for more deaths than injury and poisoning (Scott 1993). Infant mortality is higher and life expectancy lower than among non-indigenous people, largely due to such factors as poor housing and sewage (McKenzie 1993).

Mortality

Trying to assess the health consequences of alcohol on the health of indigenous Australians is hampered by a number of factors: there are no national studies, only regional analyses which provide only a partial view; Aboriginality is not routinely recorded in some data collections; and both health records and death certificates may not record the role of alcohol (Alexander 1990:15).

To overcome problems due to the under-reporting of the role of alcohol, sophisticated methods of estimating alcohol-related deaths have been developed. Within populations, deaths to which alcohol contributes can be divided into: those whose causes are wholly attributable to the effects of alcohol, such as alcoholic cirrhosis of the liver; and those causes from which some proportion of deaths can be attributed to alcohol, such as assaults, cardiovascular disease and some cancers. The latter are estimated using 'aetiologic fractions' based on studies of the contribution of alcohol to deaths from a particular cause in known populations (Holman *et al.* 1990). Caution needs to be exercised when applying this method to populations, such as those of indigenous peoples, where the contribution of alcohol to the proportion of deaths due to those causes might differ in unknown ways. Nevertheless, the method can provide broad estimates.

Studies from different parts of Australia consistently show a far greater proportion of indigenous than non-indigenous people dying from alcohol-related conditions, whether in New South Wales (Hunt 1981), the Northern Territory (Devanesen *et al.* 1986), Queensland (Trigger *et al.* 1983), the Kimberley region of Western Australia (Hunter 1989; Swensen & Unwin 1994), or Western Australia as a whole (Unwin *et al.* 1994). Alcohol is responsible for an estimated 8–10 per cent of indigenous Australian deaths (Hicks 1985; A. Gray 1990; Unwin *et al.*1994). This figure is much greater when only the deaths of middle-aged men are considered; then, it is estimated that between one-quarter and one-third of deaths are attributable to alcohol. The lower figure represents a rate three to four times higher than that for the general population. A number of regional studies reflect this result (Alexander 1990).

In the Northern Territory for the period 1979–83, deaths certified as attributable to alcohol were 3.4 times higher among indigenous males compared to the general population, and 4.8 times higher among indigenous females (Devanesen *et al.* 1986). For many parts of the north of

Australia, however, it is clear that alcohol is implicated in the deaths of many non-indigenous people as well. An analysis of the impact of alcohol on deaths in Tennant Creek revealed that the rates for both indigenous and non-indigenous people were similar (33 and 31 per cent respectively) (Brady 1988).

A New South Wales study of cause of death as recorded on death certificates indicates that 13.7 per cent were attributed to alcohol (17.1 per cent for males and 7.3 per cent for females) (Gray & Hogg 1989). This comparatively low figure is a consequence of the methodological difficulty in identifying indigenous people on death records. Using more intensive identification methods, Hicks estimated that in Western Australia, over one-third (36 per cent) of indigenous deaths in 1983 were alcohol-related (Hicks 1985). A more recent study in Western Australia indicates that indigenous men are 5.2 times more likely to die from alcohol-related conditions than non-indigenous men, and indigenous women 3.7 times more likely than non-indigenous women. The main causes of death were alcoholic liver cirrhosis, alcohol dependence and assaults (Unwin *et al.* 1994; 1995).

Another New South Wales study, using both certificates of death and death reports by Aboriginal health workers, determined that alcohol was implicated in 27 per cent of indigenous deaths, with the highest impact among the 35–44 year age group. In this population the primary cause of death was circulatory disease, and alcohol was implicated in nearly one-third (32 per cent) of all male deaths from this disease. Alcohol was seen to contribute also to mortality due to: diseases of the digestive system, particularly liver and pancreatic disease; respiratory diseases, especially pneumonia; and death by injury and poisoning (Smith *et al.* 1983 in Alexander 1990:16–17).

Just under half (46 per cent) of all deaths of indigenous people living in town camps in Alice Springs in Central Australia were attributable in part to alcohol, while elsewhere in the Northern Territory, in the town of Katherine, the impact of alcohol on mortality was only slightly less (30 to 44 per cent) (Weeramanthri, d'Abbs & Mathews 1994).

These are the stark figures, but the impact on individuals and communities, who regularly mourn the passing of a countryman or woman because of the grog, cannot be overestimated. Lyon (1990) recounts the toll for a single individual:

> Funerals also have become a feature of daily town camp life. The alcohol-related death toll within Tyapewe Rice's family alone is horrendous: his father's four sisters, two of his mother's three brothers, two of his own brothers, not to mention cousins and friends. He has had two friends die in his arms from alcohol-related disease or injury. 'A lot of people dying from grog', he said. 'Too many people dying' (1990:41).

Similarly, Brady (1990b:6–7) has documented the effects of alcohol- and drug-related mortality on a small Western Desert community of 300 people in South Australia. Between 1978 and 1989 there were 30 deaths, more than half (16) of which were alcohol- or petrol-related. Six of the deaths were of young people between the ages of 12 and 25 years, two from petrol sniffing, two from alcohol-related accidents, one after an assault and one by homicide.

Suicide

The relationship between alcohol and suicide is complex, but the statistics are telling. In a review of the general literature on the subject, Frances, Franklin & Flavin wrote that:

> . . . alcohol has been found to be associated with 50% of suicides and to increase the risk of suicidal behaviour both for alcoholic and non-alcoholic populations. Between 5% and 27% of all deaths of alcoholics are caused by suicide. The incidence of alcoholism among persons who commit suicide ranges from 6% to 30% in different studies with approximately 20% most frequently cited. Lifetime risk for suicide is 1% in the general population, 15% for major affective illness, and 15% for alcoholism (Frances, Franklin & Flavin, in Hunter 1993a:165).

In Australia it was the Royal Commission into Aboriginal Deaths in Custody (see below) that brought the issue of suicide among indigenous people to both national and international prominence. Prior to this, however, a number of reports had documented cases of suicides, many of which were alcohol-related, in various indigenous populations (Eastwell 1988; Brady 1988; Reser 1989). For instance, Kamien's (1978) study of the health of indigenous people in Bourke, New South Wales, described four suicide attempts that were precipitated by alcohol abuse. In Queensland, a study of indigenous suicides in the period 1973–88 noted a significant increase in suicide attempts from 1986. Alcohol was involved in the case of most males and half the females. The author concluded:

> It is clear that in the north Queensland data the pattern of alcohol use by a number of heavy regular and binge drinkers is placing them at a much higher risk of attempting suicide. Indeed this risk is over 18 times higher than that for those who drink only lightly, occasionally or not at all (Reser 1991:272).

The Royal Commission into Aboriginal Deaths in Custody produced an interim report in 1988, which documented the circumstances surrounding the deaths since 1 January 1980 and concluded that the excess indigenous deaths could simply be explained by the gross over-representation of indigenous people in the prison system. To explore the reasons for this, the scope of the Commission was broadened to examine the social, cultural and legal factors underlying indigenous incarceration. The Commission's massive eleven-volume report was published in 1991, and represents the most recent and exhaustive documentation of the inequalities experienced by indigenous Australians. Alcohol features prominently in the report, and the Commission found four factors that accounted for deaths in police cells: being in custody less than two hours; being confined on their own; youth (only one was over 30); and the fact that alcohol was involved in all cases (Australia, Royal Commission into Aboriginal Deaths in Custody 1991).

Details of two of the suicides from Broome, Western Australia, illustrate the depressingly familiar role of alcohol:

> Both had many previous arrests, were heavy drinkers with symptoms of alcohol dependence, and had histories of disorders of ideation and perception associated with alcohol withdrawal in the past (one had been given a diagnosis of 'alcoholic hallucinosis' by a medical practitioner). Both men were arrested for public drunkenness, one at 3.30 pm on a Saturday and the other at 6.30 pm on a Tuesday. They were found dead within three hours of incarceration, being the only inmates in the lock-up, both hanging themselves by attaching makeshift cords to the cell door. Post-mortem blood alcohol levels were similar and high, being 0.264 and 0.279. Both had been seen within two days by medical personnel, one just prior to his death, and both had sought help from a local alcohol treatment facility in the past, one within days of his demise. Finally, both had histories of problems with interpersonal relationships and one had had a recent altercation with his partner, having been arrested repeatedly and imprisoned as a result of past violence to her (Hunter 1993a:145).

A detailed analysis of indigenous suicide in the Kimberley region of Western Australia over a thirty-year period demonstrated both a dramatic increase in the number of mostly young men taking their own lives, and a changed pattern of suicide. More than three-quarters of all those who committed suicide from 1957 to 1989 were heavy drinkers from heavy drinking families (Hunter 1993a:150–1). Trying to determine the relationship between alcohol consumption and self-harmful behaviour has been methodologically complex, not least because of the complex socio-historical factors contributing to Aboriginal disease (Hunter 1991a; 1991b).

In Canada, the Task Force on Suicide (Canada, Health and Welfare 1987) noted that between 15 and 20 per cent of all violent deaths among indigenous peoples were due to suicide, which accounted for one-third of all deaths. One dramatic illustration of this is a study that reports that Saskatchewan Indian children between the ages of 0 and 14 have a suicide rate 27.5 times that of the general Canadian population, and 33.6 times that of children in the Saskatchewan region. In British Columbia, on-reserve communities had dramatically higher risks of suicide than either off-reserve indigenous groups or the general population (37 per 100,000 compared to 16 per 100,000) (Scott 1996). Indigenous suicides in Canada are associated with a number of factors apart from alcohol and other drug abuse. These include the frequent use of guns, being single, depression, financial difficulties, unstable home environment, and a family history of suicide. People were also more likely to commit suicide during the winter months. As with the prevalence of substance abuse in Canada, there is also regional variation in the suicide rate.

Morbidity

Measuring the extent to which alcohol contributes to illness and disease in the community requires data of different kinds. Reports of alcohol-related hospitalisation provide one means, while studies of the preva-lence of mental illness, suicidal tendencies and self-inflicted injury are others. On the basis of a number of disparate studies, it has been estim-ated that about one-quarter of hospital admissions of adult indigenous Australians are alcohol-related, compared to about one-fifth of the gen-eral population (Alexander 1990:18).

In Western Australia (WA), it has been shown that in the period 1981–90, hospital admission rates for alcohol-caused conditions were 8.6 times greater for indigenous than for non-indigenous men, and 12.8 times greater for indigenous than for non-indigenous women (Veroni, Swensen & Thomson 1993). Regional variations exist, as recent data from the Pilbara region of WA show. In the period 1989–93 hospital-isation for alcohol-related injuries increased significantly for indigenous men (10.7 per cent), compared to a smaller but still significant statewide increase (7.6 per cent for males and 7.0 per cent for females). Hospital-isation of non-indigenous people for alcohol-related injuries showed a significant decrease over the same period (4.3 per cent). While falls were the most common injuries recorded for non-indigenous people, assault was the most frequent cause of injury for indigenous people (Unwin & Serafino 1995:32).

Hospitalisation in the Pilbara for conditions wholly attributable to alcohol use (such as alcoholic psychosis and alcoholic liver cirrhosis) shows a significantly higher rate than in the whole of WA for non-indigenous people, but a lower than average rate for indigenous people (both males and females). Non-indigenous people had 156 hospital admissions per 100,000 person–years (compared to 84 per 100,000 for WA), while indigenous people had 979 hospital admissions per 100,000 person–years (compared to 1,308 per 100,000 for WA). Hospitalisation trends show that while non-indigenous rates are decreasing (13.5 per cent between 1989 and 1993), there is no such trend for indigenous people. If all conditions attributable to alcohol use are combined, indigenous people in the region were hospitalised at a rate similar to that for the rest of WA (3,452 per 100,000 compared to 3,492 per 100,000). This is not the case for non-indigenous people, however, with both men and women more likely to be hospitalised than others in Western Australia (520 per 100,000 compared to 350 per 100,000) (Unwin & Serafino 1995:33).

In the past, indigenous Australian women were less likely than men to present at a hospital for alcohol-related diseases (Devanesen *et al.* 1986). However, this pattern is changing, and more women are presenting for these types of conditions. In one Pitjantjatjara-speaking community, female presentations for alcohol-related injuries increased from 30 per cent of all such presentations in 1982 to 50 per cent in 1987 (Brady 1994:58). Even more striking figures are available from the Kimberley region in WA for the period 1988–92. During this time there were 313 hospital admissions for indigenous women who had been assaulted, compared to only 12 such admissions for non-indigenous women in the region (Swensen & Unwin 1994:6).

Young people are also likely to be hospitalised for alcohol- or other drug-related conditions. For instance, in the Northern Territory between 1977 and 1982, injury and poisoning was the primary cause of hospitalisation for males aged 5–14, and 15–24 years. This was also true for indigenous girls in the 5–14 age group (Brady 1990b:8). Similar findings pertain to young indigenous men in rural New South Wales (Thomson, Paden & Cassidy 1990:10).

In a Northern Territory sample over one month during 1983, 28 per cent of indigenous people attending the Tennant Creek hospital had alcohol-related complaints. Although only one-quarter of the total attendances at the hospital were by indigenous people, they made up more than two-thirds (69 per cent) of the alcohol-related incidents (Brady 1988).

In Canada, indigenous groups constitute approximately 3.7 per cent of the population, yet they make up 17 per cent of all alcohol-related hospitalisations, and their rates of admission to alcohol and drug treatment centres are 13 times the national rate. More than half of all illnesses (50 to 60 per cent) are estimated to be alcohol-related (Scott 1996).

Foetal Alcohol Syndrome/Foetal Alcohol Effects

In Canada there has been a great deal of concern over, and research on, Foetal Alcohol Syndrome (FAS) and Foetal Alcohol Effects (FAE). These are alcohol-related birth defects, which can result in noticeable growth deficiencies, central nervous system abnormalities and distinctive facial features. A conservative estimate of the incidence of FAS in the non-indigenous Canadian population is between 1 and 3 cases per 1,000 live births. There are no national figures on the indigenous population, but data from several regional studies are available. One report has cited an FAS/FAE prevalence rate of 25 per 1,000 children (0–16 years) among Métis and Indians in north-western British Columbia, and 46 per 1,000 among indigenous people in the Yukon Territories (Asante & Nelms-Matzke 1985, in Scott 1993:27–8). Even more alarming was a study that claimed to have found an FAS/FAE prevalence rate of 190 per 1,000 children in British Columbia (Robinson, Conry & Conry 1987, in Ashley 1993). For the general population in both regions, the FAS rate is 0.4 per 1,000 (Asante & Nelms-Matzke 1985, in Scott 1996). For methodological reasons – particularly the failure to consider confounding variables – the results of some of this work have been controversial and need to be interpreted with caution. Nevertheless, the results are a cause for serious concern. Far less attention has been focused on FAS/FAE among indigenous Australians, and the rates among them are not known.

Mental health

Only recently has research, at least in Australia, started to document what many community workers knew to be the case, that alcohol and other drug use are strongly implicated in the poor mental health of many indigenous people. A national survey of mental health issues among indigenous Australians identified:

> . . . the critical importance of the interrelationship between substance abuse and mental health, and that these should not be separated (Swan & Raphael 1995:5).

Of course, there are also more fundamental causes for such obvious distress, not least of which is the acknowledged harm that forced separation from family has done for thousands of indigenous people. Documenting the stories of many of these 'stolen children' is the first step in healing some of this immense hurt (Aboriginal Legal Service of Western Australia 1995).

Alcohol and other drugs exacerbate the problems of very fragile families and communities. Describing how Aboriginal children in Bourke, New South Wales, became anxious and out of control, Kamien has written:

> . . . few of these Aboriginal children possessed the building blocks commonly regarded as desirable for the development of good mental health. They came from families in which quarrelling, alcoholism and physical violence were common, and in which the moods and actions of their parents, especially

their fathers, were unpredictable and often inconsistent. . . . Poverty was chronic and often deprived them of the bare necessities of life. Separation from the parents was common owing to the repeated hospitalisation of chronically ill children (1978:135).

A study of psychiatric illness in the Kimberley region of Western Australia revealed a very strong link between alcohol use and a range of both psychological and physical illnesses and death. Indigenous people suffering a range of psychological disorders, including anxiety and depression, and complaints such as hypertension, were more likely to be frequent drinkers. Frequent alcohol consumption was also closely associated with acts of self-harm, such as self-mutilation and attempted suicide (Hunter 1990; Hunter 1993b; Hunter, Hall & Spargo 1991; Hunter, Hall & Spargo 1992; Hall, Hunter & Spargo 1993).

Summarising the literature from across Australia, Swan and Raphael concluded:

> In all these instances the complex interrelationship of substance use and misuse with depression, anxiety and other disorders is not well established. However, the relationship to adverse outcomes is clear, both in terms of direct effects on mental health of any of these substances when used to hazardous levels, and effects through social and health outcomes, especially violence, injuries, accidents and organic syndromes. Substance abuse and mental health are closely interrelated and service response in mental health must address this area (1995:90).

The Canadian Royal Commission on Aboriginal Peoples (1996) reached a similar conclusion.

Alcohol and crime

Since the days of the first European settlements in Australia, New Zealand and Canada, the introduction and wide distribution of intoxicating liquor has been seen by many observers as contributing to criminal behaviour (Cutter & Perkins 1976). While it is clear that there is no simple causal link between alcohol and crime, it is equally clear that much criminal behaviour is alcohol-related, and this is particularly true among indigenous peoples (Australia, National Committee on Violence 1990). There are significant methodological difficulties in assessing the relationship, and it is obvious that crime occurs without alcohol and that drinking occurs without crime (d'Abbs et al. 1994; Atkinson 1991; Weatherburn 1990). These qualifications aside, however, there is evidence of an important connection. It is also apparent that the methodological limitations mean that the real extent of alcohol-related crime is under-reported (d'Abbs *et al.* 1994:53). Brady's descriptions of alcohol-related incidents in Aboriginal camps illustrate the case:

> Many violent incidents occurring at the camps were never officially 'crimes' as they were not reported to the police. They merely came to the attention of the nursing sisters the next day as their victims sought medical help. There were no telephones at camp: should someone need help (either from the police or nurses) a car had to be found and driven the several kilometres into the settlement. The nearest hospital and doctor were 200 kilometres away by road. At the point at which a serious assault was brought to the attention of the community adviser (usually the next morning), there was the growing likelihood that the police would be called in to investigate, and the act became a 'crime'. The nearest police station was one and a quarter hours drive from the settlement (1986:147).

Among many indigenous people there is a clear view that alcohol causes violence. Major Sumner of the Aboriginal Sobriety Group writes:

> I have spoken with many women who grew up on reserves and they all say that alcohol brought violence to their community and not just into the community but into their homes. Even today, if you talk to a lot of older women who are married and lived with their husbands that were violent towards them they'll tell you that it was alcohol that brought the violence out. Their men became violent when they were drunk. And a lot of those people who were violent when drunk were good family men when sober; it changed their whole being when they were drunk. It changed their wives and families too. When you bring in alcohol everyone loses respect for everyone (1995:16).

Some researchers have noted that intoxicated people are unlikely to be controlled by sober people in indigenous communities. This is usually explained in terms of the individual's autonomous right to be 'their own boss'. In these circumstances police involvement is often welcomed when violence erupts after heavy drinking sessions (Brady & Palmer 1984:37). But surrendering control over community violence is a twin-edged sword, as the many indigenous complaints about the timing and severity of police intervention testify.

As Hunter (1993b:204) observes, violent behaviour has become normative in many indigenous Australian drinking settings. Reser has commented that 'in many indigenous contexts the social expectation for "being drunk" is that you will become angry and possibly violent' (1989:19). Here 'drunken comportment' (MacAndrew & Edgerton 1969) reflects both historically learned drinking patterns and more recent experiences.

One estimate is that between 60 and 80 per cent of violent crimes by indigenous Australians involve alcohol, and for remote areas police estimates are even higher, between 80 and 90 per cent for assault arrests and other arrests (Western Australia, Task Force on Aboriginal Social Justice 1994:452). This compares to an estimated 30 to 70 per cent among non-indigenous Australians (Alexander 1990:26). This figure is confirmed in studies from the Northern Territory in general (d'Abbs 1989), and Tennant Creek in the Northern Territory (Brady 1988) and Palm Island in Queensland (Barber, Punt & Albers 1988) in particular. On Palm Island it was reported that between one in three and one in four of the total population had been convicted in the Aboriginal Community Court between 1976 and 1981, and further, that:

> It is clear that with the possible exception of break and enter, alcohol is involved either directly or indirectly with almost all forms of crime on the Island. More importantly, however, the records reveal an extraordinary rate of violence and abusiveness (e.g. disorderly behaviour, assault, offensive language, etc.) occurring under the influence of alcohol (Barber, Punt & Albers 1988:97).

People taken into police custody are also more likely to have consumed alcohol. More than one-third (35 per cent) of all holdings in police cells in 1988 in Australia were for either drunkenness or, when public drunkenness had been decriminalised, protective custody. Further analysis of these holdings reveals that indigenous people were much more likely to be held for these reasons than non-indigenous people (57 per cent as against 27 per cent) (McDonald 1990b, in Alexander 1990:27). A Kimberley study shows disturbing correlations between incarceration and drinking. About half the randomly surveyed population of adult indigenous males under 50 years of age had been in prison, and the risk of imprisonment was associated with frequency of drinking. A person defined as a constant drinker (as distinct from an intermittent or episodic drinker) was 183 times more likely to be incarcerated in a police lock-up than a lifetime abstainer (Hunter, Hall & Spargo 1991).

The Royal Commission into Aboriginal Deaths in Custody, which commenced in the late 1980s in Australia, documented the ways in which alcohol was implicated in many deaths of indigenous prisoners. The Interim Report summarised the evidence, which:

> . . . suggests that both in Australia and overseas alcohol is the single factor most consistently linked with deaths in police custody. Intoxication at the time of arrest or detention plays a predominant role in ensuing tragedies. The vulnerability of an intoxicated person . . . cannot be overemphasised. There is much medical evidence and material which shows that a person who is intoxicated or suffering from withdrawal may be under a great deal of stress, both physiological and psychological, and thereby at risk unsupervised (Muirhead 1988:26).

As mentioned previously, some lawyers have attempted to use intoxication as a mitigating factor in criminal trials, and in some cases this argument has been accepted by the courts. For instance, sentence for an indecent assault upon a four year old boy by an intoxicated indigenous male was determined at 15 months, with a non-parole period of six months in 1978; the judge stated that he considered intoxication for indigenous people more of an excuse than for members of the general population (McCorquodale 1987:C224). Certainly many indigenous people regard drunken people as not responsible for their actions, but this view is being challenged both by the courts and by indigenous people (Alexander 1990:28). In 1981, in the Northern Territory, Justice Muirhead rejected such an attempt in a case of grievous bodily harm that resulted in the death of a woman, saying:

> ... I am just not prepared to regard assaults of Aboriginal women as a lesser evil to assaults committed on other Australian women, because of customary practices or life-styles, or because of what appears at times to be the almost hopeless tolerance or acceptance by some Aboriginal people to drunken assaults of this nature ... (McCorquodale 1987:C269).

In summarising the available statistical and qualitative evidence of the association between alcohol and violence among indigenous people, a report for the National Symposium on Alcohol Misuse and Violence stated:

- violence is pervasive;
- women are more likely to be victims of violence, and men perpetrators;
- violent episodes are often associated with drinking;
- the relationship between drinking and violence is not, however, a direct causal one; some researchers have suggested that drinking alcohol serves to 'enable' or 'allow' violence – by providing a socially sanctioned excuse for it – rather than causing it; and
- contemporary patterns of family violence in Aboriginal and Torres Strait Islander communities do not represent 'traditional' values and practices (d'Abbs et al. 1994:5).

Domestic violence and sexual assault

Indigenous women in Australia are nearly 40 times more likely than non-indigenous women to be victims of so-called 'spousal violence'. This risk is even higher in country areas, where they are 62.9 times more likely to be bashed than are non-indigenous women (Harding et al. 1995:131). Documenting domestic violence and sexual assault has been a very contentious issue. A provocatively titled article – 'Speaking about rape is everyone's business' – written by a non-indigenous woman with an indigenous co-author (Bell & Nelson 1991) was met with an indignant response, with some indigenous people claiming rape is indigenous women's business only (Huggins *et al.* 1991). An alternative view from an indigenous woman is that:

> Violence towards Aboriginal women is neither a private, family or Aboriginal community problem. It reflects the broader structures of racial, sexual and economic inequality in society. The level of Aboriginal male violence towards Aboriginal women reflects a breakdown in Aboriginal social order. This inference cannot be drawn when considering male violence in Australian society generally. Violence by men towards Aboriginal women is an affirmation of a particular social order (that of white males) which arises out of the socio-cultural belief that women, and in particular Aboriginal women, are less important than men and so are not entitled to respect (Atkinson 1991:4).

A 1977 report of the Australian House of Representatives Standing Committee on Aboriginal Affairs highlighted the ways in which alcohol abuse was linked to domestic violence and sexual assaults of women and children in indigenous Australia. Subsequently, a number of studies have detailed such abuse and its increase. Bolger has documented serious levels of violence against women in a number of Northern Territory communities, and examination of crime reports revealed that alcohol was involved in just less than half of all cases (1990). Devanesen and others also report that in the Northern Territory, hospital admissions associated with assault and injury have increased among indigenous women (Devanesen *et al.* 1986:222), a trend documented in other community-level studies (Brady & Palmer 1984; Lyon 1990). At the Alice Springs Hospital, nurses told one researcher of their shock at the number of indigenous women who had been assaulted by their drunken partners:

> It is not unusual for the spouses or boyfriends of these women to come into the hospital 'charged' and attempt to remove them, frequently to collect pension cheques or supporting mothers' benefits. Some of these intoxicated men have even attempted to beat their spouses in their hospital beds. Some turn on hospital staff. In 1988, the hospital recorded 37 incidents in which staff were physically abused, including being bitten, hit (in one incident with a chair), kicked, punched and scratched (Stevens 1989:1–2). In the first four months of 1989, 19 such incidents already had been recorded. The vast majority of these incidents involved inebriated patients or visitors (Lyon 1990:88).

Judy Atkinson, an indigenous researcher, has documented both the problem of domestic violence – estimating that almost all families in Queensland trust communities are touched by it in some way – and alcohol misuse. However, she cautions about attributing all blame to alcohol alone, and, like Bolger, cites cases of domestic violence in which alcohol was not involved. She notes that as alcohol and violence have been used to subjugate indigenous people, so too have some indigenous people appropriated those tools and used them against their own (Atkinson 1990).

Alcohol-related injuries of women in a Pitjantjatjara community were shown to be culturally patterned, with women more likely to receive head injuries, while male injuries were more likely to be to the thigh (Brady 1990b). This has raised the contentious issue of whether assaults on indigenous women can be interpreted as traditional punishment, and some lawyers have attempted to defend charges of assault against women on the basis that the violence was customary practice. However, this has been vigorously resisted by indigenous women, who assert that violence is not acceptable in any form (Langton *et al.* 1991).

Counting the economic costs of 'grog'

> They sit under the gumtrees
> waiting for the Post Office to open
> looking cleaner than any other day
> Some yarn and laugh
> while others sit silently
> They don't say what
> they are gonna do
> with their money
> There's no need
> They all end up at
> the club
> laughing, drinking and fighting
> It's Pension Day
>
> ('Pension Day', Charmaine Papertalk-Green
> 1988, in Gilbert 1988:76)

A report prepared on behalf of the Australian Council on Alcohol and Other Drugs found that:

1. Aboriginal people are generally paying the costs but not reaping the benefits from the alcohol economy.
2. In general, Aborigines are poor and live in a welfare economy. The purchase of alcohol thus diverts money away from sustenance expenditure.
3. Reciprocity and obligation underlying traditional patterns of sharing protects some heavy drinkers from the economic consequences of their activities at the cost of compromising the minimal sustenance income of the groups as a whole.
4. The practice of certain business people (including those involved in alcohol sales) of extending informal credit to Aboriginal drinkers, often in

conjunction with cashing social security cheques, may contribute to increased expenditure on alcohol (Alexander 1990:33)

Alcohol is big business – for governments, which charge taxes, excise and customs duties; for members of the wider community who are employed in the production, sale and promotion of alcohol; and especially for the often small, licensed outlets and ancillary businesses which deal with alcohol in local indigenous communities. In 1991–92, gross revenue from excise, customs and sales tax to the Australian Commonwealth government and liquor taxes to state and local governments in Australia was $2,563 million, or 1.9 per cent of all government revenue (Australia, Department of Human Services and Health 1994:28). While the alcohol industry generates very significant revenues at all levels, it also produces health and associated social problems whose cost is more difficult to calculate (Alexander 1990:28). Government assessment of the cost of alcohol misuse in Australia in 1990 was $6.9 billion; this includes the costing of loss of workplace productivity, property crime and theft, and the treatment of alcohol problems (Australia, Department of Human Services and Health 1994:25).

In those areas where the supply and sale of alcohol are in the hands of non-indigenous people – by far the most common situation in Australia – it is clear that few indigenous people reap any monetary gain from alcohol, and many suffer considerable costs to their health, local economies and social well-being (Langton *et al.* 1991; Lyon 1990). While a few studies have sought to measure the effects of heavy drinking in such situations, there are none that do so in situations where indigenous communities themselves control liquor outlets, and it is clear that more research in both areas is required.

It should be stated that not all investigators have viewed alcohol as a uniformly negative economic influence. Collmann (1979), for instance, describes the way in which alcohol is used as a medium of social credit among some indigenous people in Central Australia. For these people, sharing alcohol ensures future inclusion in reciprocal exchanges, an important strategy for poor households. However, such positive exchange functions of drinking cannot obscure the fact that money spent on alcohol is money not spent on other household items, such as food (Alexander 1990:29).

Figures are available that indicate that the proportion of income spent on alcohol in many indigenous households is significantly greater than the national average – reported in 1992–93 to be 3.4 per cent, down from a high of 5.1 per cent in 1985 (Australia, Department of Human Services and Health 1994:25). Studies in the 1970s and 1980s in rural and remote indigenous communities in Australia suggest that expenditure on alcohol amounted to between one-quarter and a half of disposable income (Kamien 1978; Australia, House of Representatives Standing Committee on Aboriginal Affairs 1977; Brady & Palmer 1984).

More recently, Hunter has assessed the length of time for which money lasted after pay day for drinkers and non-drinkers in the Kimberley region of Western Australia. While there was no significant difference in fortnightly income between non-drinkers and drinkers, non-drinkers and episodic drinkers reported being able to make their money last for a median of 13.6 days, compared to only 7 days for intermittent drinkers and 5.1 for constant drinkers. This fortnightly economic cycle, described as one of 'abundance' immediately after pay day followed by deprivation, is powerfully evoked by Papertalk-Green's poem cited above. As Hunter notes, the burden of economic support for drinkers falls upon their non-drinking kin (Hunter 1993a:117).

As the so-called 'availability hypothesis' predicts, those people in communities where alcohol is less freely available appear to spend far less on it. In a remote outstation in the Northern Territory, only 4 per cent of income was spent on alcohol, as locals were able to extract alcohol as payment in kind from other indigenous people crossing their land. The community was also protected to some extent by their hunting and gathering activities, which were significant supplements to their food source (Altman 1987).

As the Australian Council on Alcohol and Other Drugs report points out, understanding the economic impact of alcohol on indigenous communities requires knowledge of the distinctive ways in which indigenous economies throughout Australia are structured (Alexander 1990:30–2). Overwhelmingly, indigenous people are poor, un- or under-employed, and dependent upon a range of state-provided welfare benefits. Those people living in rural and remote regions are further burdened by the much greater costs of basic items such as food, which may be as much as 40 per cent higher than metropolitan prices (Sullivan, Gracey & Hevron 1987). Expenditure on relatively expensive consumer items, such as television sets and video-recorders, which require maintenance, can also have an adverse effect on other expenditure. In the Fitzroy Valley, Western Australia, indigenous 'families of children who grew adequately had fewer consumer goods such as televisions and refrigerators than those whose growth was worse' (Gracey et al. 1989:323).

In these circumstances, the economic pressures from insistent demands to purchase alcohol can become very onerous. Anecdotal accounts of grog trips that cost hundreds of dollars in transport alone, and staggeringly high consumption levels in some areas, illustrate the seriousness of the problem (Alexander 1990; d'Abbs et al. 1996). The National Aboriginal Health Strategy Working Party (1989:205) was told of 'sly grog merchants' in Queensland who in 1987 were charging indigenous people $10 for a can of beer and $50 for a cask of wine. At the same time, however, the fine for the illegal sale of alcohol was only $100. In many communities some indigenous people are themselves profiting from the heavy drinking of others. Brady (1986) describes the way in which people with serviceable vehicles hire these as 'taxis' for carting of wine, the driver covering the costs of the trip and making enough profit to buy his own drink.

As well as the costs to individuals and families, the economic costs of excessive drinking to the wider communities are also considerable. In Alice Springs, Central Australia, Lyon (1990:13–14) was able to document some of these:

> An estimated 60% or more of the funds allocated for housing repairs and maintenance go toward alcohol-related damage and other problems, such as overloading of septic systems. In 1988/89, a year in which there were few funds for repairs and maintenance, that amount was approximately $73,254.
>
> Nearly half (46.6 per cent) of staff hours and more than half (55.3 per cent) of the cost of the six programs in the Community Services Department go toward addressing grog issues . . . or dealing with the myriad domestic problems posed to home-makers, old people, school children, youth and women by the heavy-drinking way of life in the camps. The dollar cost to Community Services in 1988/89 was an estimated $205,488.
>
> The Tangentyere Works Department, which builds houses on the town camps and carries out all repairs and maintenance, estimates its 30 workers and office staff spend up to 66 hours per week – at a cost of approximately $4,700 per week, including materials – repairing grog-related damage to houses and appliances or being harassed by drunks on the job.

These examples illustrate 'what everyone knows' (Lyon 1990) about the effects of alcohol, that is, that the costs to families, communities and the nation go far beyond simply excessive allocations from household budgets for the purchase of 'grog'.

Costs to families and children

> The cost to the community is high. When the man is gaoled the wife suffers, the kids suffer, we all suffer. The kids have no role models when their mothers are being bashed by their husbands or boyfriends. And the kids can drift into the same kinds of behaviours that they experienced when they were growing up, drinking, having babies too young, being unable to cope with the responsibility, bashing their wives and even in some instances their babies. This destroys people's lives and their future (Sumner 1995:17).

Heavy drinking in indigenous communities places great strains on child rearing and everyday family life. More than 20 years ago, Kamien described the link between family breakdown and excessive drinking in Bourke, New South Wales. Children often left home to escape the physical violence associated with parental drinking, and of those who did remain, many exhibited antisocial behaviour (Kamien 1975). Children from drinking families are more likely to suffer from malnutrition, either because food money is diverted to alcohol, or because of neglect of meals; and they receive little day-to-day care or encouragement to attend school (Kahn *et al.* 1990:358). Submissions to the Royal Commission on Aboriginal Deaths in Custody express vividly the way in which drinking becomes part of many children's socialisation:

> Even the new generation coming on, when they finish school they got nothing to do because they haven't got work to go for. . . . All they do is go drinking with their Mum and Dad down the streets, getting drunk and some of them getting killed. It's the young people we are losing; alcohol is bad for the Aboriginal people (Edmunds 1990:41).

Details of the disruptive influence of heavy drinking on children's lives are available from both indigenous and non-indigenous accounts. Domestic routines of feeding, clothing and caring for children can be quite different in drinking and non-drinking households, and many children grow up not knowing the rudiments of care which other children take for granted. Many of the people Brady (1995a) spoke to about giving up grog spoke of the need to provide for children – either their own or their children's children. Other studies have documented the growing number of children being raised by people other than their parents because of heavy drinking. In the Kimberley region, for instance, Hunter (1990:20) found that nearly one-third (30 per cent) of his sample group aged 16 to 30 years had been raised by people other than their parents. In traditional circumstances it would be expected that child rearing would be shared among a number of extended kin, but the contemporary situation where some children experience total neglect by their biological parents cannot simply be explained in terms of these arrangements.

There are suggestions that these impacts on indigenous children are strongly gendered. Hunter's (1993a) Kimberley studies include some discussion of the greater vulnerability of Aboriginal boys because of the relative absence of male parental figures or other positive role models as a result of drinking. Characteristics of the drinking-affected family include emotional, physical and educational deprivation for children, a drinking role model, and an unavailable or absent parent, who is more often the father (1993a:197). In one school surveyed, 70 per cent of all absentees were from heavy drinking or gambling families. While both sexes suffer educationally as a result of such absenteeism, it seems clear that girls are more able to form securely realistic identities because of their relationships with female kin. Primary school girls, asked about their ambitions after school, cited work as teachers' aides, health workers or mothers.

The boys' answers were quite different, apparently informed both by television and everyday life. They were more likely to cite karate or boxing champion, or predict, even more pessimistically, that 'they'd pick up their (social security) cheque at the office' (Hunter 1993a:231). This point about male identity is explored further below.

Children in heavy drinking families are exposed early to alcohol and the range of behaviours associated with its use. Evidence from indigenous groups elsewhere indicates that not only are these children more likely to experiment with drinking at an early age, they are also more likely to have similar drinking careers to their parents (Oetting *et al.* 1989). As one man from Alice Springs said after he had realised his drinking was a problem:

> The way I drank was normal to me. . . . My family, my friends, almost everyone I knew drank like I did. . . . I drank the way my father taught me to drink – all night and all day (Lyon 1990:36).

Workers with indigenous people in the Alice Springs area in the 1980s described drunken seven year old children, and groups of children early in the morning, 'full drunk' (Wynter & Hill 1988:1). Although parents may not approve of this, their own drinking behaviours make it unlikely that illicit drinking by children or adolescents will be punished in any serious way. In communities where petrol sniffing is a problem, some parents have welcomed children's interest in alcohol, which is seen by some as the lesser of the two evils (Hunter 1993b).

Indigenous children's schooling is frequently affected by heavy drinking, either their own or that of their families. In Alice Springs, for instance, almost half (44.4 per cent) of the contacts made by non-medical community services with children under 15 years of age were alcohol-related. Children presented with problems of anxiety, low self-esteem, difficulty in maintaining friendships with peers, refusal to go to school or obey any adult instructions, and symptoms such as bed-wetting. At the local school nearly one-third (29.1 per cent) of children's contacts with nursing sisters, community police or counsellors were believed to be alcohol-related. Indigenous youth homelessness, estimated to be at least 40 on any given night in 1988–89, was precipitated by alcohol problems in every case during the survey period (Lyon 1990:91–6).

Community life

In western social settings, an individual's problem drinking is often masked by the privacy of the nuclear household and the clear separation between family and work life. However, problem drinking in indigenous communities is often more noticeable because the communities themselves tend to be more open physically, drinking itself is more likely to be a communal activity, and the much lower workforce participation rate means there is much more opportunity to drink. Because much of indigenous life is experienced within the larger communal group, the negative effects of heavy drinking are correspondingly felt by that larger community. This is clear to indigenous councils, which are concerned about places like the Alice Springs town camps:

> To Tangentyere (Council), the human cost of the grog-saturated life on the camps has always seemed huge, inescapable and requiring urgent attention. Fathers (and mothers) have severe difficulty getting or keeping jobs. Mothers have difficulty feeding their children. Children have difficulty with school. All attempts to raise the standard of living in camps through jobs, training, education or community development programs are seriously undermined by excessive drinking. Lives are destroyed. People are sick and dying (Lyon 1990:12).

Despite such problems and the concerns that have been expressed, there are clearly ambivalent and conflicting attitudes to alcohol and its effects on communities. Attempts by some communities to declare themselves 'dry' and maintain that status are frequently contested by others in the communities who are equally determined to drink. One illustration of the volatile nature of this conflict occurred in 1989 in the Northern Territory, when a group of non-drinkers in one community who were frustrated at the effects of excessive drinking took the law into their own hands and physically tore down the licensed club (Alexander 1990:24).

It is not simply alcohol-related activities that are the focus of conflict in indigenous communities, but also the fact that excessive drinking impedes the whole range of community development initiatives and service provisions. Maintaining everyday life, encouraging children to go to school, assisting in health programs, and participating in community employment schemes are difficult when, in the words of one community leader, 'World War 3 breaks out every night' (Western Australia, Task Force on Aboriginal Social Justice 1994:453).

Threats to culture and tradition

'Grog kills the cells in the body but it also kills the traditions and the culture – everything' (Australia & Western Australia, Royal Commission into Aboriginal Deaths in Custody, transcript, One Arm Point, 1991:741).

Members of many indigenous Australian communities have argued that alcohol poses a serious threat to the maintenance of traditional customary and religious beliefs and practices, or the 'Law' as it is often called.

In Wiluna, Western Australia, indigenous people spoke to Sackett (1977) of their concern at the damage drinking caused to the social obligations set down by the Law and – as elsewhere (Langton *et al.* 1991) – to the neglect of religious ceremonies. In some communities, such concern about the impact of drinking on religious observance has led to the suspension of liquor sales while 'Law business' is in progress (Alexander 1990).

Other work, however, demonstrates that no simple causal link can be made between drink and drug taking and 'losing' culture. The situation in one community was described by Brady in this way:

> The three hundred members of the indigenous community studied . . . strongly maintained their language, social organisation and ceremonial life. They expended much energy and commitment in order to pursue these socially meaningful activities – driving long distances to attend ceremonies or funerals, planning and executing bush trips and hunting expeditions, and visiting relatives. Some sections of the community also devoted much energy and initiative to the obtaining and consuming of alcohol. . . . Younger people engaged from time to time in petrol sniffing in order to get high, and took part in subsequent escapades which usually resulted in appearances at the Children's Court. These adolescents, however, also participated with skill and interest in hunting and gathering activities, in living out bush away from the settlement, and were fluent primarily in their own language, with English very much a second language (1986:141).

In this community some controls over the excesses of alcohol were maintained by non-drinkers calling upon people to maintain the Law in what was called a 'growl'. This was a ritualised speech 'in (Aboriginal) language' by a senior man, often stripped to the waist to demonstrate his anger, and assisted by the rattling of boomerangs and spears he carried. In the speech, the man would castigate the drunken offender and '. . . urge the need to keep the law strong, to uphold the law of the land, and the difficulty of doing so when wine was so important for people' (Brady 1986:145).

A call to action

In this chapter, drawing mainly upon Australian data, we have documented the harms attributed, by mostly non-indigenous observers, to the excessive consumption of alcohol in indigenous communities. While some specific problems attributed to such misuse are the subject of dispute, it is abundantly clear that excessive drinking takes a heavy toll at all levels within indigenous communities. Certainly in Australia, non-indigenous observers who spoke of the misuse of alcohol in indigenous communities risked being labelled as 'racist' – as some of them undoubtedly were – and accused of singling out indigenous people for criticism when problems of alcohol misuse were clearly more widespread. However, the disproportionate impact of excessive alcohol consumption on indigenous peoples cannot be ignored, and studies such as those discussed above have helped to make that impact clear. Importantly, as we documented in Chapter 2, many indigenous people themselves are increasingly speaking out about the issues and, as we will see in the next chapter, are calling for, and taking, action to address them.

CHAPTER 8

What's being done?

The harm caused by alcohol misuse among some segments of indigenous populations is increasingly acknowledged by indigenous and non-indigenous peoples alike. As we discussed in Chapter 5, there is considerable variation in the way this 'problem' is conceptualised. Often such conceptualisations are either taken for granted and regarded as 'common-sense', or they are not made explicit. However, it is important to identify and understand them, as the way in which 'the problem' is conceptualised plays an important role in the response to it; and the extent to which these explanations mirror reality affects the outcomes of interventions based upon them. In the discussion of interventions that follows, we have grouped them into four broad categories: treatment, harm minimisation, supply reduction, and demand reduction. The narrow range of strategies we have grouped in the category 'harm minimisation' is purely for convenience. In fact, we regard all of these strategies as being aimed at the minimisation of harm associated with alcohol misuse. Before going on to examine them in detail, it is necessary to consider the crucial role that governments play in funding them.

The role of government

In the past, governments played a paternalistic role in dealing with problems of alcohol misuse among indigenous peoples, as attested by the legal prohibitions they imposed upon alcohol consumption by indigenous people. With the failure of such prohibitions and the recognition of their inherent inequality, governments have utilised a two-pronged approach to dealing with alcohol misuse, based on the regulation of supply, and the provision of various treatment and prevention services. In Australia, state and territory governments have largely been responsible for the delivery of these latter services through mainstream agencies (or through special branches or units within them), although some have also provided funds to community organisations for the provision of services. The Australian federal government has played a less direct, but no less important, role as funder of services. As part of the National Drug Strategy, the Department of Health and Family Services has directed funds to both state government agencies and indigenous community organisations for the provision of services. Until 1995, when responsibility for all indigenous health programs was transferred to the Office of Aboriginal Health within the Department of Health and Family Services, the federal government also provided funds for alcohol and other drug misuse projects to indigenous community organisations through the Aboriginal and Torres Strait Islander Commission.

In Canada the situation is somewhat different. As part of its treaty obligations, the federal government provides both services and funds to 'status Indians' living on reserves. These are provided through the National Native Alcohol and Drug Abuse Program (NNADAP) within Health and Welfare Canada (Scott 1993). The Royal Commission on Aboriginal Peoples reported that:

> NNADAP provides funds for about 400 community-based prevention and treatment programs, 51 regional residential treatment centres, and basic training to prepare Aboriginal staff to deliver most of these services. Budget estimates for 1994–95 show about $59 million allocated to NNADAP (Canada, Royal Commission on Aboriginal Peoples 1996).

Services to 'non-status Indians' and Métis are provided by provincial government agencies, which are assuming an increasingly important role in the delivery of health services to indigenous peoples (Waldram, Herring & Young 1995).

In New Zealand, which does not have a federal system, so-called 'reforms' of the health care system in the early 1990s have led to a changed role for government, which has stepped back from the direct provision of health services. Health policy and objectives are set by the Ministry of Health, which reaches agreements with Regional Health Authorities (RHAs) as 'purchasers' of health services. In turn, the RHAs enter into service agreements with service 'providers' (Durie 1994; New Zealand, Manatu Hauroa, Ministry of Health 1996). This system has provided the opportunity for Maori organisations to contract for the provision of services to Maori communities. Although this splitting of funding, purchasing, and provision of service functions has gone furthest in New Zealand, it should be noted that in Australia some state health departments have attempted, with mixed success, to implement similar arrangements, and such arrangements are also proposed in Canada (Waldram *et al.* 1995).

Despite the variations in the roles played by government agencies in the direct provision of services, in all three countries governments provide the overwhelming bulk of funds for alcohol misuse programs. The policies and resource allocations made by government agencies, and the extent to which they are responsive to indigenous demands, sets the overall framework within which intervention strategies can be implemented.

Treatment

Whatever approach one takes to the explanation of alcohol misuse, it is clear that individuals with alcohol-related problems require some kind of assistance or 'treatment' in overcoming them. While some drug-based treatments are available – such as the administration of disulfiram to cause an aversion to the consumption of alcohol (Cawte 1982) – most treatment is based on some form of counselling. Such counselling may take place in a variety of settings, including residential treatment facilities, clinics, community centres, and prisons. It should be noted that some indigenous Australians distinguish between 'treatment' and 'counselling', using the former term to refer to the counselling and other services provided in residential facilities, and the latter to describe counselling which takes place in non-residential settings. One of the advantages of providing treatment in a residential setting is that people are removed from drinking environments, and have the opportunity to physically recuperate from the ravages associated with alcohol misuse. Indeed, O'Connor (1988) has cited this 'time out' period as the most beneficial aspect of indigenous residential treatment programs.

Counselling is generally of two types, namely therapeutic and life skills counselling. Therapeutic counselling is aimed at healing psychological trauma and/or other factors underlying the misuse of alcohol by individuals. It may take place on a one-to-one basis between client and counsellor, or in group where people meet, with the aid of a counsellor, to discuss the events and situations that led to their alcohol problems and successful ways to negotiate either abstinent or controlled drinking lives. People may also receive individual counselling, which allows them to talk about general issues contributing to their substance problem, but also more intimate triggers, like that of child sexual abuse, which has become a significant issue for many indigenous people (Gray & Morfitt 1996:58). While therapeutic counselling is overtly psychological in orientation, life skills training is more educative in focus, and is usually facilitated by a drug and alcohol educator in a 'classroom' setting. Here the aim is to inform people about the properties and effects of alcohol, let them know of ways to avoid or minimise harm associated with its use, and to provide other skills that will enable people to lead lives in which alcohol is not a major focus. Usually the clients' own experiences are woven into such training sessions. In practice, many treatment programs are based on some combination of both these types of counselling, and many are based on the Alcoholics Anonymous approach (Gray & Morfitt 1996:58).

Incorporating indigenous culture into treatment programs

Certainly in Australia, for many years, mainstream health agencies have offered places in treatment programs to indigenous people. However, they have not been particularly successful in terms of attracting large numbers of clients, or in achieving positive outcomes for those they have attracted. Thus, for over 20 years, there have been increasing calls for the establishment of culture- and need-specific programs that acknowledge that program models developed for white, mostly middle-class males may not suit indigenous clients (United States, National Clearinghouse for Alcohol Information 1985:4). Accordingly, treatment programs have been developed by indigenous community organisations that are based on indigenous values and customs and/or which incorporate both folk medicine and indigenous healing alongside, or sometimes instead of, standard western treatments. In many cases these cultural understandings have been used to 'Aboriginalise' treatment programs whose underlying philosophies are European in origin. For example, most indigenous programs in Canada have:

> . . . adapted and indigenised the AA approaches for self-help and member support. These programs are shaped by Native cultural and spiritual values– with liberal sprinklings of 'tough love', compassion, and mutual support (Hazlehurst 1994:102).

This approach is typified by the Poundmaker's Lodge program in Canada (discussed in detail below). This program has attracted enthusiastic attention worldwide, and leading figures such as Eric Shirt have been brought out to Australia to encourage the development of similar indigenous alcohol and drug programs. However, the program is not without its critics. One very experienced indigenous alcohol counsellor in Canada told us of his concerns about the superficiality of the traditional elements incorporated in the treatment program, which he saw as a largely non-indigenous United States model onto which indigenous elements had been grafted. Traditional healing, in our informant's view, requires traditionally qualified healers and, according to him, these people were largely absent from the permanent staff at Poundmaker's.

It is not possible to explore this charge here, but such criticisms are not unusual wherever attempts have been made to blend aspects of western healing with traditional indigenous culture. Australian readers may remember the debate in the Northern Territory about the appropriateness of so-called 'two-way medicine', which attempted to incorporate traditional Aboriginal medicines and healing practices into mainstream health care delivery to Aboriginal groups. Some Aboriginal people were strongly opposed to this on the grounds that it would weaken traditional medicine and confuse the different roles of traditional healers and western health professionals (Nathan & Japanangka 1983).

Underlying these criticisms are a number of contested assumptions about the nature of traditional culture and its place in the contemporary world. At one extreme are people who have maintained links to their traditional culture and who wish to keep as much as possible of what they regard as whole systems of health beliefs and behaviours. At the other extreme are people who, because of colonial policies of dispossession from land and separation from family, are trying to regain contact with a culture with which they have little familiarity. In between are individuals and groups who, while not maintaining continuous association with their own country, still have kinship ties that allow them access to people and places of significance.

Targets of treatment – the individual versus the collectivity

A core issue with regard to indigenous alcohol treatments is the level at which they should be directed – whether to the individual or the group of problem drinkers. In the past few years in Australia a thoughtful debate has emerged that examines notions of indigenous selfhood and the ways in which these notions impact on drinking patterns and treatment options. On the one hand there are rich ethnographic descriptions of indigenous drinking in which the collectivity takes clear precedence over the individual (Bain 1974; Sansom 1980; O'Connor 1984). On the other hand are descriptions that have articulated a strong sense of individual autonomy, where people are 'bosses for themselves' (Bell 1993; Myers 1986; Brady 1990a, 1992a).

The first situation describes drinking environments in which the non-drinker is set apart as being different. These are settings in which 'The choice is simple: drink and belong, or abstain and remain outside' (O'Connor 1984:181). For O'Connor (1984) drinking in these settings defies conventional descriptions of alcohol addiction or dependence, as individuals seem perfectly able to control their drinking while apart from the collectivity. It is when they return to the group, newly sober, that the struggle to exist with a completely transformed way of life proves too difficult for most. This is a style of drinking termed 'contingent drunkenness' (O'Connor 1984:180), as it is intimately connected to the communal drinking lifestyle, rather than any particular individual susceptibility to alcohol.

In these circumstances, it is argued, treatment programs that target the individual, as Alcoholics Anonymous programs do, are misdirected because they fail to differentiate between drinking in indigenous communities, where heavy drinking is the norm, and drinking in other settings, where the problem drinker is the alienated outsider. Instead what is required are programs in which social control mechanisms within indigenous groups may be strengthened to reduce alcohol-related harm. If, as it is claimed, in many of these groups '[T]he pressure of kinship in Aboriginal society is extremely intense, so much so that individual choice can be almost eliminated' (Bain 1974:46), surely these same social pressures can be constructively used to support moderate drinking. We know, for example, that in all indigenous communities there are significant groups of non-drinkers, mostly women, who could presumably lead such a campaign.

Tempering such optimism, however, is the evidence of the limits to the collectivity, at least in the indigenous Australian context. This has been usefully discussed by Rowse (1993), who cites Brady's research documenting the sentiment in indigenous communities of the 'deeply felt respect for the autonomous right of an individual to conduct his/her life in a particular manner, even if this involves harm' (Brady 1990a:216). In these settings, Brady claims that traditional social controls may actually facilitate drunkenness, and that individual autonomy more often than not allows individuals to maintain their drinking rather than enabling them to stay sober. However, Rowse cautions against such generalisations, pointing to the places where non-drinking is normative, like the 'dry' communities where alcohol is prohibited, and places where mostly senior women choose not to drink. These diverse indigenous subcultures where drinking is not part of everyday life provide a possible place for hard-drinking individuals who want to give up the grog – a place where both individual autonomy and the strength of the collectivity can be expressed in mutually supportive ways (1993:397).

A Canadian example: Poundmaker's Lodge

In Canada, many indigenous alcohol and other drug programs are funded by the National Native Alcohol and Drug Abuse Program (NNADAP), and since the 1980s more than 60 treatment centres have been established, most of which offer residential care for a period of at least 28 days (Brady 1993:410). All of these programs combine western and indigenous treatment models, most of them based on training provided by the Nechi Training Research and Health Promotions Institute, based in Edmonton, Alberta. Nechi is funded by both the Medical Services Branch of NNADAP and the Alberta Alcohol and Drug Abuse Commission (AADAC). Its mission statement includes a list of beliefs that makes clear their ideological approach to drug use:

> Nechi and the communities it serves are involved in the healing process. Healing must be a component of training. The approach to training and healing must be comprehensive, addressing the individual client/trainee in the context of the Aboriginal community. Healing of the individual contributes to healing of the family and the community.

> The client/trainee must be honoured: individual people know what they need and can contribute to their own healing.

> Our approach to training and healing must be holistic and balanced, focusing on the mental, emotional, physical, and spiritual aspects of the person.

> The cultural context for training and treatment of Aboriginal people is critical to success; so the process of Nechi training must embody Aboriginal ways of knowing, healing, and learning.

> Alcoholism, drug, and gambling dependencies, like other addictive/dependency behaviours, are diseases which can be treated and from which recovery is possible.

> Each person has the ability to make a commitment to personal well being, which is a natural state of being.

> The vision and spiritual development of Nechi's staff and Board are rooted in the well being of the collective Aboriginal community.

> Every person is a teacher, a learner, and a healer. We believe in serving our community through voluntarism (Jock *et al.* 1996:19).

Embedded in the above statements are notions of individual and community responsibility, and alcohol misuse as an addictive behaviour. These notions are illustrated in many of the indigenous drug programs in Canada.

One of the best known indigenous treatment centres – both in Canada and overseas – is the Poundmaker's Lodge Alcohol and Drug Treatment Centre, which is based upon the principles of, and shares some accommodation with, the Nechi Institute. One of its publications states that:

> Poundmaker's Lodge treatment philosophy and treatment approach is based on the belief that alcoholism is a disease. We also believe that the disease of alcoholism and other drug addiction is of epidemic proportions in the Indian community and that the Native client will respond most positively to a specialized treatment approach that embodies Indian cultural awareness and the philosophy of Alcoholics Anonymous (Poundmaker's Lodge n.d.).

A key symbol for the Centre, and an important part of the treatment, is the sweatlodge. This consists of a circular tent-like structure with a doorway facing east, in which a circle of people sit around heated rocks to pray, sing and relax. Other traditional symbols, such as the drum, sweetgrass, eaglefeather, and the natural elements of fire, rock, air and water, are used as a focus throughout the treatment program.

Poundmaker's Lodge operates facilities in three locations: their main centre and 54-bed residential in-patient facility in St Albert, Edmonton; an adolescent treatment facility in St Paul; and an out-patient program in downtown Edmonton. Treatment staff include elders, treatment directors, counsellors, psychologists, and medical personnel, including a dentist. An Executive Director manages the 50 staff. All staff are required to be abstinent – in their terms to not only 'talk the talk' but also 'walk the walk'. Most staff are indigenous Canadians, many of them having been previously alcohol- or drug-dependent.

Treatment in the highly structured 28-day residential program consists of four components, through which Alcoholics Anonymous and Narcotics Anonymous philosophies are interwoven: education (about the nature of drugs and their consequences); skills development (life skills such as communication, assertiveness and problem solving); counselling (encouraging the expression of feelings); and Native culture (sweatlodge and pipe ceremonies, sweetgrass ceremonies, and lectures by Elders). Clients follow a structured timetable from 6:30 am wake-up to 11:00 pm lights-out.

In the last week of the client's treatment, family members are encouraged to join a residential family program, which includes details on Al-Anon, the AA group for family members of alcohol-dependent people. Family counselling is also offered in an attempt to resolve past conflicts and help equip family members to deal with the client in the future. During the 28-day period, medical and dental care are available to clients, and psychological assistance is provided for staff to deal with the client's emotional concerns. A wide range of physical activities (organised sport and a fully equipped gymnasium) and recreational pursuits such as dancing are provided. In addition, an annual three-day Pow Wow for people who have given up drinking attracts around 5,000 people.

As a supplement to the in-patient treatment, clients may return for a 14-day follow-up program of lectures, films and counselling, which are designed to help them deal with the stresses attached to a sober lifestyle. For entry, people must not have used alcohol or other drugs since leaving the 28-day treatment program. If they have done so, they are encouraged to participate again in the 28-day program.

The Adolescent Treatment Program is designed for indigenous young people between the ages of 12 and 17, and provides an intensive, 90-day addictions program. It currently has 30 beds for residential males, and plans a future capacity for 20 males and females attending the Centre on a daily basis. Referrals include offenders from the Solicitor General's Department. The addictions treatment component of the program is based on the AA 12-Step Program, and incorporates individual, group and family therapy; life skills; information on alcohol and other drugs; and recreation – all interwoven with traditional culture taught by a cultural adviser and consultant elders. A wilderness program involving survival skills includes fire-making, canoeing, hunting and tracking techniques (with ice fishing in winter), building a sweatlodge, and compass expeditions.

An accredited school education program follows the Alberta high school curriculum, and students are required to attend for about four hours a day, throughout the entire year. As in the adult treatment program, families are encouraged to participate in a one-week residential program. Young people who leave the Centre are followed up by staff once a month for six months.

Poundmaker's Lodge also offers out-patient programs for people not requiring residential treatment, and aftercare for anyone who has undergone treatment. Aftercare includes accompanying the client to AA meetings, to sober functions and to any local native ceremonies. Counsellors and elders are also used as part of a case management team for Native offenders. The team assists in the pre-release planning, including the provision of treatment if required. People in prison receive assistance with communication difficulties with staff, and may take part in a range of programs such as life skills, job readiness, community support networks, and alcohol and other drug programs. Elders also provide spiritual and cultural services to inmates, including sweatlodge, pipe and sweetgrass ceremonies.

The Poundmaker's Lodge program is important, not least because of its influence in other countries, particularly Australia. While the program has certainly helped some indigenous people to achieve their goal of complete abstinence, it is not clear that in this regard it is any more successful than other treatment approaches. Furthermore, many indigenous people, particularly in Australia, believe that abstinence is not the only or most desirable treatment outcome. An alternative approach that emphasises controlled drinking is exemplified by the following New Zealand example.

A New Zealand example: Tu BADD (Brothers Against Drunk Drivers)

In 1994 Paul Stanley, a Maori researcher for a health research unit in Auckland, and Nick Pataka, a social worker, helped to set up Tu BADD at the Hoani Waititi in West Auckland. The program was directed at a rugby league team, Kia Toa, comprised of members from various local gangs – Black Power, the Headhunters, the Nomads, and the Mongrel Mob. Like many young Maori men, gang members frequently had long histories of drinking, often starting earlier than 14, interspersed with stints in gaol.

Using mentors from the gang and others who had transformed their heavy drinking lives, the program aims to give simple messages about the harm that excessive drinking in general, and drink-driving in particular, can do. This was to be no easy task in a drinking culture in which alcohol is seen as an essential ingredient for most social occasions, where workers at a *marae hui* (a meeting at a ceremonial place) would be rewarded with kegs of beer, where the dead (the *tupapaku*) are farewelled accompanied by much drinking, and where brewery companies target Maori men in advertising campaigns costing $40 million annually.

Instead of sobriety, the program focuses on moderation: stopping at one or two beers instead of drinking to oblivion. Men were encouraged to substitute family outings, trips to gather *kaimoana* (seafood), barbeques, and football for their drinking with the mates. The coordinators claim that most of the Brothers in the program had their first dry Christmas after the year-long program. Program members also targeted alcohol consumption at traditional Maori gatherings, for instance encouraging people to serve beer in glasses rather than bottles to reduce consumption (Harawira 1996).

The no-treatment option

While no-one seriously questions the need to provide treatment options for people with alcohol and other drug problems, there is also evidence that many people simply give up on their own. In Australia, Brady's research over the past few years has begun to document this phenomenon (1993; 1995a). Her most recent publication, *Giving Away the Grog* (1995a), documents the stories of indigenous people throughout Australia who, for a variety of reasons, either stopped drinking altogether, or drastically reduced their consumption. When asked what prompted their decision, people's responses were diverse. Many had been warned by their doctors that they faced severe illness or even death, and this frightened them sufficiently to stop. Others were concerned about the effects of the drinking lifestyle on the lives of their children and grandchildren. For some, marriage and other intimate relationships were threatened; for others it was the risk to their employment that forced the issue. Becoming Christian for many people meant giving away the grog, and in many communities the term Christian and non-drinker are synonymous.

These examples provide some support for Rowse's (1993) suggestion that indigenous cultural traditions of individual autonomy may assist in the recovery of people from alcohol and other drug dependence. They are also timely reminders that, just as there is no one reason for people's drinking excessively, there is no single treatment that will suit all people.

Harm minimisation

As we have shown in Chapter 7, there are a range of consequences associated with the misuse of alcohol. Recognising that it is extremely difficult in the short term to change patterns of drinking behaviour, a number of strategies have been employed to address some of the short-term consequences of misuse. As we indicated above, while we believe that all intervention strategies are ultimately aimed at minimising the harm associated with alcohol misuse, for the purpose of this book, we have categorised these short-term interventions as harm minimisation strategies.

Acute interventions

Acute interventions are those that aim to prevent intoxicated persons from harming themselves or others. They include patrols, sobering-up shelters, refuges and detoxification facilities. Some communities provide only one of these services, while others employ some combination of them.

Patrols, also known as night patrols or warden programs, are generally community initiatives run by teams of local indigenous people. At the time of writing, there are approximately 24 of these operating in different parts of Australia. Most do not attempt to stop the use of alcohol, but patrol members seek to minimise harm by removing intoxicated persons from situations that put them or others at risk. For example, the Numbud Patrol in Derby is run by volunteers using a roster system. The service is offered six days a week, from early evening until licensed premises close. Depending on staff availability and how busy the local drinking spots are, a group of up to seven workers will patrol the streets and licensed premises. The workers encourage drinkers to slow down their consumption, help settle drunken disputes, and place intoxicated people in safe environments by returning them to their communities or homes, or moving them away from roadsides (Gray & Morfitt 1996:57).

Sobering-up shelters provide a temporary haven for, and supervision of, intoxicated persons who are at risk of causing immediate harm to themselves or others. Importantly, they provide a more appropriate alternative to placing intoxicated persons in police custody. Across Australia there are over 20 established sobering-up shelters, and others are being developed. Roebourne Sobering-up Shelter in Western Australia is a typical example of how such shelters function. It is a 10-bed facility open between 3:00 pm and 8:00 am from Tuesday to Friday, this being the high consumption period in the town. The shelter is staffed by four workers, rostered in two shifts of two persons; where possible both a male and a female worker are rostered. Intoxicated persons are self-referred or referred by the hospital, police, local store or community members. The shelter provides the client with a bed, showering facilities, clean night clothes while his/her clothes are being washed, first aid, and a meal on departure (Gray & Morfitt 1996:57).

Most refuge services are not specifically designed as part of alcohol or other drug programs. However, the reality is that alcohol figures in a large proportion of domestic disputes. Refuges offer short-term accommodation to women and children who are the subjects of domestic violence. They also offer support and counselling, and assistance in finding alternative accommodation, financial aid and legal advice. While most refuges are special facilities, some organisations have used alternative approaches. For instance, the Numbulwar Substance Misuse and Recovery Team in the Northern Territory consists of a group of women who offer their own homes as refuges and personal support for women at risk from alcohol-related domestic violence (Gray & Morfitt 1996:57).

Detoxification is the supervised withdrawal of individuals from alcohol. In Australia, most indigenous organisations do not regard detoxification as a treatment *per se*, but as a prerequisite for entry into treatment programs. Detoxification is commonly carried out in one of three settings: residential treatment centres; bush camps, where clients are taken away from their community and access to alcohol; and community settings, in which the onus is sometimes placed on individuals to detoxify themselves as a prerequisite to entering a treatment program (Gray & Morfitt 1996:57).

Personal injury prevention

One very practical strategy is being employed to prevent alcohol-related injury in a number of communities. It is common in hospital emergency rooms and health centres to see patients who have been injured by broken glass, either in accidents or in fights in which broken glasses and bottles are used as weapons. In order to reduce such injury, indigenous community organisations in towns such as Wiluna and Fitzroy Crossing in Western Australia have reached agreements with the operators of liquor outlets whereby alcohol for both on-premises and take-away consumption is sold only in non-glass containers such as aluminium cans or casks. No formal evaluation of the impact of these measures has been undertaken, but informal reports suggest that they have been effective.

Support services

Support services aim to improve the lifestyle and health of indigenous people who are currently experiencing, or are at risk of experiencing, alcohol- and drug-related problems, without directly addressing alcohol or drug use. Such services include health and medical services, accommodation, after-treatment care, and other crisis care and support. It is difficult to identify how many support programs are offered, due to the diversity of the services. However, in Australia, we have identified at least seven hostels that specifically target indigenous people who have experienced alcohol- and drug-related problems, and all of the approximately 90 community-controlled indigenous health services provide health and medical care for those directly or indirectly affected by alcohol and other drugs (Gray & Morfitt 1996:58).

Demand reduction

Health promotion

Health promotion aims at changing the behaviour of target populations by giving them the knowledge to make informed choices, in this case about alcohol use. In Australia, both mainstream health agencies and indigenous organisations are making extensive use of media campaigns and health education to promote positive health and to increase awareness of alcohol and drug issues. At the time of writing, approximately 40 indigenous health promotion campaigns were being conducted in Australia at local, regional, state and national levels.

The types of media used in health promotion include television, radio, posters, pamphlets, T-shirts and caps – media that receive considerable exposure. Often they are targeted at quite specific audiences. For example, the Port Lincoln Aboriginal Health Service in South Australia has a one-hour program on the local prison radio station during which a drug and alcohol worker with the Service talks about a wide range of alcohol- and drug-related topics. Another innovative strategy has been the use of theatre to promote health by the Kimberley Aboriginal Medical Services Council (KAMSC) in the north of Western Australia. KAMSC's Health Promotion Unit has produced a number of short plays incorporating health themes, including one on alcohol. The plays are staged in Aboriginal communities throughout the Kimberley region, and include local people as supporting cast members. As much as possible, local languages are incorporated into the scripts so that local audiences can more readily identify with the plays and their messages (Gray & Morfitt 1996).

Many argue the need to direct preventive educational approaches at young people. Indigenous populations in Australia, New Zealand and Canada are comparatively young, over 40 per cent being aged less than 15 years. It is among this group, particularly those aged around 13–15 years, that the uptake of alcohol is most marked. This group is also more familiar with western education, and, it is argued, more receptive to it (May 1986); the group is also accessible through the school system. Thus, for example, Dunjiba Community Council in South Australia conducts a youth drug and alcohol education program that incorporates the use of written materials, videos, lectures and group activities to educate youth about the types of drugs, their effects, the harm they can cause, and strategies to minimise this harm (Gray & Morfitt 1996).

While some claim that young people have either insufficient or erroneous information about the deleterious health effects of alcohol, our own research and that of others indicates that this cannot be assumed. Young Aboriginal people in Albany, Western Australia, knew about the health risks of both smoking and excessive alcohol use. Older children also had reasonably good knowledge of the dangers of other illicit drugs as well. However, there was no association between knowledge about the possible ill effects of a range of drugs, and consumption of them. Children with high consumption levels of alcohol and other drugs knew just as much as those who consumed less (Gray *et al.* 1996). While knowledge about alcohol and its effects is important, often education is seen as a quick fix and is seized upon, particularly by governments, because it is relatively inexpensive and creates the impression that something is being done to address alcohol misuse and related problems.

Recreational activities

Another strategy that has been advocated to reduce the demand for alcohol – particularly among young people – has been the provision of recreational activities (Australia, Royal Commission into Aboriginal Deaths in Custody 1991; Brady 1992a). The rationale for this approach has included the observation that daily life for many indigenous young people lacks sufficient activity and excitement. More than 20 years ago Brody described what life was like for Inuit young people in northern Canada:

> Time weighs heavily on the young. Those who feel unable or disinclined to hunt and trap must spend many hours trying to amuse themselves, by meandering here and there in the villages, visiting, gossiping, sitting, dreaming. In such a monotonous round, it is not surprising that they welcome the diversion of drink and the soft drugs that occasionally find their way even into the remotest settlements, and that they sometimes experiment with alcohol-substitutes, such as drinking aftershave lotion and sniffing gasoline. It is still rare to hear of excesses in such entertainment, but as settlement life develops

these, opportunities will increase. There is a growing interest in being intoxicated or high (1975:208–9).

As the health statistics for Canada show, Brody's predictions have proven accurate. There are similar descriptions of life for Australian indigenous youth. In her work on petrol sniffing – which applies equally well to issues of alcohol misuse – Brady describes the situation for those living in remote communities, which have:

> . . . no basketball, no recreation hall, poor ovals, no BMX tracks, no swimming pool, no television, no musical instruments and no rock groups (1992b:178).

She goes on to criticise funding priorities that permitted adults to purchase vehicles, attend Bible Camps, establish outstations, develop traditional arts and ceremonies, and even to travel overseas, while capital expenditure on youth activities was poorly supported.

This type of criticism resonates with intuitive understandings that young people with plenty of interesting things to do are less likely to have the time or inclination to drink excessively or use other drugs. Accordingly, many communities have instituted recreational activities for young people. In Esperance, Western Australia, for example, the Bay of Isles Aboriginal Corporation runs a drop-in centre for young people and organises different outings, such as camping, motor-bike riding, and sporting events (Gray & Morfitt 1996). At Weipa, in northern Queensland, the local community, with the Weipa Aboriginal Council and joint funding from the mining company Comalco, set up a youth centre. The centre, which is open between 1:00 and 10:00 pm, has its own library, homework centre, disco and other recreational activities, in an alcohol-free zone. In addition, a bus and boat are used to provide recreational outings for young people (Hazlehurst 1994:150).

These recreational initiatives are an important and necessary part of providing equality of opportunity for indigenous people, and their provision appears to reduce some antisocial behaviour, such as juvenile offending. However, health professionals and communities are becoming aware that boredom alone cannot explain alcohol and drug use by young people. In Albany, Western Australia, our own research has shown that access to, and participation in, a wide range of recreational opportunities does not necessarily divert indigenous young people from alcohol and drug taking (Gray *et al.* 1996).

Cultural initiatives

During the assimilation period, there was a concerted effort by Australian federal and state governments, with the support of some missionary churches, to break down indigenous cultures; this included the forcible removal of children from their parents and a denigration of indigenous cultural values and institutions (Aboriginal Legal Service of Western Australia 1995; Haebich 1988). This has left a legacy of fragmented family life, and mental health and other social problems. This legacy is seen by communities as both a cause of alcohol and other drug misuse, and a factor that limits the effectiveness of intervention programs. Thus in Australia (as in New Zealand and Canada) there is a widespread and explicit acknowledgement of the importance of strengthening traditional culture and cultural values as a means of resisting excessive alcohol consumption, and as a means of making treatment and other interventions more effective. Thus a cultural initiative proposed by Woolkabunning Kiaka, a Western Australian organisation, involves re-establishing mutual self-respect and cooperation between adults and their children, in turn strengthening the family as a problem-solving unit that can deal with the alcohol misuse and other problems faced in an often hostile urban environment (Gray & Morfitt 1996). In Canada, too, traditional culture is interwoven into healing strategies:

> A central component of the Poundmaker's treatment program involves the strengthening and renewal of 'Indian culture'. An elder works full-time at the Centre, holding pipe ceremonies, sweat lodges, and other sacred ceremonies. With meditation, prayer, ceremonies, and elder counselling, patients are given spiritual assistance in overcoming their afflictions (Hazlehurst 1994:133).

Again, however, while such initiatives are important for many reasons, there is little documentation of their effects in reducing alcohol misuse and associated harm. It is also important to note that those communities where there are strong continuities with traditional cultures are themselves not exempt from alcohol-related problems.

Supply reduction

Prohibition

At various times and in various places, governments have sought to eliminate problems attributed (rightly or wrongly) to the use of alcohol by prohibiting its use. There have been two rationales for such prohibitions. When applied to broader, non-indigenous populations, the justification has been that *the drug itself* is the cause of misuse – for example, that it has irresistible 'addictive' properties. When applied specifically to indigenous minorities, the rationale has been that they are incapable of controlling the use of alcohol.

Although alcohol consumption is prohibited in many Islamic countries, there are no western industrialised countries that have blanket prohibitions on alcohol use. However, early this century, there were strong temperance movements in many such countries, and they succeeded in having prohibition enacted at local and regional levels. The only one of these countries that prohibited alcohol use on a national scale was the United States, which introduced it in 1919. There, hard-headed business people supported utopian moralists who argued that prohibition would solve most of the social and economic ills of the country, improving worker discipline and productivity.

In the United States, prohibition was not popular with large segments of the population, and there was widespread evasion of the law. Although popular opinion has it that during the prohibition era the supply of alcohol was controlled by 'crime bosses', the evidence suggests otherwise. While organised crime distributed some of the illicit alcohol in the big cities, most production and distribution were carried out by thousands of small-time operators (Levine & Reinarman 1993:170–2).

Given this widespread evasion and prohibition's unpopularity, various arguments were mustered against prohibition, including the fact that it was difficult to enforce, and that it infringed upon the rights of individuals. Also, in the climate of the 'great depression' and widespread social upheaval, it was argued that repeal would help calm the masses. United States Senators heard that:

> Beer would have a decidedly soothing tendency on the present mental attitude of the working men. . . . It would do a great deal to change their mental attitude on economic conditions (Gordon 1943, in Levine & Reinarman 1993:164).

After being in force for 14 years, national prohibition was repealed in 1933, although it was maintained in some state and local jurisdictions.

Prohibition in the United States is generally regarded as having been unsuccessful. There is little evidence to suggest that consumption levels among the general population during prohibition were any lower than in the period subsequent to it during the late 1930s and 1940s (Levine & Reinarman 1993:168–9). Furthermore, there is also some evidence that prohibition led to the illicit consumption of beverages with a higher alcohol content. Beer consumption in the United States fell during prohibition years but the consumption of illegal wines and spirits rose, in part because it was more profitable to make and distribute drinks with higher alcohol content (Levine & Reinarman 1993:170).

Following the failure of the United States experiment, prohibition on a large scale has lost favour as a means of reducing the consumption of alcohol (though not of other drugs, such as heroin and cocaine). Nevertheless, prohibitions on the use of alcohol by indigenous peoples are still employed. These are of two kinds: those imposed by government authorities; and those imposed by indigenous people themselves, often with support from government. In Australia, particularly in rural and remote areas, it is still common to hear some segments of the non-indigenous population expressing the view that indigenous alcohol consumption should be prohibited. However, this is a minority view, and in any case it would breach both federal and state anti-discrimination legislation. Nevertheless, local and state governments have passed by-laws and legislation that prohibit consumption in certain locations. Perhaps the best known example of this is what is known as the Northern Territory's 'Two Kilometre Law', which prohibits public consumption within two kilometres of a licensed liquor outlet. While this ostensibly applies to all citizens, it is widely considered to be an attempt to 'clean' the streets of indigenous people, who for a variety of reasons are more likely to consume alcohol in public.

Some geographically discrete indigenous communities have themselves prohibited the consumption of alcohol within their boundaries. In some instances, such prohibitions have been informal. In others, state or territory governments have enacted legislation that enables indigenous communities to declare themselves 'dry' and make it an offence to take alcohol into, or consume alcohol in, those communities. There have been few formal evaluations of these measures, and reports of their effectiveness are mixed. On the one hand, community members report reduced levels of social disruption and violence, and improvement in the health and well-being of children. On the other hand, there are frequent attempts to smuggle alcohol in – a practice known as 'sly grogging'. In some cases, this sly grogging is small in scale, but in others it involves considerable quantities of beverages and large profits are made. Generally, most communities are not equipped to enforce prohibitions, and the police are often reluctant to commit resources to the enforcement of prohibitions on indigenous lands. It has also been suggested that prohibition simply transfers many problems associated with alcohol misuse to other locations, as people move either permanently or intermittently to fringe camps on the outskirts of towns – locations in which drinking is often excessive and in which there are a variety of other social and health problems. In these situations, there has also been loss of life and severe injury as people drive considerable distances on poor roads to obtain alcohol and are involved in accidents while returning under its influence.

We do not have any information about prohibitions initiated by indigenous peoples in New Zealand and Canada. However, review of the effects of prohibition on indigenous people in the United States indicates that the evidence for its effectiveness is mixed. Prohibition tends to lead to less frequent drinking and slightly lower consumption levels on reservations, compared to the drinking of tribal groups in urban settings. But prohibition does not prevent people from purchasing and consuming alcohol; those who want to do so will generally find some middleman willing to sell to them. It also incurs other costs such as border-town drinking, binge drinking and the like (Weibel-Orlando 1990).

Despite the equivocal nature of the evidence for the effectiveness of prohibition, in Australia, the Royal Commission into Aboriginal Deaths in Custody agreed with the conclusion of Larkins and McDonald that:

> It would appear that, if desired by the community and adequately enforced, dry area legislation can be a qualified success and is thus worthy of further support (Larkins & McDonald 1984:61, in Australia, Royal Commission into Aboriginal Deaths in Custody 1991, vol. 4:278).

Regulation

That alcohol is a potentially dangerous drug is recognised by most societies, and they generally have some set of customary or legal rules to regulate aspects of its consumption. Of course, there are different, and contested, views, both between and within societies, about the potential dangers posed by alcohol (especially when compared to other drugs), and these views shape the regulatory legislation and procedures that are put into place. At the minimum, legislation attempts to specify one or more of the following: who may or may not produce or sell alcoholic beverages; the public places in which such beverages may be consumed; the days and times at which alcohol can be sold; those to whom consumption is to be restricted or denied, such as minors or intoxicated persons; and, of not least importance to governments, taxes or levies to be imposed on the production or sale of alcohol.

Such regulation of supply has been seen to have two advantages over prohibition as a means of controlling alcohol consumption. First, unlike prohibitions (both state-regulated and those operating in 'dry' indigenous communities), regulations are usually obeyed. That is, trading hours are generally observed, as are the myriad of other laws to do with amenities, space, and the like, although this is much less the case with minimum-age drinking laws, which are more likely to be both openly and inadvertently flouted. Compliance with liquor licensing regulations is assisted by policing, but also by the fear associated with the potential loss of a liquor licence for infringements. The second advantage is that most consumers take alcohol regulations for granted, and few agitate for change (Levine & Reinarman 1993:178–9).

A more contentious aspect of liquor licensing regulation has to do with the extent to which it is used to reduce consumption. Until recently – considering the direct revenues to be gained and disregarding the costs

– governments have generally agreed with the alcohol industry that level of consumption is an *individual problem*, that most harm is attributable to a relatively small number of problem drinkers, and that prevention is the province of education and health agencies (Levine & Reinarman 1993:179). Thus in Australia, Canada and New Zealand, as elsewhere in the world, there have developed both government and private agencies whose main task is dealing with the harmful effects of alcohol (and other drugs).

However, as we have seen, there is a direct correlation between the level of consumption and a number of harm indicators, and that most harm is contributed by 'moderate' drinkers rather than just 'heavy' drinkers (Stockwell 1995:126). Given this, there have been increasing demands that liquor licensing regulations should be used to control levels of consumption and to reduce the associated harm. Not surprisingly, such calls have been resisted by the liquor industry. Nevertheless, there is evidence that some governments are prepared to experiment with stronger controls on supply.

In Australia, just as some indigenous communities have used provisions of various pieces of legislation to prohibit alcohol consumption, others have used such legislation to regulate it. For example, discrete communities have obtained licences to operate their own liquor outlets. In such cases, they have then limited the hours of trading, the type and strength of beverages available for sale, and the amounts of alcohol that can be purchased, for example limiting purchases to two cans of beer per person per day.

While such use of liquor licensing laws has met with some success in discrete indigenous communities, it has been much more contentious in communities where indigenous groups have applied to liquor licensing authorities to impose restriction in communities consisting of both indigenous and non-indigenous people. A case study from Tennant Creek, in the Northern Territory of Australia, is illustrative. In July 1995, the Northern Territory Liquor Commission agreed to a trial restriction on the sale and supply of alcohol for a period of six months. The trial was in response to community complaints about high levels of alcohol consumption and public drunkenness, and consequent property damage, personal injury, effects on health and nutrition, and low employment and school attendance rates. Indigenous people complained of the impact of 'the alcohol culture that grips many families in the town'. The effects of the trial on public order, health and welfare, and the economic impact on licensees, were to be evaluated and the results submitted to the Northern Territory Liquor Commission for a decision regarding the continuation of restrictions (d'Abbs *et al.* 1996:8).

The trial was conducted in two 13-week phases. The most significant of the restrictions were as follows. In the first phase, on Thursdays ('pension day', or the day on which various social security payments are made) all take-away sales of alcohol were prohibited, as were sales from the front bars of hotels (though not other bars or restaurants). In the second phase, on Thursdays, take-away and hotel front bar sales were permitted only between 3:00 and 9:00 pm. In both phases, on all days except Thursdays, front bar sales were permitted only between 10:00 am and 9:00 pm, before noon only low-alcohol beer could be sold, and wine could only be sold if accompanied by a meal. In an attempt to reduce take-away sales and associated problems, sales of riesling or moselle wine in casks of more than two litres were prohibited; sales of those wines in casks of less than two litres were restricted to one per person per day; sales of wine in glass containers of more than one litre were prohibited; and sales to taxi drivers believed to be purchasing for others were banned (d'Abbs *et al.* 1996:7).

The restrictions provoked intense debate, both before and during the trial, because of some fears of the economic costs to local businesses, infringements of individual rights, and heightening of racial tensions as some non-indigenous people perceived themselves to be disadvantaged because of the drinking excesses of indigenous people. While most people in the town acknowledged the social disruption caused by excessive drinking, some were unhappy with the proposed solution. As might be expected, the outcomes of the trial were not straightforward. However, the Liquor Commission found, after reading the evaluation report, that the trial had resulted in 'civic' improvements, in terms of fewer police incidents and reduced disturbance to public order; and improved health and welfare, in terms of fewer alcohol-related hospital presentations and admissions to the women's refuge. Improvements were more marked during the first phase of the trial but even Phase 2 produced positive outcomes when compared to the previous year. The economic impact of the measures was varied, with a downturn in alcohol sales in the town of Tennant Creek offset to some extent by increases in sales at roadside inns. While wine sales fell, purchases of full-strength beer increased. However, the effects on work practices were positive. Absenteeism and numbers of days lost through sick leave declined, particularly on Thursdays and Fridays (d'Abbs *et al.* 1996:1–4,77).

After reviewing the evaluation report, the Liquor Commission found that although liquor controls could not solve alcohol problems in the town, there was general community support for restrictions similar to those implemented in Phase 1 of the trial. It also noted favourably the change in drinking practices, with an increase in lounge bar patronage, where dress and behaviour standards are higher and food is served. It further suggested that licensees whose front bar sales had fallen during the trial period upgrade their facilities so that they are more similar to those in lounge bars (d'Abbs *et al.* 1996:81). As we discuss later, these comments gloss over a wide range of social and cultural issues to do with the drinking environments of indigenous and non-indigenous people.

In spite of the threat that such controls are perceived to pose for individual and community liberty, in Australia at least, small communities are showing they are prepared to sacrifice some freedoms for a reduction in alcohol-related harm. In part, this approach reflects the widely held view in Australia that controlling excessive drinking is a more practical means of intervention than simply promoting abstinence. However, this view is quite controversial among indigenous advocates of complete abstinence in Australia, New Zealand and Canada. On a recent visit by one of us (SS) to treatment centres in Alberta, Canada, for example, workers were baffled by descriptions of controls over the availability of alcohol in Australia, claiming it was the right of any business to sell alcohol. As they regard control over alcohol to be an individual decision, and the notion of controlled drinking foolish, it made no sense to them to prohibit or restrict the sale of any legal substance. A similar attitude exists in many indigenous Australian communities that have declared themselves 'dry'.

Treatment versus prevention

As we have seen, the various preventive approaches – harm minimisation, demand reduction and supply reduction – aim to positively intervene at the individual and community levels before health and other problems emerge. For agencies working within an abstinence model, this means preventing the original use of alcohol. For those supporting moderate use, it means alerting users to the harm associated with excessive use.

For indigenous people in Australia, prevention of alcohol and other drug problems has had a practical focus:

> Primary prevention is when a community decides to do something about their problems. It focuses upon the social and personal factors which lead people to abuse alcohol, tobacco, drugs and petrol fumes.
>
> Primary prevention focuses on good health issues. It focuses on developing and maintaining healthy lifestyles. This program goes hand in hand with all other areas of community development.
>
> Local people identify their own problems, and are responsible for finding their own solutions. If we have ownership of problems we have control of our own destiny (Jean Jans, drug and alcohol counsellor, in Hazlehurst 1994:151).

However, despite such statements, of 284 projects being undertaken by 155 organisations in Australia in 1995, 50 per cent were providing treatment services, either alone or in concert with other projects. While figures on the total funding such projects received are not available to us, it appears that the bulk of such funding has been spent on treatment rather than prevention services (Gray & Morfitt 1996).

Similarly, in Canada, indigenous communities have produced a comprehensive framework that recognises the various levels at which substance abuse occurs, and aims at both treatment and prevention. Strategies to counteract misuse are directed at the person, the community, and the drug, and include:

- INFLUENCE – (education and persuasion programs, positive peer pressure, role modelling, and counter advertising);
- CONTROL – (developing and enforcing laws, policies and rules, limiting availability of alcohol and other drugs, reducing promotional messages to use substances, raising alcohol and drug prices, and placing warning labels on substances);
- SKILLS DEVELOPMENT – (teaching life skills, teaching traditional values, parent education programs, and teaching people to resist negative peer pressure); and
- COMMUNITY DESIGN – (bringing change to elements of the community culture and structure that tend to support or promote heavy drinking, intoxication or other abusive behaviours) (Canada, Health and Welfare 1993:3).

As set out, this framework is balanced in that it acknowledges the complexity of drug use and misuse at the individual and structural levels. It also acknowledges the differences in opinion about how to tackle substance abuse, between those arguing for abstinence and those urging moderate consumption. However, our own limited experience of indigenous drug and alcohol programs in Alberta, Canada, did not indicate that such flexibility exists on the ground, with particular programs, such as that at Poundmaker's Lodge, strongly wedded to disease-oriented views of alcohol misuse and to treatment.

The differences that exist between the approach of the advisory group that produced the Prevention Framework for First Nations Communities, a body supported by the NNADAP, and that of the premier organisation conducting indigenous alcohol and drug training, Nechi, raises the question of the effectiveness of these approaches.

In principle, few would disagree with the old adage that prevention is better than cure, although most are in agreement that some form of 'treatment' should be available for those who are misusing alcohol. However, it appears that in both Australia and Canada, considerable resources are put into treatment at the expense of preventive activities.

A structural view

Clearly, a wide range of intervention strategies have been applied to the misuse of alcohol among some segments of indigenous populations.

Various claims have been made for the success, or otherwise, of these interventions. However, generally speaking, there have been few comprehensive attempts to evaluate their relative effectiveness, and it is difficult to
distinguish accounts of real gains from partisan pleading. Nevertheless,
despite the range of intervention strategies that have been applied, and
despite the limited success claimed for some of them, there is little
evidence that there has been any significant reduction in alcohol misuse
and related harm among indigenous peoples in the past two decades. Why
is this so?

As indicated earlier, levels of alcohol consumption are a function of both
demand and supply. Yet most attempts at exploring indigenous alcohol
misuse have focused on explaining high levels of demand. That is, they
seek to identify the conditions that cause indigenous people as individuals,
or as a collectivity, to misuse alcohol. The demand for alcohol is generated
by both structural and personal factors. Marginalisation from the dominant society, which becomes apparent during the transition from primary
to secondary school for children, and subsequent unemployment are
powerful predictors of alcohol misuse (Gray *et al.* 1996). But indigenous
societies have also provided models of autonomy that allow individuals to
be 'bosses for themselves' (Bell 1993; Rowse 1993). Many have demonstrated this autonomy by giving up the grog, either by entering into a
treatment program, or simply quitting by themselves. This is no mean feat
when they have to live in communities where grog often reigns supreme,
and the one who abstains or is moderate is the outsider.

Similarly, most attempts to deal with the problem of excessive consumption and its consequences in indigenous communities have attempted to reduce demand. They have done this through treatment, which
aims to bring about either abstinence or significantly reduced consumption, and those demand-based strategies that emphasise education. To a
large extent, both of these approaches are based upon liberal notions of
individualism and individual responsibility, whether the programs have
been provided by government or indigenous agencies.

There is no doubt that treatment has helped some individuals, but
there are patently too few treatment programs available. We are currently
working in a rural Western Australian town where indigenous drinking is
a serious concern, and where a night patrol has funds to operate three
nights a week from 9:00 pm until 1:00 am. But there is no sobering-up
shelter, so drunks are simply returned home where they create a
disturbance for others; there is no women's refuge, so battered women
and children are forced to remain at home with their abusive family
members; there is no local detoxification centre, apart from a couple of
occasional beds at the local hospital; and there is no long-term residential treatment centre for people wishing to quit. Indigenous community

organisations in the town want all of these facilities, but the indigenous health service still hasn't been able to attract doctors to work in the town.

However, it is probable that more indigenous people have given up excessive consumption without treatment than as a consequence of it. Similarly, there is no doubt that knowledge about alcohol and its effects is essential to enable individuals to make decisions about whether or not they will use alcohol, and if so, how they will use it. However, indigenous people have long been exposed to information about the effects of alcohol, and there is no evidence to suggest that they are any less aware of this than are most non-indigenous people. Furthermore, such knowledge is not the only factor affecting decisions about drinking behaviour; as well as by rational knowledge, behaviour is also affected by a range of emotional, cultural and social factors. This is not to deny the role of individual agency, and the fact that individuals can actively work to change their social circumstances. It is, however, to indicate that such individual agency is constrained by broader social structures.

On the basis of the limited evidence available, most success in reducing excessive consumption and related harm appears to have been the result of structural interventions. That is, interventions that aim to change the social environment, which facilitates high levels of consumption. Such interventions include both demand reduction strategies, which provide alternatives to the excessive consumption of alcohol, and supply reduction strategies, which seek to limit the availability of alcohol. These strategies confront liberal notions that attribute alcohol problems to individuals, whether or not those attributions are made on the basis of genetic predisposition, moral weakness, or physical or psychological disease.

If, as we propose, structural approaches to intervention are more likely to be successful than treatment and educative approaches, why then have they not led to greater reductions in levels of alcohol misuse and related harm? The answer to this question is that these strategies do not address the underlying issue of colonialism. The consequences of this have been well documented by the Australian Royal Commission into Aboriginal Deaths in Custody (1991) and the Canadian Royal Commission on Aboriginal Peoples (1996), and its continuing legacy is well illustrated by contemporary events in Australia. At the time of writing, in Australia the federal Liberal–National Party coalition government (with support from conservative state and territory governments and only half-hearted opposition from the federal Labor Party) is seeking to legislate to overturn the High Court's *Wik* decision, which extended the previous *Mabo* decision recognising limited indigenous land rights. In the face of such actions, the intervention strategies we have described merely tinker with existing political and economic systems that marginalise and exclude indigenous peoples, and perpetuate the inequalities they face.

This situation has led some indigenous people to eschew concern with addressing alcohol-related problems as focusing on the symptoms. Instead, they have focused their attention upon broader-based strategies aimed at improving the overall social, political and economic well-being of indigenous peoples. Among these broad-based strategies are attempts to regain land, 'return to country', establish business enterprises, create employment opportunities, and re-assert control over their own lives.

Given all this, one might ask, despairingly, whether it is worthwhile supporting the attempts of indigenous people to directly intervene to change patterns of drinking behaviour in their communities. We believe that it is. Elsewhere we have written of Australia, and it also applies to New Zealand and Canada, that no government has acted in a manner that would significantly alter existing power relationships or address the structural inequalities faced by indigenous people (Saggers & Gray 1991:417). Improvements that have taken place have been hard fought for by indigenous peoples, and the concessions made to them have generally been limited; and this pattern of incremental change seems likely to continue for the foreseeable future.

Under these circumstances there is a need to identify which intervention strategies, or combination of them, are likely to be most effective. Doing so is not an easy task, however, and there are many reasons why it has not been adequately undertaken. This point will be taken up in the next chapter.

CHAPTER 9

Determining what works: Program evaluation

In the previous chapter, we have outlined the range of actions being undertaken to deal with problems of alcohol misuse among indigenous peoples. In the light of what we have said about the continuing levels of alcohol misuse and its consequences, it is reasonable to ask 'Which of these interventions work?' However, answering this question is not an easy matter. First, there is a paucity of published reports on the evaluation of indigenous substance misuse interventions (Gray, Saggers, Plowright & Drandich 1995). Second, evaluation of such interventions is beset with a range of difficulties, including contestation over objectives and the criteria against which success is to be measured, methodological difficulties, and, importantly, the issue of cultural appropriateness.

Over the past 25 to 30 years, governments in Australia, New Zealand and Canada have launched various plans to achieve equality of health status for indigenous peoples (Saggers & Gray 1991; Comeau & Santin 1995). Despite considerable expenditure and significant improvements in particular areas such as the reduction of infant mortality, bridging the gap between indigenous and non-indigenous health seems as difficult as ever. As a consequence, concern has been expressed that resource allocations are insufficient, services are inappropriate, and resources are used less than optimally; and there have been calls for increased program monitoring and evaluation. These calls have come from different quarters, including: indigenous people who feel they are not being adequately served; indigenous affairs departments critical of the performance of mainstream agencies; technocrats who appear to believe that rational management techniques are the solution to all social problems; and conservative politicians seeking to reduce government spending and specialised services for indigenous peoples.

It is in this context that we wish to explore the monitoring and evaluation of indigenous substance abuse programs, largely in Australia, but drawing upon our more limited overseas experience, particularly in Canada. This chapter builds upon a project undertaken for the Western Australian Aboriginal Affairs Department, which was concerned with an absence of culturally appropriate models for evaluating indigenous programs (Gray, Saggers, Plowright & Drandich 1995; Gray, Saggers, Drandich, Wallam & Plowright 1995). Our research team for that project included members of indigenous community organisations who had first-hand experiences of trying to maintain programs and satisfy government and community concerns for accountability.

At the outset, it is important to understand that most interventions, including those conceived and conducted by indigenous community organisations, are funded by national and state- or provincial-level governments through both special indigenous affairs and mainstream agencies. Various governments are responsive in different degrees to the voices of indigenous peoples, and this responsiveness is reflected to a greater or lesser extent in their indigenous affairs and health policies. However, in the absence of resources of their own, indigenous community organisations must conduct their efforts at intervention within the framework of government policies and the programs that flow from them. In attempting to assess which interventions work, it is crucially important to evaluate the policies and programs that provide the overall context within which particular interventions are conducted. As a consequence, much of what follows will focus on the evaluation of government programs, although it is also of direct relevance to those interventions conducted by indigenous organisations.

Evaluating the success of interventions

Those who are interested in which interventions 'work' to reduce the level of alcohol misuse and related harm in indigenous populations are bound to be disappointed by the paucity of well conducted evaluative studies that report program or project outcomes. As we indicated previously, most interventions are funded by government agencies. However, in Australia, although there has been much informal or general comment upon them, there have been no comprehensive reviews of government alcohol misuse intervention programs for indigenous peoples. (Note, however, that at the time of writing, the Commonwealth Department of Health and Family Services is conducting a review of its programs.)

Similarly, there has been little comprehensive evaluation of the interventions conducted by indigenous community organisations. Of 205 indigenous community projects that we have identified in Australia: 39 per cent had no evaluation component at all; 31 per cent collected data only on the administration of the projects; and only 30 per cent conducted any formal evaluation. In the latter group, only about half of the evaluations were being conducted as intended. Spokespersons for the organisations involved expressed concern at the inadequacy of resources and other supports provided by funding agencies to enable them to conduct adequate project evaluations.

Of the various interventions, most attention has been focused on the evaluation of 'treatment'. There is general agreement among health professionals, and to some extent the general public, that those who are dependent on alcohol should have access to some form of treatment. However, much more contentious is the question of what that treatment should consist of, and what effects should be expected of it. Not surprisingly, many of those operating treatment centres claim to be successful – claims which are sometimes accepted uncritically – but others are much less confident and their scepticism seems to be supported by the evidence.

There are many reasons why evaluating the success of treatment is difficult. For one thing, people undergoing treatment will differ with respect to many social factors and the severity of their substance use. More than 30 years ago Bruun (1963) identified four criteria by which evaluations of alcohol treatment could be simply judged: a sample of at least 150 is required; each individual in the sample needs to be adequately followed up for a designated period; the type of treatment must be specifically described; and categorical definitions of success must be articulated. Then, as now, few evaluations meet these criteria, and the methodological weaknesses of many treatment follow-up investigations continue to be cited (Sargent 1979:167; Weibel-Orlando 1989). Further, a review of several evaluations of alcohol treatments utilising a wide range of therapies (hypnosis, group therapy, drug therapy, aversion treatment, incarceration and probation) found, after controlling for treatment setting, no statistically significant differences in results, and this has been confirmed by other studies (Weibel-Orlando 1989).

One reason for this is that the performance indicators for judging the success of alcohol programs are 'various, unreliable and value-laden' (Sargent 1979:167). Those whose programs aim at abstinence will regard participants' being alcohol-free as a primary indicator of a program's success. In contrast, programs based on the harm minimisation model may use reduced incidences of alcohol-related morbidity, interaction with the law, or similar indices. Some agencies combine an ideology of abstinence with more practical goals of reduced harm. For instance, the Canadian Poundmaker's program states that its mission is to 'reduce the prevalence and harmful consequences of alcohol and other drug abuse among Native peoples', while its goal is 'abstinence through counselling and through providing peer support, information, and opportunities for spiritual growth' (Poundmaker's Lodge n.d.)

As mentioned previously, lifelong sobriety is the sole criterion of success of the AA-oriented programs throughout the world, but the impracticality of tracing clients over this period has led to selection of arbitrary periods after treatment, for example three months or twelve months, over which a client's sobriety is monitored. Another suggested intermediate measure of outcome for treatment programs has been the length of stay in treatment.

In Australia and Canada, most indigenous alcohol and other drug treatment centres are based on the Alcoholics Anonymous model, being run by recovering ex-substance-dependent staff with little formal training in either treatment or rehabilitation (Brady 1991a:206). An analysis of Australian treatment centres found poor success rates in both these indigenous centres and national rates of rehabilitation (Wilson n.d., in Brady 1991a:206).

In Canada, completion of the treatment (usually residential programs of between four and six weeks' duration) appears to be one of the few criteria by which treatment centres are assessed. Across that country, about two-thirds (68 per cent) of all those entering treatment actually complete the program; terminations are mainly initiated by the clients themselves (Canada, Health and Welfare 1991). A follow-up study of those leaving treatment found that more than one-third (36 per cent) had been residents of treatment programs previously. This finding is supported by one from an analysis carried out among indigenous people in the United States, where a two-year follow-up study revealed that 47 of 50 clients interviewed reported a drinking relapse (Kivlahan *et al.* 1985). Similar poor rates of recovery are cited elsewhere for the United States (Flores 1985).

The report on the evaluation of the Central Australian Aboriginal Alcohol Programs Unit (CAAAPU) noted that some clients were less likely than others to stay in treatment. Consequently the evaluators suggested that those 'who reside less than 150 kilometres from CAAAPU, who reside in town camps and riverbeds, and who do not have English as their first language' should be targeted for longer stays. (Miller & Rowse 1995:31).

A clear difference between indigenous treatment centres in Canada and Australia (with the exception of CAAAPU in Central Australia) is the incorporation of traditional healing practices into Canadian treatment programs. Poor recovery rates of indigenous clients of treatment centres have been attributed to the relative absence of indigenous cultural values in programs in the United States (Flores 1985). It is clear that indigenous people prefer programs that incorporate their understandings of the world (McKenzie 1993). According to Scott, describing Canadian programs:

... consistently what seem to work best are treatment interventions that emphasize strengthening from the inside out (where communities direct the healing process and tap into internal and external resources as necessary) and the essential balance between physical, mental, emotional and spiritual elements (1996:7).

However, the absence of any systematic form of evaluation of these methods means that 'We still do not know if any sort of alcoholism intervention, conventional or indigenous, works at all or for long periods of time' (Weibel-Orlando 1989:152).

Throughout Australia, Canada and New Zealand, indigenous communities have seen the control of the availability of alcohol, in particular, as central to their overall strategy to combat dependence and abuse. This has involved both prohibition (as in the 'dry' communities) and restrictions on sales and supply. In Ontario, Canada, isolated communities have benefited in the short term from prohibition (Smart 1979). In a review of prohibition policies in that country, McKenzie (1993) notes that although prohibition restricts the supply of alcohol, other substance abuse problems associated with gasoline sniffing, marijuana or cocaine use, particularly among the young, seem to be becoming more frequent.

In Australia, as we discussed in the previous chapter, a number of indigenous communities have experimented with both prohibition and regulation of the supply of alcohol, but there have been very few rigorous evaluations of these. An evaluation of a trial period of restrictions in Tennant Creek found fewer offences against the public order, fewer alcohol-related hospital admissions, and declines in the number of admissions to the women's refuge (d'Abbs *et al.* 1996:1–2). Anecdotal evidence suggests that while prohibition has had positive consequences in some remote communities, problems might simply have been transferred to other locations as heavy drinkers move to other communities.

The paucity of well conducted and well documented evaluations does not enable us to provide definitive answers to the question of what works. However, there is a considerable literature on the issues involved in the evaluation of indigenous programs. This and our own experience indicate that a number of conditions must be addressed and satisfied before meaningful evaluation of indigenous alcohol misuse interventions can be undertaken that will provide more certain answers.

Evaluation and political self-determination

Indigenous peoples are insisting that governments deliver on their promises of self-determination, ensuring local community control and participation. The extent to which demands for self-determination are accepted by various levels of government determines how well indigenous peoples are enabled to: formulate policy and programs; participate in the delivery of services that meet their perceived needs; and themselves evaluate the effectiveness of those programs and services.

In part, the extent to which the promise of self-determination has been met has been determined by national political frameworks. In Canada, there are important differences between policy and service delivery to those indigenous peoples covered by treaties (so-called 'status Indians') and those who are not. In recent years, policy in New Zealand has been framed with reference to the obligations to indigenous people provided by the Treaty of Waitangi in 1840. These legal frameworks provide indigenous peoples (or at least some of them) with advantages that indigenous Australians do not enjoy – although it is possible to argue that a de facto distinction is increasingly made in Australia between so-called 'traditional', remote-dwelling, 'real' Aboriginal people, and urban, more politicised people, whose claims to Aboriginality are contested, both by some Aboriginal people and by many non-Aboriginal people.

In Australia and Canada, differences in treaty obligations are compounded by the tension that exists between federal and state or provincial governments. In both countries, federal governments have generally made greater concessions to indigenous demands for self-determination than state and provincial governments. In both countries, indigenous peoples are concerned that even where provincial governments have made 'in principle' concessions to self-determination, often this is not reflected in the program objectives and activities of mainstream government agencies; and that concessions to 'states' rights' have been at the expense of local indigenous control (Australia, ATSIC 1995; Long, Boldt & Little Bear 1988).

Concern with self-determination is not an issue for abstract political theorising. The literature on self-determination and indigenous–government relations contains an implicit view that from self-determination will flow the development and implementation of effective policy and programs (Little Bear, Boldt & Long 1984; Tonkinson & Howard 1990). This view is supported by a comprehensive US review, which found that real improvements in the socioeconomic status of indigenous Americans are directly attributable to political changes of the 1970s that led to 'increased Indian control over, and participation in, the formulation of Indian policy' including agenda setting, and policy development, implementation and evaluation (Gross 1989).

Recasting self-determination into accountability

Although the notion of self-determination was initially coined to express the desire of indigenous peoples to have control over significant aspects of their lives, increasingly the term has been recast to refer to issues of accountability. For example, in Australia in the mid-1970s, the Commonwealth government's official policy was changed from 'self-determination' to 'self-management'. At the political level, in the context of indigenous health and substance abuse programs, much of the demand for increased evaluation has been driven by concerns about financial accountability (Kumpfer *et al.* 1993).

Few people seriously oppose the need for either government agencies or indigenous community organisations to be financially accountable. All too often, however, insufficient attention is paid to the provision of the skills and resources required to meet reporting requirements. While the staff of many of the larger indigenous organisations now include accountants and administrators, many small agencies are inadequately resourced to complete the often complex administrative and financial tasks associated with external funding, especially when such funding comes from multiple sources.

In the cautious 1990s, no-one should be surprised that governments and citizens are more closely monitoring how public monies are spent. However, while not discounting its importance, many indigenous people are concerned that a narrow focus on financial accountability overlooks the broader issues of what one prominent indigenous Australian has referred to as 'social accountability' (O'Donoghue 1995).

Social accountability includes the demand that those who provide services for indigenous peoples – be they government or indigenous organisations – should be directly accountable to the people who receive them. Unfortunately, however, this demand for direct accountability is at odds with the indirect accountability provided for in the Westminster system of government. In this system, services are provided by so-called public servants, who are responsible to the ministers of their respective departments who, in turn, are responsible to elected parliaments and the law (McInnes & Billingsley 1992). This system severely limits the influence of local indigenous populations and, in conjunction with the stringent financial accountability requirements and conditions imposed on indigenous organisations, severely constrains indigenous self-determination (Dyck 1985; Powderface 1984).

The constraints imposed by the Westminster system mean that complaints to a government agency about the perceived shortcomings of a particular program in a community may take months to receive a response. It can be quicker and more effective to complain to the media and/or local politician – particularly if the community is in a marginal electorate and there is an election on the horizon. This means, however, that resources are often provided on the basis of political expediency rather than a rational consideration of community needs.

In Canada, federal self-government legislation allows some indigenous groups greater social and economic responsibility and autonomy (McInnes & Billingsley 1992). It has been argued that the creation of the Aboriginal and Torres Strait Islander Commission (ATSIC) in Australia was an attempt to similarly satisfy indigenous demands for greater self-determination, while reconciling it with government attempts to improve accountability (Sanders 1993). Currently there are calls to disband ATSIC and, at least in part, these are in response to the perceived failure of ATSIC to satisfy accountability requirements. In New Zealand, and now in parts of Australia, the contracting out of health care services from government to indigenous community organisations has provided the possibility of greater autonomy in the operation of services – although some would argue that government agencies still exercise control through their determination of what services they will purchase. The challenge in all of these arrangements is to build in some measure of accountability to funding agencies without usurping control and accountability at the local level.

Putting health visions into practice

Appropriate evaluation is only one aspect of, and not a substitute for, the planning of programs that respond effectively to the needs of indigenous peoples. Much of the dissatisfaction with alcohol misuse intervention programs for indigenous peoples – and hence the calls for more stringent evaluation – stems from shortcomings associated with the planning and implementation of such programs. Translating a vision for a substance abuse program into practice requires attention to a number of factors, the most important of which is probably the recognition of the heterogeneity of indigenous communities and the need to incorporate different needs into program design (Canada, Task Force on Program Review 1985; Australia, National Aboriginal Health Strategy Working Party 1989; Hawkes 1991). Even within national borders, indigenous peoples in Australia, New Zealand and Canada have different traditional cultures and colonial histories, which in turn have contributed to diverse contemporary social positions and experiences. For example, Noongar people from the southwest of Western Australia experienced alienation from their land soon after European settlement in the nineteenth century, while many groups in northern Australia continue to either reside on or have access to traditional country. Such differences have been incorporated into the Australian High Court's historic *Mabo* decision of 1992, which recognised native title in Australia, privileging the land rights of those people who had maintained continuous association with their land over those who had been dispossessed (Australia, High Court 1992).

Effective program outcomes are dependent upon the setting of clear objectives. While this might seem straightforward, it is apparent from the literature and our own experiences that this is often not achieved (Australia, ATSIC, Office of Evaluation and Audit 1991a; Daly 1993). At the same time, however, plans for programs and particular projects need to retain the flexibility to incorporate changed objectives. For instance, an intervention program aimed at reducing alcohol misuse among young people by offering recreational and other activities may need to be modified to include provision of education and employment opportunities in response to young people's requests for skills that will allow them to enter the workforce. Such changes need to be documented and taken into account during any evaluation.

As well as being clear, program objectives also have to be achievable. Again, while this seems simple enough, it is a point on which many programs have floundered. Program staff have to avoid objectives that are more 'wish lists' than attainable goals. For instance, while lifelong sobriety for all clients might be the long-term goal of an alcohol treatment program, a more realistic goal might be sobriety three months after treatment. This has important implications for evaluation because it is upon success in attaining stated goals that programs and projects are ultimately judged by funding agencies.

Both government and indigenous community agencies must also have the ability and resources to implement goals. In Canada, lack of field experience by Department of Indian and Northern Development personnel was identified as creating difficulties for program design (Nicholson 1984); and in Australia, reviews of ATSIC programs found that levels of staffing and other resources were often well below those approved for similar government programs (Australia, ATSIC, Office of Evaluation and Audit 1991a, 1991b, 1993). As government agencies are sometimes under-resourced and ill-equipped to implement program goals, so too are many community organisations that have taken on the responsibility for particular health programs. In Canada, a review of program delivery reported that effectiveness and efficiency would improve if communities were given more responsibility for program management (Canada, Task Force on Program Review 1985) but that this increased level of responsibility required higher levels of support.

Many bureaucrats are unaware that administrative procedures that they regard as everyday are unfamiliar to the members of many indigenous communities. To some extent this has been recognised by governments. For instance, in Australia, the Office of Evaluation and Audit's evaluations of ATSIC programs stress the need to document program procedures and educate communities about them (Australia, ATSIC, Office of Evaluation and Audit 1991a, 1991b, 1993).

Clearly, evaluation and monitoring procedures must be an integral part of program planning. This axiom has implications for the monitoring and evaluation of programs by third parties such as indigenous affairs departments. Such departments are not adequately resourced to evaluate the outcomes of the many government indigenous programs; nor is this desirable, given the need for integrated program development and evaluation. To most effectively oversee indigenous programs, indigenous affairs departments should provide other agencies with 'best practice' guidelines for indigenous program planning and evaluation, and monitor their compliance with those guidelines. Given the importance of self-determination, such monitoring should include review of:

- indigenous participation in policy formulation;
- the match between program objectives, and the needs and priorities of indigenous peoples;
- the extent to which indigenous peoples are involved in the delivery of services, including the contracting of service delivery to community organisations; and,
- the opportunity for indigenous peoples to participate in the evaluation of program effectiveness.

The political context of program evaluation

In recent years the political and ideological nature of program evaluation has received some attention (Carr-Hill 1985; Duigan & Casswell 1989). Definitions of the 'problems' that programs are designed to address, and the perceptions of the underlying causes of those problems, are inherently political. Indigenous people have argued that cultural differences lie at the heart of political differences in problem definition by their own communities and government agencies. They maintain that while government agencies continue to compartmentalise services into boxes called 'health', 'education', 'land' and 'welfare', indigenous people perceive their needs holistically, and insist that their programs be evaluated in this light (O'Donoghue 1995; Canada, Development Indicator Project Steering Committee 1991). The division of the public service into various departments, each having its own aims and objectives, works against intersectoral cooperation, and it is rare for evaluators to take into account the impact one program may have on other sectors in a community (United States Senate, Select Committee on Indian Affairs 1992).

This definitional problem for program development is compounded by the quality of analysis applied by policy makers to the understanding of social problems such as the misuse of alcohol. This is often unsophisticated, and based on what Chen and Rossi have described as 'the current folk-lore of the upper-middle-brow media' (1983:285). The ideological assumptions that underlie such analysis are rarely questioned. They carry weight because of the political power of those holding them, rather than any inherent explanatory value, and they hold sway over the views of other groups, including indigenous peoples.

Program evaluation is a site for political contestation for other reasons as well. For both pragmatic and ideological reasons, indigenous groups may use programs to achieve objectives not considered by the funding body. For example, one community organisation with which we have worked required funds to support family-based activities as a means of reducing alcohol misuse among youth. To comply with restrictive funding agency guidelines, the organisation prepared an application for funds for a project to provide alcohol education for youth, and then sought to use the money for the organisation's original purpose. In another example, gaps in services provided by government agencies may necessitate the redirection by community organisations of money from projects funded for other purposes to fill those gaps. These kinds of activities make sense at the community level, and lead to positive outcomes unintended in terms of the original programs (Dyck 1985; Cain, Davidson & McGrath 1981). However, they may lead to accusations of misuse of funds when programs are externally audited.

For these reasons, it has been argued that the evaluation of programs for indigenous peoples must incorporate indigenous assessments of both the programs and their broader effects, using criteria that reflect the broad range of indigenous social needs (Australia, ATSIC 1995; Cobbin & Barlow 1993). In Canada, indigenous people have taken the initiative in this regard, attempting to construct development indicators that can be used to measure the wider effects of new programs at the community level (Canada, Development Indicator Project Steering Committee 1991). The use of such indicators requires political support from sources outside communities, as governments driven by economic rationalism seek to narrowly define how communities should spend their allocated monies.

Just as political and ideological assumptions underlie decisions about what is to be evaluated, they also underlie the choice of methodology. Again, such assumptions are rarely openly discussed or questioned. Debates such as that between Garbutcheon Singh (1990) and Keefe (1990) over the relative merits of economic rationalist and culturalist approaches to evaluation are rare. However, in reports such as that of the Office of Evaluation and Audit review of ATSIC's Community Infrastructure Program (Australia, ATSIC, Office of Evaluation and Audit 1991b), it is possible to identify an implicit economic rationalist drive for financial accountability that contrasts with broader social development approaches to program evaluation. Evaluators need to make explicit the theoretical assumptions underpinning their work, so that a more open debate about those assumptions and their degree of fit with those of indigenous communities can be conducted. In the absence of such openness, indigenous communities cannot be blamed for regarding decisions about methodology as motivated by narrow political considerations (Owston 1983; Long, Boldt & Little Bear 1988; Fleras & Elliot 1992).

Much of the evaluation literature assumes rational decision-making models, which are based on the fictional notions of a stable environment, unambiguous program objectives and resourcing at a level sufficient to undertake detailed assessments of program outcomes. This model ignores evidence from the real world, in which program decisions and evaluations are made in response to political manoeuvring between groups within organisations (Hennessy & Sullivan 1989). This is particularly so in many indigenous communities, where rival groups are often forced to compete for scarce public resources. Perhaps more striking is the evidence that in spite of the public clamour for evaluation, policy making appears not to be influenced by it in any clear way (Duigan & Casswell 1989; Miller & Hester 1986; Peele 1991). This reinforces suspicions that evaluation is often undertaken primarily to reassure political constituents that accountability is being taken seriously.

Among many indigenous organisations there is a perception that evaluation is used by program funding agencies to impose unreasonable accountability requirements on them, or to justify political and/or bureaucratic decisions to cut funding. Some believe that the performance of indigenous organisations is subjected to more scrutiny than other programs of funding agencies (Bartlett & Legge 1994; Moodie 1989). This is not to argue that program evaluations are of no practical value. In the right hands they can improve service delivery and inform public debate about political processes. However, ultimately major program decisions will be based on political considerations and relative power, not on the basis of evaluation reports alone.

Evaluation methodologies

Just as there have been contentious debates about the role of evaluation, so too have there been debates about how evaluations should be carried out. At one extreme there are claims that only experimental or quasi-experimental research designs can properly evaluate outcomes. At the other extreme are those who argue the need for the most flexible of qualitative evaluation. Both claims need to be treated with scepticism.

Objections to experimental design in evaluation are considerable, the most important being the ethical difficulties of assigning potential program recipients to experimental and control groups. Among groups whose need for services are demonstrably great, it is difficult to justify withholding some services from one group for any purpose. This type of evaluation is also expensive, requiring more time and resources than alternatives. Outcomes from experimental research designs are also dependent upon variables such as the choice of the control group and the time chosen as the benchmark for measurement. A more practical limitation is the difficulty of replicating experimental evaluations in whole populations or other environments, especially the socially and culturally complex settings of many indigenous communities (Daly 1993). Integral to experimental designs is the exclusion of stakeholder participation, whereas this is the most fundamental criterion for many indigenous communities. Unlike more flexible approaches, experimental designs cannot include any criteria of program effectiveness that may have arisen when the program was implemented (Broughton 1991). This is a serious shortcoming for many indigenous alcohol and other drug programs, where positive unintended consequences, such as increased levels of community activity in a number of areas, may result. Furthermore, a comprehensive review of standardised instruments for the evaluation of substance abuse prevention programs in the United States found that none were sensitive to cultural difference between populations (Kumpfer *et al.* 1993).

To overcome these limitations, evaluators have explored non-experimental and more qualitative approaches, variously termed 'naturalistic' or 'fourth-generation' evaluation (Hébert 1986; McEvoy & Rissel 1992). Such designs employ a more descriptive approach, and rely on qualitative techniques of data collection and analysis – such as participant observation and in-depth interviews – used to good effect in cross-cultural research by anthropologists and sociologists. Some evaluators demonstrate a relatively unsophisticated understanding of qualitative techniques (McEvoy & Rissel 1992). However, others have shown how they can be used sensitively, rigorously and successfully in evaluation research (Brooks 1994; Patton 1980). In Australia a number of reports recommend on-site visits, allowing observation of programs in action and discussions with participants, for the most reliable and valid data (Australia, ATSIC, Office of Evaluation and Audit 1992; Martin 1988; Baume 1992).

Qualitative evaluation has attracted such strong support in some quarters that a claim has been made that this is the only appropriate way in which to evaluate indigenous programs. Based on the notion that many indigenous communities operate on a group-centred, consensus model of decision making, Hébert (1986) claims that the individually

focused nature of quantitatively based surveys and sampling are methodologically inappropriate. Hébert's understandings of indigenous social
organisation and political decision reflect a stereotype that neglects the
myriad of individually focused actions that occur at the community level
and cut across attempts at group consensus. The evidence suggests that
researchers should not dismiss the possibility of conducting quantitatively oriented research among indigenous people. Research among
indigenous groups in the United States has been conducted by the use of
telephone surveys (Sugarman *et al.* 1992), and in Australia the use of tele-
conferencing has been suggested as a way to reduce the costs of research
in remote locations (Bourke *et al.* 1991). The ease with which indigenous
communities have adopted new technologies, including computers and
tele-conferencing, supports their use in research. We argue that rigorous
evaluation requires a pluralistic methodology that includes a range of
techniques and data sources (documentary, interviews, questionnaires,
group discussions, participant observation, case studies, and so on), and
as many stakeholders as practicable.

In the last decade or so there has been increasing pressure to include
specific performance indicators in program planning, and then to use
them to assess the extent to which programs have met their objectives.
However, the selection of performance indicators requires careful
consideration. They should realistically reflect the impact of the program
and the processes involved, from the viewpoints of both administrators
and recipients. However, the literature abounds with examples of where
this has not been achieved. For example, simple counts of patient visits –
proposed in the past as one measure of the performance of Aboriginal
health services – provide no information about outcomes achieved by
particular services, say nothing about the severity of problems dealt
with, and are too general to be of any use in process evaluation; and the
collection of the data is wasteful of resources (Moodie 1989). Furthermore, when data from individual health services are aggregated, they
provide no information on either the efficiency or the effectiveness of
the program as a whole.

Given the difficulty of developing appropriate performance indicators
and the costs involved in the collection of data, the use of existing data
collections for program evaluation has obvious attractions (Australia,
Department of Finance, Management and Information Systems and
Evaluation 1992). There are problems with this, however, not the least of
which is the fact that the purposes for which routine data are gathered
are often different from those required for the assessment of the success
of programs (Alati 1993). The suggestion that health indicators such as
census, morbidity and mortality statistics be used to measure program
success ignores the complex economic, social and political foundations

of ill health (Moodie 1989; Saggers & Gray 1991). Furthermore, such indicators take no account of the adequacy of the resources allocated to address the problems.

These limitations have been widely recognised, and there have been various calls for the establishment and maintenance of specialised databases (Canada, Task Force on Program Review 1985; Australia, ATSIC, Office of Evaluation and Audit 1991b, 1992). Our own experience has shown some of the problems with these databases, which require heavy staff and resource commitments to establish and then maintain. The computing technology is expensive and time-consuming, with constant problems arising from the lack of fit between hardware and software, and the reliance on specialised computing personnel when things go wrong. Those suggesting that multi-functional databases be established for planning and evaluation purposes (Western Australia, Task Force on Aboriginal Social Justice 1994) have not been able to demonstrate that these will not have the same limitations as existing data collections, or that the data gathered will be sufficiently comprehensive to measure program outcomes.

There is clearly a need for expanded data collection systems to facilitate the evaluation of programs for indigenous peoples. However, the impact of these must be carefully considered. Sackett (1993) has been critical of the call by the Australian Royal Commission into Aboriginal Deaths in Custody for the collection of more data on Aboriginal and Torres Strait Islander peoples. He has argued that the response to this call by federal and state governments will 'extend the scrutiny of Aboriginal lives' and increase bureaucratic control of indigenous peoples with little likelihood of benefit to them. For these reasons, the Canadian Development Indicator Project Steering Committee (1991) has argued that performance indicator development and data collection should be undertaken by indigenous communities themselves, thus promoting indigenous autonomy and responsibility, and responding to community heterogeneity. This, of course, requires a commitment by governments to providing the necessary training and resources to carry this out.

Cultural appropriateness

In the 1990s when so-called 'political correctness' is attacked by the political right in most western countries, cultural appropriateness is a term some see as a survival from the 1970s. However, for indigenous groups it remains an important concern, and it is necessary to engage in debates about what indigenous people understand by the term and how it can be implemented. When indigenous people talk about the need for cultural appropriateness, they are demanding that all programs and the evaluations of those programs incorporate indigenous understandings of history, society and culture. That is, they want acknowledgement of indigenous and colonial histories, of indigenous social organisation and activities, and of continuing language and cultural traditions. One of the difficulties with this demand, in terms of implementation, is that these understandings are varied because of the heterogeneity of indigenous peoples' experiences in Australia, Canada and New Zealand.

In spite of this difficulty, there is widespread recognition that both programs and the means by which they are evaluated must be culturally appropriate. What is more problematic, however, is translating this principle into something more than simple rules for better intercultural communication. In particular, we must ensure that programs meet the needs of individual communities. Even when reviews stress the importance of cultural appropriateness – as was the case with that by the ATSIC Office of Evaluation and Audit in Australia (1993) – guidelines for achieving this are absent.

As with program development, the best way of ensuring that program evaluation is culturally appropriate is to involve indigenous stakeholders in the evaluation process. Indigenous groups in Canada and New Zealand are more likely to be consulted than those in Australia because of their greater power, which is based on the widespread recognition of self-government in those countries, and the stronger tribal and national organisation of their indigenous peoples (Gross 1989; Owston 1983; Jull 1992).

The inclusion of indigenous people is more likely to occur at the data collection stage, when clients may be approached for their views of the success of particular programs. They are much less likely to be consulted when the evaluation is being planned, or during the analysis of the results. As with all research, the findings from an evaluation require interpretation, and there may be differences between the ways in which researchers and the indigenous stakeholders view the evidence, and hence the recommendations flowing from that evidence (Australia, ATSIC, Office of Evaluation and Audit 1992; Hébert 1986; Owston 1983). Here the sometimes competing interests of indigenous and other stakeholders have to be balanced. For example, an evaluation of a moderate drinking campaign may recommend stronger controls on the availability of alcohol which, if implemented, could adversely affect the financial viability of local liquor suppliers.

Even within indigenous communities there may be contentious debates about what constitutes cultural 'truths'. For example, some indigenous Australian men and their lawyers have claimed that sexual assault and violence towards one's spouse are part of traditional 'Law', a claim vehemently rejected by some indigenous women, who have called this 'bullshit Law' (Bolger 1990). With respect to the evaluation of the CAAAPU treatment centre, there were differences of opinion about issues such as the mixing of men and women in therapeutic groups, and the cultural details of the style of training (Miller & Rowse 1995:24). Describing one 'truth session' in one of the training modules, one of the evaluators wrote:

> The males sat in a circle surrounded by the females; they then completed a 'naming ceremony' (an Indian custom [introduced by a Native Canadian consultant to the program]) where a feather was passed around the circle and each male stated full name and family ties. Several items had been placed on the floor in front of them – two items were then chosen and an explanation as to why these items were chosen (that is, what the items reminded them of) was then given. Participants described this session as 'very personal' and 'intimate', together with 'culturally inappropriate' specifically because session(s) were conducted in mixed gender groups (Miller, in Miller & Rowse 1995:25).

The selection of indigenous stakeholders in evaluation can itself be a complex procedure. In small communities it may be feasible to speak with all the adult members, but in most communities it will be necessary to select a sub-sample of the total population (Hébert 1986). For many indigenous communities, statistically based random selection, or western, democratic notions of representation are not considered acceptable (Weaver 1984). In these communities, authority to speak is not universal, being vested in those whose age and/or gender renders them appropriate spokespersons in particular contexts. This may be especially problematic when those authorised to speak present a position at odds with that of significant numbers of other community members. In the past, indigenous Australian women have claimed that their views have not been heard, with non-indigenous people preferring to rely exclusively on the testimonies of senior men (Bell & Ditton 1980; Bell 1993). In such situations, evaluators need to exercise great caution and sensitivity.

Just as there are age and gender divisions in communities, so too there are differences in power between stakeholders; often these are more acute between indigenous and non-indigenous stakeholders. These power differentials need to be understood by evaluators when setting objectives, determining data collection techniques, or interpreting the results. Evaluators need to ensure that the opinions of indigenous people are not overshadowed by those of other stakeholders, by clearly artic-ulating in evaluation guidelines procedures that ensure that indigenous voices are heard. At another level, sensitive analysis of community-level indigenous politics and strategic political alliances will reveal the folly of stereotypical notions of community egalitarianism.

Inclusion of all stakeholders is seen as being important to best professional practice in mainstream evaluation (Owen 1993; Palfrey 1992). However, it is *essential* in indigenous communities, where power holding is more diffuse and where exclusion of some can cause social disruption. Among the advantages accruing from community involvement in evaluation are the identification of unforeseen problems, improvements in both program efficiency and effectiveness, and the allaying of community suspicion and hostility that can undermine evaluation (Australia, ATSIC 1995; National Centre for Research into the Prevention of Drug Abuse 1989; Australia, Second Task Force on Evaluation 1992).

While indigenous stakeholder involvement is essential, it will not ensure the cultural appropriateness of program evaluation if the cultural chasm that often separates non-indigenous evaluators and indigenous peoples is not given adequate recognition. Central to this are issues of language and communication. Among non-indigenous people there is often little understanding of the varieties of non-standard English spoken, and the wide range of non-verbal communication used, by indigenous peoples (Eades 1992; von Stürmer 1981). Without such understanding, the integrity of the evaluation process can be compromised. It should be noted, however, that even indigenous people themselves are not immune to criticism of this kind. Participants in the Aboriginal-run CAAAPU program told the evaluators that the level of English used in lectures was too difficult for them to follow; this led to recommendations that rather than conduct training in English only, Arrente and other Central Australian languages should be used (Miller & Rowse 1995:27–31).

Evaluation and the reduction of misuse

The economic rationalism that, in the 1980s and 1990s, has driven governments to cut public expenditure and demand greater levels of accountability, has contributed to the healthy state of the evaluation industry. Despite such agendas, it is reasonable to expect that all organisations purporting to offer services to reduce levels of alcohol misuse and its consequences should be evaluated in terms of their effectiveness. However, the evaluation of such interventions is not a simple matter – as attested by the fact that there are so few successful studies – and, because of the complexity of the issues, we need to be wary of the uncritical application of general evaluation theories and methodologies to programs for indigenous peoples.

The literature and our own research and community-based experiences indicate the existence of a chasm between the expectations of funding agencies and those of indigenous peoples about health and substance abuse program evaluation. While there are no ideal, culturally appropriate models that can guide the kind of evaluations that are needed, there are a number of principles that must be contextualised within a framework of self-determination, where indigenous peoples negotiate with government agencies to decide what programs they need, how the programs might be implemented, the outcomes they believe are desirable, and how those outcomes can be evaluated. These issues are political as well as financial.

Evaluation methodologies need to incorporate a wide and flexible array of qualitative and quantitative techniques that are sensitive to the social and cultural differences existing in indigenous communities, and to the paucity of administrative, technological and information infrastructure available to support evaluation. Indigenous peoples must be consulted at each stage of the evaluation process, from the determination of objectives to the interpretation of evaluation results. We also need to be sure that indigenous alcohol misuse programs that are poorly resourced are not unfairly bearing the brunt of evaluation attention, while programs for healthier, non-indigenous communities escape the bureaucratic gaze.

Finally, a word of caution is required. More systematic evaluation of the interventions we have described is, in our view, likely to demonstrate their necessity and importance in ameliorating the effects of alcohol misuse. However, as we have argued earlier, the higher rates of alcohol misuse and associated harm among indigenous peoples are a consequence of colonisation and its continuing effects, and ultimately will not be adequately dealt with until these underlying issues are addressed.

CHAPTER 10

Where to from here?

Throughout this book we have documented the role that alcohol plays in indigenous communities in Australia, New Zealand, and Canada, and the responses by mainstream health authorities and indigenous groups. For many years now, indigenous people have risked intensifying negative public attention by speaking out about the devastation that alcohol has wreaked on their communities. Violence within and between families, job loss, absent or poor parenting, threats to culture and tradition, sickness and premature death are all part of the drinking cultures embedded within many indigenous communities. Indeed, for many non-indigenous people, these characteristics have come to stereotypically define indigenous life, while those who abstain or drink moderately, hold down jobs, raise their children responsibly and otherwise contribute positively to society are less likely to be noticed.

Understanding why alcohol and other drugs hold such a powerful position in some segments of indigenous communities necessitates consideration of the place these drugs have had in human societies in different times and places. All known human societies have exploited mind-altering substances available to them, choosing some substances and rejecting others in a wide variety of cultural patterns. The effects of those drugs is also extremely variable, depending upon the drug itself, the state of mind of the user, and the physical and social context in which drugs are consumed (Zinberg 1984:6). In this context, indigenous use of alcohol is not unique.

Alcohol is the most commonly used drug among the non-indigenous peoples of Australia, New Zealand and Canada, despite some declines in its use in the past decade. Although, epidemiologically speaking, tobacco is the drug that takes the greatest toll on their health, alcohol is of far greater concern among indigenous people because of the social disruption it causes in addition to its health consequences. For these reasons, we have concentrated on alcohol in this book. However, it is clear that the use of tobacco, solvents and, increasingly, pharmaceuticals and illicit drugs, by indigenous people will require greater attention in the future.

Our focus has been on Australia. However, by making comparisons with New Zealand and Canada we have tried to show that, although there have been some variations, the colonial histories of the three countries have led to similar patterns of marginalisation of indigenous people, and resulted in very similar health and social profiles. As we have argued, this marginalisation exacerbates the misuse of alcohol and its consequences.

Understanding the political economy of indigenous health and the role that alcohol and other drugs play within this economy is fundamental to our theoretical approach to substance abuse. As we have shown, there are several competing theories of alcohol and other drug use, which draw upon biological, social and cultural factors to attempt to explain why some individuals and groups appear to be more prone to misuse than others. While not denying the various contributions of these factors, we have emphasised the importance of structural conditions such as lack of economic resources, limited political power, and social marginalisation, which have their origins in the history of British colonialism and the dispossession of indigenous peoples.

Theories of political economy may satisfactorily explain the continuation of poor health and high rates of substance abuse. However, they are less able to explain why some communities and individuals have successfully struggled against this scenario. Alkali Lake, in British Columbia, is often cited as such an example. Of a community where almost all residents were reputedly heavy drinkers, 95 per cent became abstinent. Bootlegging of alcohol was eliminated and completion of alcohol treatment rewarded by employment. Most of this transformation was attributed to the efforts of the chief, who persuaded the council that drastic measures were required (Smart 1979). Remarkable too have been the efforts of individuals who have been able to simply quit, while still retaining membership of heavy drinking communities (Brady 1993, 1995a). These examples demonstrate the value of theories that allow for dynamic interactions between individuals and groups, and for the structural conditions and institutions within which their lives are negotiated.

As our research on local-level political economies of alcohol shows, however, individual and community efforts to curb alcohol-related harm can be more effective when combined with an understanding of the ways in which the supply and promotion of alcohol occurs, particularly in small communities. In depressed rural economies, and in a context of declining consumption of alcohol among the general population, competition for drinkers among the owners of liquor outlets is fierce, resulting in an array of promotional strategies designed to increase, or at least maintain, high levels of consumption (Boffa, George & Tsey 1994; Saggers & Gray 1997). The evidence suggests, however, that some compromises are possible. Concern by indigenous organisations and health professionals has led to agreements between licensees to restrict hours of trading, limit sales of particular high-risk items such as cask wine and bottled beer, and to encourage more moderate drinking by the provision of higher-quality drinking environments (d'Abbs *et al.* 1996). Maintaining these agreements requires delicate negotiations and continued vigilance as segments of the alcohol industry attempt to maintain profit levels in the face of declining consumption in the wider population.

These increases in regulation have come about because of the devastation that alcohol misuse has wrought – devastation which is especially evident in the many small communities where indigenous people comprise a significant proportion of the population. While precise epidemiological studies of alcohol misuse might not always be available, no community in which heavy drinking occurs can ignore the personal and community toll of related hospital admissions, road accidents, suicides, fights, domestic violence, child abuse and sexual assault, and disruptions to work, family and social and cultural life (Durie 1994; McKenzie 1993; Swensen & Unwin 1994). It has been estimated that between one-quarter and a half of all illness and deaths among indigenous people in Australia, New Zealand and Canada are alcohol-related (Alexander 1990; Scott 1993). In some regions these proportions are even higher, with few families escaping some direct experience of these consequences.

Whether prohibiting or regulating alcohol, governments and organisations tread a fine line in assessing the risk to society from the drug-related harm, and the risks to individual liberties posed by regulations and treatments. However, in spite of occasional ideological statements to the contrary, many indigenous communities have been prepared to compromise individual liberties in order to achieve communal gains from such restrictions.

Besides limiting the supply of alcohol, an array of therapeutic interventions are available for alcohol- and other drug-dependent indigenous people. Canada has more than 20 years' experience in the provision of such programs, and the establishment of the National Native Alcohol and Drug Abuse Program (NNADAP) in 1975 provided a national focus for the treatment of substance abuse. Here residential treatment is the focus, most based on the AA model with indigenous cultural elements added (Scott 1993). Australia and New Zealand have fewer residential treatment centres but, like Canada, offer a range of prevention programs in education and health promotion, recreation and cultural initiatives (Gray & Morfitt 1996).

While there is some evidence that controlling the availability of alcohol and other drugs reduces consumption, the success of treatment for dependent individuals remains ambiguous at best. Very few evaluations of indigenous treatment programs have been carried out, and most regard length of stay in treatment as a criterion of success, rather than using the more ambitious criteria of sobriety or reduction of harm after a specified period.

To adequately assess their effects, program objectives need to be clearly defined, with criteria for success standardised. Follow-up of clients to assess their ability to sustain themselves outside a program is essential. It seems to us that the most useful indicators of success are those related to reduced incidences of harm – hospitalisation, accidents, violence, crime. AA-based programs obviously regard sobriety as the ultimate goal of their treatment, although some are happy with harm minimisation as a medium-term objective. This is perhaps more realistic, for as Weibel-Orlando (1989) points out, life histories of drinkers tend to show cycles of abstinence, moderation, and heavy drinking followed by abstinence, rather than lifelong sobriety.

We have stressed the need for more rigorous evaluation of treatment outcomes. However, evaluation must not be used as a blunt instrument with which to bludgeon under-resourced indigenous organisations and programs. In Australia, the new catch-phrase of 'self-empowerment' puts more emphasis on community responsibility and accountability at the same time as the federal government is reducing public spending wherever possible. It is important that in this climate any calls for more rigorous evaluation of indigenous substance misuse programs be examined critically.

The determinants of health

Some observers are encouraged by the evidence that there are proportionally more indigenous non-drinkers than among the non-indigenous population, and by the numbers of people who have recovered from alcohol and other drug dependence on their own (Brady 1993, 1995a; Rowse 1993). But an analysis of drinking and other drug-taking trends in indigenous populations provides little comfort. Children are experimenting with alcohol and other drugs at earlier ages, with 10–13 years being the greatest risk period (Scott 1996; Gray *et al.* 1996). Children as young as five are sniffing solvents, and trying marijuana and other illicit drugs (Okwumbabua & Duryea 1987). Because more women than men abstain from drinking, they have been seen by some as models of restraint (Rowse 1993). But many of the abstainers are middle-aged or elderly women; they are much less likely to be young. This is also the case for men. This indicates that, despite the effort that has gone into the treatment and prevention of alcohol-related problems, while some important successes have been achieved, overall this effort has had, and is having, limited impact.

In part, this lack of success is a consequence of the fact that, although considerable resources and energies have been devoted to both prevention and treatment, the magnitude of the response has been inadequate. There are many towns and communities where there are no sobering-up shelters, no refuges and no residential treatment for those who desire it. Those programs which have been established need more skilled, trained staff and suitable accommodation and other resources.

To understand why these interventions have had limited success, we also need to examine the problematic use of alcohol in the broader context of other health problems. We sometimes need to be reminded that while good health and medical services (including alcohol and other drug treatment services) may influence who gets better after becoming sick, it does not determine who remains well or gets sick in the first place (Stoddart 1996; Saggers & Gray 1991).

Alcohol and other drug dependence and their associated illnesses are often grouped with other diseases that are termed 'lifestyle' diseases, that is, are said to originate in the behaviours and ways of life of particular populations. For this reason, much health promotion and lay opinion stresses the responsibility of individuals to take better care of themselves, by drinking moderately or not at all, giving up smoking, and eating nutritious foods. Research among indigenous groups indicates that these health messages have been heard – most people understand the risk to their health that smoking, excessive alcohol and some illicit drugs pose (Gray *et al.* 1996). However, this seems to make little difference to their health behaviours.

Much research has been conducted on the general determinants of health, and it is now generally well known that the improvements in health over the past two centuries occurred well before the development of effective medical therapy. Prosperity and improved standards of living, made possible by the industrial revolution, are strongly correlated with declining mortality rates (McKeown 1979). A striking contemporary example of this relationship comes from Russia, where between 1987 and 1993 life expectancy for men has fallen from 65 to 59 years. Increased death rates for children and adults are due to rises in the rates of infectious diseases, accidents, suicides, poisoning and violence. These declines are attributed to the economic and social crises that accompanied the dissolution of the USSR. Maintaining a very basic standard of living is beyond the means of increasing numbers of Russian citizens (Hertzman & Ayers 1993).

The very strong relationship between economic status and health is complex, however, as another example helps to illustrate. Japanese life expectancy has overtaken that of Canada, the United States, the United Kingdom and much of the rest of the developed world in the past 30 years. In 1955 Japanese men could expect to live 63.6 years, while women could expect to live 67.8 years. By 1991 life expectancy had risen to 76.1 years for men and to 82.1 years for women. Along with these improvements, Japan enjoys the world's lowest infant mortality rate and one of the lowest perinatal mortality rates (Marmot & Smith 1989).

Although Japan places much importance on maternal and child health, the overall health care system, representing about 6–7 per cent of GDP, is not rated as highly as those in, for instance, Canada and the United States, where greater national resources are invested in health care. Instead, observers point to a constellation of factors contributing to rising good health. These include the importance of education, strong family support systems (reliant on contributions from women, which many people see as oppressive), and a pervasive sense of 'belonging' throughout all levels of Japanese society. Overshadowing all these factors, however, has been the dramatic economic development of Japan, with growth rates faster than those of other countries in the OECD for much of the last 45 years. However, it is not simply that Japan has become more prosperous. Income in that country is much more equally shared than in most other developed nations, and it is this *narrow distribution* of income, rather than *absolute levels* of income, that has been closely associated with higher life expectancy there and elsewhere in the world (Stoddart 1996).

It is this complex interaction of material factors such as income, and psychosocial factors associated with people's relative position in social and economic hierarchies, that appears to be a critical determinant of health. The notion of hierarchy is important here, as the differences in health are not simply those between the rich and the poor, but are graduated so that as people occupy higher positions in the socioeconomic order, so too does their health improve. These socioeconomic gradients:

> . . . are common to all developed nations, persist over time, are unaffected by changes in the leading causes of death in societies, and do not appear to be sensitive to the provision of health care (Wilkinson 1994). They suggest that income and social status may be markers for more fundamental processes that occur in all societies (Stoddart 1996:16).

These gradients have been demonstrated among retirees and infants in Canada (Wolfson *et al.* 1993; Mustard 1993), and among populations in Britain (Black *et al.* 1988; Marmot 1986). A British study of civil servants showed a 3.5 times higher cumulative mortality rate among the lowest-ranking civil servants than among the highest-ranking administrative workers. Of more direct relevance for our purposes was the further finding that these gradients were applicable as well for diseases associated with individual risk factors such as smoking, blood pressure and cholesterol, and lifestyle choices. These risk factors could explain only one-quarter of the gradient for coronary heart disease (Marmot 1986 in Stoddart 1996:16).

The implications of this research are twofold. First, focusing on specific health problems such as alcohol-related illness obscures the relationship between socioeconomic gradients and health. As one disease retreats among socioeconomically vulnerable groups, it will be replaced by others (Comeau & Santin 1995:106). For example, infant mortality rates among indigenous populations have been falling steadily, particularly in the past three decades. Instead of dying during the first year of life, more children now live but often suffer from 'failure to thrive', among a host of other illnesses requiring significant hospitalisation. Second, it implies that healthier lifestyles in themselves can have only limited effects on the health of populations unless they are accompanied by improvements in socio-economic status.

In examining the details of the social environments that are known to be associated with good health, the vulnerability of indigenous populations becomes more clear. According to Stoddart, the areas on which we need to focus are:

> . . . how people work and play; how they care about, support, condition, or even harass others; how they nurture and teach successive generations to develop self-esteem and competencies for living; and how the resources for dealing with the stresses of daily life (resources like support, income and power) are distributed across groups and individuals. High-quality social environments can reduce vulnerability to ill health at all stages of the life cycle, through both material pathways (e.g., better nutrition) and psycho-social pathways (e.g., avoidance of depression) (Stoddart 1996:17).

Key elements of the social environment that are known to influence health are work, the nurturing of infants, experience in early childhood, and social support.

Work

People who are unemployed experience more stress and suffer higher mortality rates than those with secure jobs. The unemployed are also more likely to smoke and drink excessively. The type of work environment also affects health with diseases like coronary heart disease higher among those whose jobs are:

... characterized by a high degree of psychological demands and a low degree of control, latitude for decision-making and discretion over use of skills (Stoddart 1996:17).

Throughout Australia, New Zealand and Canada, indigenous people suffer higher rates of unemployment than any other groups, and consequently receive the lowest incomes. However, some qualifications are necessary before considering official statistics. Unemployment rates in particular are likely to be very conservative, as most record only those registered as unemployed. For a variety of reasons, including toughening of conditions allowing registration, many people who are not working do not appear in these figures.

In 1994 the unemployment rate for indigenous people in Australia was 38 per cent, compared to 10 per cent for the total Australian population. Those living in what are called 'other urban' areas (that is regional cities and towns) were most likely to be unemployed (46 per cent), followed by those in capital cities (36 per cent), and rural areas (29 per cent) (McLennan 1996:103). Whereas just over one-third of all unemployed Australians had not had a job for more than a year, about half of all indigenous people had been out of work for more than a year. For the same period, 58 per cent of the indigenous population was in the labour force, compared to 62.7 per cent for the total population. Indigenous men had a labour force participation rate similar to that of non-indigenous men (72.3 and 73.4 per cent, respectively), but indigenous women were less likely than the general population to be in the labour force (44.4 compared to 52.3 per cent) (McLennan 1996:101).

While unpaid work such as traditional hunting and gathering or voluntary work for community or sporting associations is not recognised in standard labour force definitions, the Australian Bureau of Statistics notes the importance of this type of activity to indigenous people, recording a participation rate in voluntary work of 28 per cent (McLennan 1996:103-4).

Not surprisingly, indigenous income in Australia is comparatively low. Indigenous people are more likely than non-indigenous people to have incomes less than $12,000 per year (59 compared to 46 per cent), and they are much less likely to earn more than $25,000 (11 compared to 28 per cent). The average income for indigenous people of $14,000 per year is 30 per cent less than that for the total population. While indigenous households are less likely to have combined incomes below $16,000 (20 compared to 25 per cent in the general population), this can be explained by the significantly larger size of indigenous households and the younger age structure of the indigenous population (McLennan 1996:124-5).

The importance of government support for indigenous people becomes clear when the main source of personal income of people is noted. Almost two-thirds (64.1 per cent) of all indigenous women's main source of income is through government payments, with just under half (45.3 per cent) of indigenous men reliant on government sources. Less than one-third of indigenous men and even fewer women had earned income (30.1 per cent and 18.5 per cent). Government-sponsored employment through the Community Development Employment Program provided for 12.5 per cent of indigenous male income and 4.7 per cent of indigenous female income. In capital cities, 51 per cent of indigenous people were reliant on government payments as their main income, compared to 52 per cent in rural areas and 60 per cent in other urban areas (McLennan 1996:122–3).

One of the reasons for the lower participation rate in employment, and consequently lower average income, is the lower level of education of indigenous people in Australia. In 1994 only 18 per cent of indigenous people between the ages 15 and 64 who were not attending school had completed a post-school qualification, compared to 41 per cent of the total population. Indigenous people are also more likely never to have attended school (3.0 compared to 0.1 per cent for all Australians) (McLennan 1996:75–6).

As a consequence of lower educational attainment, greater unemployment and lower average incomes, indigenous Australians are much less likely to own their own homes than those in the general population. More than two-thirds (70 per cent) of the indigenous population lived in rented accommodation in 1994, compared to less than one-third (28 per cent) for the total population (McLennan 1996:142).

In New Zealand, according to 1991 census data cited by Workman, Maori socioeconomic standing included:

- 23.8 per cent male unemployment.
- 24.7 per cent female unemployment.
- Between 15 and 24 years 36.7% of Maori were unemployed.
- Maori are over-represented in manual, unskilled occupational groups.
- Annual median income for Maori over 15 was $11,001.
- Income less than $20,000 received by over 75% of Maori.
- Over 85 per cent of Maori women receive less than $20,000.
- One parent families (14.4% among Maori) had a median annual income of $14,525 compared to $35,050 for two parent families.
- 66.8% of Maori women over 15 had no educational qualification.
- 63.6% of Maori men over 15 had no educational qualification.
- Fewer than 50% of Maori adults own their own home (c.f. 75% non-Maori) (Workman 1996:5).

A review of socioeconomic indicators for the decade 1981–91 revealed a deterioration of Maori socioeconomic status relative to non-Maori in

New Zealand. This has been exacerbated by restructuring by the state, which has resulted in high levels of job losses within production, transport, labouring and manufacturing sectors of the state, areas of over-representation for Maori workers (Workman 1996:5).

For indigenous people in Canada the story is similar. Figures from the 1986 and 1991 censuses reveal that:

- 25 per cent of those over 15 were unemployed – versus 10 per cent for the total population (1991).
- Of those unemployed 54 per cent report incomes below $9,999 – 35 per cent for total population (1991).
- Average income for registered Indians living off-reserve was $11,000–$18,188 for total population (1986).
- Average income for those on-reserve was $9,300 (1986).
- 21 per cent of indigenous people over 15 have less than Grade 9 education – versus 9 per cent for the total population (1991).
- only 20 per cent of indigenous children complete secondary school – 75 per cent for the total population (1991) (Comeau & Santin 1995:56–7).

These figures disguise regional variations, and differences between on-reserve populations, where unemployment rates are much higher, and off-reserve groups. For instance, in 1991 more than two-thirds (66 per cent) of working-age people on reserves were either unemployed or on some kind of government assistance. This percentage rose for isolated reserves (Comeau & Santin 1995:40).

Indigenous communities and successive governments have recognised the importance of creating meaningful work. In Australia, New Zealand and Canada, attempts have been made to establish a range of economic development programs funded and managed by both government and non-government sectors. However, many of the government programs established since the late 1960s have not accomplished their stated goals of greater economic independence for indigenous people. For example, in Saskatchewan, Canada, the Canada/Saskatchewan Northlands Agreement (1974–79; 1979–83) and the Northern Economic Development Subsidiary Agreement (1984–89) received more than (Canadian) $212 million for capital improvements such as housing, roads and communication systems, and recreation centres. Once these developments had been completed, however, there was still no local economy to provide employment for the burgeoning indigenous populations (Comeau & Santin 1995:96). As with similar developments in Australia, stories such as these tend to reinforce non-indigenous notions of the economic hopelessness of indigenous communities.

Nevertheless, there are some success stories. In Canada:

> The Quebec Cree own an airline, Creebec Air. The Pas band in northern Manitoba is the area's second largest employer, operating a successful

multimillion-dollar shopping complex across the river from The Pas, a non-native community. Alberta Indians operate Peace Hills Trust, a trust company in western Canada. The Squamish Indians of British Columbia have turned lucrative land holdings adjacent to Vancouver into a multimillion-dollar operation. Indians offer these ventures as proof that, with control of funds, they can survive and thrive without welfare or Ottawa's misguided and wasteful programs (Comeau & Santin 1995:99).

These examples show indigenous initiative, but they also obscure the very uneven distribution of indigenous wealth in Canada, with resource-rich groups able to diversify economically, while resource-poor groups rely overwhelmingly on government support. On a recent visit to Canada, one of us (SS) visited two very different reservations in Alberta, the Lake Beaver community at Lac la Biche, and Hobbema, south of Edmonton. Lake Beaver is a small reservation with no current economic development activities or income from natural resources. The school, health centre, and alcohol treatment centre are the main sources of employment and all are funded by government. In contrast, Hobbema is the centre for four bands, the registered members of which have an annual income from oil resources on tribal lands. Besides the school, medical centre, and other government-sponsored services, the Cree council own and administer a number of businesses, including a shopping centre, which provide employment for band members.

In New Zealand, the Maori Development Corporation has consolidated monies from Maori trusts and authorities, and now has more than $12 million in investments, owns a successful chain of stores and a major company, and is branching out into tourism investment. Profits from the corporation are used for language and cultural maintenance (Western Australia, Task Force on Aboriginal Social Justice 1994:105).

Australia's indigenous people have limited access to income generation from land and its resources because – unlike Maori and indigenous Canadians – before the High Court's 1992 *Mabo* decision, they had no legal recognition of their prior ownership of land. Various pieces of land rights legislation in Australia's states and territories have enabled Aboriginal groups to occupy traditional country, some of which had been converted to pastoral stations which indigenous groups now operate. Much of this land is marginal economically, however, and provides limited employment opportunities. Consequently, economic development schemes in Australia have overwhelmingly focused on the role of the public sector.

Care of infants

The children of parents who are socioeconomically well off are more able to recover from stress suffered in the perinatal period. One study showed that at 20 months, children from higher socioeconomic status families who experienced such stress suffered little or no developmental disadvantage compared to a similar group from unstable or low socio-economic status families (Werner & Smith 1989 in Stoddart 1996:17).

Indigenous children are more likely to be raised in single-parent families, where incomes are significantly less than those of two-parent families. Even where both parents are present, family income will be lower than in the wider population. The health consequences of this are apparent in the increased rates of death and illness among indigenous children. Infant mortality rates, although dramatically reduced over the past 30 years, are still much higher than in the wider population. In Canada, for example, between 1984 and 1988 the overall infant mortality rate was 7.8 deaths per 1,000 live births. Among the Inuit, however, the rate was 19.0 per 1,000 live births, and 17.7 per 1,000 live births among the registered Indian population (Comeau & Santin 1995:106). If indigenous children do survive, they are more likely to be lower in birth weight, suffer poorer nutrition, and subsequently be more subject to repeated gut and respiratory infections with consequent growth retard-ation than their contemporaries in the wider population (Western Australia, Task Force on Aboriginal Social Justice 1994:325).

Experience in early childhood

The social environments in which children are reared are known to have lifelong impacts on their health and social development. Studies of children from socioeconomically disadvantaged homes demonstrate that this early relative deprivation remains throughout life. Children who have received extra support during the crucial preschool years, through programs such as Head Start, are much more likely to perform better across the board in later life (Schweinhart *et al.* 1985, cited in Stoddart 1996). Schools and communities can protect disadvantaged children by providing care and support, having high expectations of children, and allowing them to participate in a meaningful way (Bernard 1991).

Indigenous groups are responding to this situation by the creation of preschool programs that are designed to equip children with an under-standing and appreciation of their own culture, and to provide a culturally appropriate introduction to formal education. In New Zealand, such pre-schools are known as *Kohanga Reo*, and more than 600 of them provide Maori children with culturally rich experiences (Western Australia, Task Force on Aboriginal Social Justice 1994:98). In Australia, a range of programs based on the Head Start approach exist for children in the 0–5 age group, although these are by no means available to all indigenous children.

Social support

The epidemiological data demonstrate what most of us intuitively understand – that having strong social supports is good for your health. As the level of social support increases, the relative risk of mortality decreases (House, Landis & Umberson 1988). Lacking social support increases the relative risk of mortality to levels similar to those of traditional individual and lifestyle risk factors. The economically vulnerable are also those most socially vulnerable as job and income insecurity are exacerbated by declining state support for families (Stoddart 1996:18).

With some variation, kinship formed the basis of social organisation in the traditional indigenous societies of Australia, New Zealand and Canada. Since European colonisation, these kinship networks and the social support they provide have been under assault from a variety of factors including the loss of members as a result of violence and disease, the taking of indigenous children from their families and placing of them in institutions or non-indigenous foster care, and as a result of high rates of imprisonment of indigenous peoples. Nevertheless, in modified form, these kinship networks have survived, and they, and the support they provide, have enabled indigenous people to adapt to the changes wrought by colonialism.

Future directions

Building resilient individuals and communities

In Canada and the United States, in particular, researchers have over the past few years used the concepts of vulnerability and resilience to explore both the negative factors that are associated with the uptake of alcohol and other drugs, and the protective factors that allow some children to seemingly beat the odds and achieve better individual outcomes than their family circumstances would predict. In Australia, this has also recently been taken up by Brady (1995b). Prevention research is increasingly focusing on the characteristics of these resilient children. For instance, one often hears that while one of every four children of 'alcoholic' parents will develop alcohol problems, three will not. What has occurred in the lives of these children to allow them to achieve in spite of early deprivation (Bernard 1991)?

Generally three levels of factors are recognised: those at the individual, family and wider community levels. Resilient children are those who have some or all of the following characteristics: social competence, problem-solving skills, autonomy, and a sense of purpose and future. Protective families are those that provide consistent care and support, have high expectations for their children, and encourage children to participate in a responsible, meaningful way in the family, school and community.

It is these same factors that characterise schools that provide:

> . . . a protective shield to help children withstand the multiple vicissitudes that they can expect of a stressful world (Garmezy 1991, in Bernard 1991:9).

Favourite teachers may provide positive role models, particularly for those children with absent or dysfunctional parents. Positive peer support also protects many children from risky behaviours, such as excessive alcohol and other drug use (Tobler 1986; Bangert-Drowns 1988). Schools that expect their students to do well and provide support for them to achieve this have high rates of academic success (Rutter 1979). The research clearly shows the negative impact of stereotypical labelling: children labelled 'children of alcoholics' attract lower expectations from health professionals and their peers, and it takes a very resilient child to resist internalising these low expectations (Burk & Sher 1990).

At the community level, competent communities are those that provide support for families and schools, have high expectations and set clear standards for citizens, and encourage the participation of people at all levels of society. Fundamental to this care and support are the resources all humans require for healthy development: education, training, employment, child care, health care, housing and recreation (Long & Vaillant 1989; Garmezy 1991). Those living in poverty, who lack equal access to these basic services, experience the single biggest risk factor to their health. It is the task of governments to address the inequalities within the community, but the political will necessary to effect adequate transferrals of wealth is unlikely to develop unless individuals and groups agitate for such change.

Cultural norms about alcohol and other drug use are powerful determinants of the uptake of drugs by young people. When children are taught the social contexts in which responsible alcohol use is appropriate, they will be less likely to drink excessively than if they were forbidden alcohol altogether. In a similar fashion, a society that tolerates drunkenness will in turn promote excessive drinking among its young people (Vaillant 1986). Indigenous children growing up among heavy drinkers learn to drink from an early age, and soon understand that social acceptance is easier when one drinks.

All the prevention programs in the world will be ineffective against the pervasive influence of alcohol promotion, which transmits glamorous messages about the positive effects of drinking (Room 1990). Beer advertisements, for instance, continue to project an image associating healthy masculinity with drinking, while messages promoting responsible drinking are produced only by sectors of government, whose interests can be dismissed as those of an over-protective 'nanny state'. It is the values and actions of the wider community with respect to the supply, sale, promotion and use of alcohol and other drugs that will convince young people that excessive drinking and other substance abuse are viewed with concern (Bernard 1991).

It is not enough to say to young people that they should not waste their lives misusing alcohol; they also need opportunities to participate in their communities in meaningful ways. Unemployment represents a primary risk factor with respect to substance abuse, and the very high rates of youth unemployment in indigenous communities (and the wider society) are exacerbating health and social problems among this group. Commitment to a whole-of-government approach to this structural inequality is difficult to achieve in the present political and economic climate. With reference to contemporary New Zealand, transformations to the political economy crucially impact on Maori:

> Firstly, the impact of the market ethos, and the application of pure economic theory to complex, real-life communities, has encouraged a general disregard for the social consequences of public policy. The fundamentals of the reform program – market liberalisation, free trade, limited government, a relatively narrow monetarist policy, a deregulated labour market, and fiscal restraint, are assumed to be 'givens', and beyond challenge. It assumes that there exists strong community structures to care for the mentally ill, the elderly and the young. Maori are expected to have tribal and family support systems to fall back on (Workman 1996:16)

For Maori, Cooper suggests that what is important is:

> . . . an integrated and harmonious balance of socioeconomic factors in a way that serves Maori social, cultural, material, environmental and spiritual needs. It is sourced in traditional values of reciprocity, a source of collective responsibility that endures through past, present and future generations, and a spiritual relationship that binds people, nature and cosmology together. Its form constantly adapts to, and takes advantage of, changing times (in Workman 1996:16).

In Australia, the demand that indigenous people empower themselves accompanies shrinking budgets and attempts to transfer responsibility for what were once considered to be state obligations onto communities, families and individuals. This trend is not without some attraction for indigenous groups eager to take financial and social control over their lives. For instance, in New Zealand, some Maori groups are keen to participate in the contracting out of health services because of the opportunities to become 'purchasers, providers, planners and developers of positive Maori health policies' (Workman 1996). Maori ability to take advantage of these developments is dependent upon structural changes in New Zealand, which acknowledge Maori rights to self-determination and economic development. However, currently, Maori are not optimistic that the New Zealand state is able to formulate policy or provide services that recognise Maori realities and priorities. In order for this to occur, Durie has suggested the creation of a National Maori Assembly for the development of Maori policy, and according to Workman:

> The development of an environment in which Maori policy can comfortably co-exist within the mainstream requires . . . a set of minimum conditions, including the development of a comprehensive policy on biculturalism within the Public Service. That policy should:
> • define biculturalism, and set clear goals and structures in order to achieve realistic outcomes;
> • hold Chief Executives accountable for developing organisations which are responsive to Maori;
> • ensure that issues of responsiveness to Maori address the core business of government organisations;
> • identify the government agency or agencies responsible for providing leadership in the development of responsiveness and monitoring the performance of Chief Executives;
> • develop a comprehensive Maori workforce development strategy for the Public Service . . .;
> • acknowledge the development rights of indigenous people;
> • develop the expertise of public service staff in understanding Maori policy issues and analysis, recognising the unique characteristics of Maori policy (Workman 1996:17–18).

Similar calls are also being made by indigenous people in Australia and Canada.

Conclusion

In the preceding chapters, we have shown that the pattern of alcohol consumption among indigenous populations in Australia, New Zealand and Canada is remarkably similar. This pattern, which includes high levels of consumption among a significant proportion of drinkers, entails much related harm to the health and social well-being of indigenous people. For many years, it was not common for indigenous people or their non-indigenous supporters to speak out about these problems, as to do so was regarded as providing further ammunition for those intent upon blaming indigenous people for the problems in their midst. Increasingly, however, attention has been directed to the magnitude of the problem, and indigenous people themselves are increasingly concerned to address it.

Over the past two decades, a range of strategies have been put into place to address these problems. These have been initiated by both governments and indigenous people themselves. The funding for most of these programs has been provided by governments, which thus ultimately control the direction and extent of interventions. Much of the intervention effort has gone into the treatment of individuals who are misusing alcohol, into education and recreation programs aimed at reducing the demand for alcohol, and into strategies aimed at reducing the immediate consequences of misuse to both users and their communities. On the supply side, while prohibition has had limited effects in some communities, especially in Australia some success is being achieved through strategies aimed at more closely regulating the availability of alcohol.

Despite some successes, however, indigenous communities continue to be plagued by alcohol misuse and associated problems. Why have the various interventions had limited success? We believe it is, in part, because of the way the problem has been conceptualised. Many of the intervention strategies that are employed are based on views that the problems of misuse are the problems of individuals or arise from aspects of indigenous cultures. However, as we have shown, the best explanation of these patterns of misuse among indigenous peoples is their common experience of colonialism and its continuing consequences, and the fact that the psychological problems of many individuals and the nature of contemporary indigenous cultures cannot be adequately conceptualised without taking account of those broader political and economic forces. In this regard, the factors underlying alcohol misuse and alcohol-related harm are the same as those underlying other health problems. Despite the best efforts of indigenous people themselves, these problems will not be adequately addressed until the wider non-indigenous societies and their governments take more concerted action to address the structural inequalities faced by indigenous peoples. That they have not yet done so is clearly attested by the findings of Royal Commissions in both Australia and Canada.

As well as addressing the structural inequalities faced by indigenous peoples, there is also a need to strengthen those aspects of indigenous societies that promote good health in general. Attention to these factors will in turn make alcohol-specific intervention activities more effective. These steps will not be easy, but they are essential if the continuing toll of alcohol misuse is to be significantly reduced.

We have examined the issue of alcohol misuse and associated harm from a non-indigenous perspective. We believe that much of our analysis is congruent with that of many indigenous people themselves. However, indigenous people have their own visions for better health. These visions incorporate their understandings of the basis of indigenous ill health and the ways in which communities, and the wider social contexts in which they are situated, will need to be transformed for health improvements. We do not offer our analysis as a substitute for such indigenous visions, but as a complement to them. We firmly believe that, *most importantly, indigenous people themselves must be enabled to determine their own goals and strategies for their achievement* – not only in the alcohol and health areas, but in all aspects of their lives. In this process, non-indigenous governments and peoples must work in partnership with indigenous peoples, specifically to eliminate the problems caused by alcohol misuse and, more generally, to the end of achieving real equity for indigenous people.

Bibliography

Aboriginal Legal Service of Western Australia (1995) *Telling Our Story: A Report by the Aboriginal Legal Service of Western Australia on the Removal of Aboriginal Children in Western Australia.* Perth: Aboriginal Legal Service of Western Australia.

Addiction Research Foundation (1993) *Moderate Drinking and Health: A Statement Based on the International Symposium on Moderate Drinking and Health,* April 1993, Toronto, Canada. Toronto: Addiction Research Foundation.

Adrian, M., Layne, N. and Williams, R.T. (1991) Estimating the effects of Native Indian population on county alcohol consumption: the example of Ontario, *International Journal of the Addictions* 25(5A/6A):731–65.

Alati, R. (1993) *Evaluation of the Koori Alcohol and Drug Prevention Program: Final Report.* Melbourne: Koori Health Unit, Department of Health and Community Services, Victoria.

Albrecht, P.G.E. (1974) The social and psychological reasons for the alcohol problems among Aborigines, in B.S. Hetzel, L. Dobbin, L. Lippmann and E. Eggleston (eds) *Better Health for Aborigines?* St Lucia: University of Queensland Press.

Alcohol Advisory Council of New Zealand (1995) *Upper Limits for Responsible Drinking: A Guide for Health Professionals.* Wellington: Alcohol Advisory Council of New Zealand.

Alexander, K. (ed.) (1990) *Aboriginal Alcohol Use and Related Problems: Report and Recommendations Prepared by an Expert Working Group for the Royal Commission into Aboriginal Deaths in Custody.* Phillip, Australian Capital Territory: Alcohol and Drug Foundation.

Ali, R., Miller, M. and Cormack, S. (eds) (1992) *Future Directions for Alcohol and Other Drug Treatment in Australia.* National Campaign Against Drug Abuse Monograph Series No. 17. Canberra: Australian Government Publishing Service.

Altman, J. (1987) *Hunter-Gatherers Today: An Aboriginal Economy in North Australia.* Canberra: Australian National University Press.

Angus, G.F. (1874) *Savage Life and Scenes in Australia and New Zealand.* London: Smith Elder.

Ashley, M.J. (1993) Alcohol-related birth defects, in D. McKenzie (ed.) *Aboriginal Substance Use: Research Issues.* Ottawa: Canadian Centre on Substance Abuse.

Ashley, M.J. and Rankin, J.G. (1988) A public health approach to the prevention of alcohol-related health problems, *Annual Review of Public Health* 9:233–71.

Ashton, T., Casswell, S. and Gilmore, L. (1989) Alcohol taxes: do the poor pay more than the rich?, *British Journal of Addiction* 84:759–66.

Atkinson, J. (1990a,b) Violence in Aboriginal Australia: Parts 1 & 2, *Aboriginal and Islander Health Worker Journal* 14(2):5–21, 14(3):4–27.

Atkinson, J. (1991) 'Stinkin' thinkin': alcohol, violence and government responses, *Aboriginal Law Bulletin* 2(51):4–6.

Australia and Western Australia, Royal Commission into Aboriginal Deaths in Custody (Dodson, P., Commissioner) (1991) *Regional Report of Inquiry into Underlying Issues in Western Australia*, 2 vols. Canberra: Australian Government Publishing Service.

Australia, ATSIC, Aboriginal and Torres Strait Islander Commission, Office of Evaluation and Audit (1991a) *Evaluation of Enterprise Program*. Woden, Australian Capital Territory: Aboriginal and Torres Strait Islander Commission.

Australia, ATSIC, Aboriginal and Torres Strait Islander Commission, Office of Evaluation and Audit (1991b) *Community Infrastructure Program Evaluation: Phase II and III*. Woden, Australian Capital Territory: Aboriginal and Torres Strait Islander Commission.

Australia, ATSIC, Aboriginal and Torres Strait Islander Commission, Office of Evaluation and Audit (1992) *Impact Evaluation, Land Acquisition Program*. Woden, Australian Capital Territory: Aboriginal and Torres Strait Islander Commission.

Australia, ATSIC, Aboriginal and Torres Strait Islander Commission (1993) *Program Evaluation Handbook*. Woden, Australian Capital Territory: Aboriginal and Torres Strait Islander Commission.

Australia, ATSIC, Aboriginal and Torres Strait Islander Commission (1995) *The National Aboriginal Health Strategy: An Evaluation*. Woden, Australian Capital Territory: Aboriginal and Torres Strait Islander Commission.

Australia, Department of Finance, Management and Information Systems and Evaluation (1992) *Evaluation Papers No 2*. Canberra: Department of Finance.

Australia, Department of Health and Family Services (1995) *National Drug Strategy Household Survey: Urban Aboriginal and Torres Strait Islander Peoples Supplement 1994*. Canberra: Australian Government Publishing Service.

Australia, Department of Health and Family Services (1996) *National Drug Strategy Household Survey: Survey Report 1995*. Canberra: Australian Government Publishing Service.

Australia, Department of Human Services and Health (1994) *Statistics on Drug Abuse in Australia, 1994*. Canberra: Australian Government Publishing Service.

Australia, High Court (1992) *Mabo vs The State of Queensland*. Published Judgements FC 92/104. Canberra: High Court Registry.

Australia, House of Representatives Standing Committee on Aboriginal Affairs (1977) *Alcohol Problems of Aboriginals. Final Report*. Canberra: Australian Government Publishing Service.

Australia, National Campaign Against Drug Abuse and National Drug Education Program (1986) *An Australian Guide to Drug Issues*. Prepared by the Centre for Education and Information on Drugs and Alcohol. Canberra: Australian Government Publishing Service.

Australia, National Aboriginal Health Strategy Working Party (1989) *A National Aboriginal Health Strategy*. Canberra: Australian Government Publishing Service.

Australia, National Committee on Violence (1990) *Violence: Directions for Australia*. Canberra: Australian Institute of Criminology.

Australia, Race Discrimination Commissioner (1995) *Alcohol Report. Racial Discrimination Act 1975. Race Discrimination, Human Rights and the Distribution of Alcohol*. Canberra: Australian Government Publishing Service.

Australia, Royal Commission into Aboriginal Deaths in Custody (Johnson, E., Commissioner) (1991) *Royal Commission into Aboriginal Deaths in Custody: National Report*. 4 vols. Canberra: Australian Government Publishing Service.

Australia, Royal Commission into Aboriginal Deaths in Custody (Muirhead, J., Commissioner) (1988) *Interim Report of the Royal Commission into Aboriginal Deaths in Custody*. Canberra: Australian Government Publishing Service.

Australia, Second Task Force on Evaluation (1992) *No Quick Fix: An Evaluation of the National Campaign Against Drug Abuse*. Canberra: Ministerial Council on Drug Strategy.

Australian Bureau of Statistics (1995) *National Aboriginal and Torres Strait Islander Survey 1994: Detailed Findings*. Canberra: Australian Bureau of Statistics.

Australian Institute of Health and Welfare (1994) *Australia's Health*. Canberra: Australian Institute of Health and Welfare.

Awatere, D., Casswell, S., Cullen, H., Gilmore, L. and Kupenga, D. (eds) (1984) *Alcohol and the Maori People*. Auckland: Alcohol Research Unit, School of Medicine, University of Auckland.

Babor, T., Mendelson, J., Greenberg, I. and Kuehnle, J. (1978) Experimental analysis of the happy hour: effects of purchase price on alcohol consumption, *Journal of Psychopharmacology* 58:35–41.

Bain, M.S. (1974) Alcohol use and traditional social control in Aboriginal society, in B.S. Hetzel, L. Dobbin, L. Lippmann and E. Eggleston (eds) *Better Health for Aborigines?* St Lucia: University of Queensland Press, 42–52.

Bakalar, J.B. and Grinspoon, L. (1988) *Drug Control in a Free Society*. Cambridge: Cambridge University Press.

Bangert-Drowns, R. (1988) The effects of school-based substance abuse education – a meta-analysis, *Journal of Drug Education* 18(3):243–65.

Barber, J., Punt, J. and Albers, J. (1988) Alcohol and power on Palm Island, *Australian Journal of Social Issues* 23(2):87–101.

Bartlett, B. and Legge, D. (1994) *Beyond the Maze: Proposals for More Effective Administration of Aboriginal Health Programs*. National Centre for Epidemiology and Population Health, Working Paper No. 34. Canberra: Australian National University.

Basedow, H. (1929) *The Australian Aboriginal*. Adelaide: F.W. Preece and Sons.

Baum-Baiker, C. (1985) The psychological benefits of moderate alcohol consumption: a review of the literature, *Drug and Alcohol Dependence* 15:305–22.

Baume, F. (1992) Moving targets: evaluating community development, *Health Promotion Journal of Australia* 2:10–15.

Beauvais, F. and Segal, B. (1993) Drug use patterns among American Indians and Alaskan native youth: special rural populations, *Drugs and Society* 7:77–94.

Becker, H. (1953) Becoming a marihuana user, *American Journal of Sociology* 59:235–42.

Beckett, J. (1964) Aborigines, alcohol and assimilation, in M. Reay (ed.) *Aborigines Now*. Sydney: Angus & Robertson.

Bell, D. (1993) *Daughters of the Dreaming*, 2nd edn. Sydney: Allen & Unwin.

Bell, D. and Ditton, P. (1980) *Law: The Old and the New: Aboriginal Women in Central Australia Speak Out*. Report prepared for the Central Australian

Aboriginal Legal Aid Service, Darwin. Canberra: Australian National University, Department of Prehistory and Anthropology.

Bell, D. and Nelson, T.N. (1991) Speaking about rape is everyone's business, *Women's Studies International Forum* 12(4):403–16.

Bernard, B. (1991) *Fostering Resiliency in Kids: Protective Factors in the Family, School, and Community.* Oregon: Western Regional Centre for Drug-Free Schools and Communities.

Berndt, R.M. and Berndt, C.H. (1964) *The World of the First Australians.* Sydney: Ure Smith.

Bhatia, K. and Anderson, P. (1995) *An Overview of Aboriginal and Torres Strait Islander Health: Present Status and Future Trends.* Canberra: Australian Government Publishing Service.

Biskup, P. (1973) *Not Slaves, Not Citizens.* St Lucia: University of Queensland Press.

Black, D., Morris, J.N., Smith, C., Townsend, P. and Whitehead, M. (1988) *Inequalities in Health: The Black Report. The Health Divide.* London: Penguin.

Black, S. and Casswell, S. (1993) Recreational drug use in New Zealand, *Drug and Alcohol Review* 12:37–48.

Blackshield, S. (1991) Alcohol test case, *Aboriginal Law Bulletin* 2(51):22.

Blum, K., Noble, E., Sheridan, P., Ritchie, T., Jagadeeswaran, P., Norgami, H., Briggs, A. and Cohen, J. (1990) Allelic association of human dopamine D_2 receptor gene in alcoholism, *Journal of the American Medical Association* 263: 2055–60.

Boffa, J., George, C. and Tsey K. (1994) Sex, alcohol and violence: a community collaborative action against striptease shows, *Australian Journal of Public Health* 18(4):359–66.

Bolger, A. (1990) *Aboriginal Women and Violence: A Report for the Criminology Research Council and the Northern Territory Commissioner of Police.* Darwin: Australian National University, North Australia Research Unit.

Bourke, E., Farrow, R., McConnochie, K. and Tucker, A. (1991) *Career Development in Aboriginal Higher Education.* Canberra: Australian Government Publishing Service.

Brady, M. (1986) A social analysis of drinking and its aftermath in a remote Aboriginal community, in R. Bush (ed.) *Exploring the Alcohol and Drug Crime Link: Society's Response.* Canberra: Australian Institute of Criminology.

Brady, M. (1988) *Where the Beer Truck Stopped: Drinking in a Northern Australian Town.* Darwin: Australian National University, North Australian Research Unit.

Brady, M. (1990a) Indigenous and government attempts to control alcohol use among Australian Aborigines, *Contemporary Drug Problems* 17(2):195–220.

Brady, M. (1990b) Alcohol use and its effects upon Aboriginal women, in J. Vernon (ed.) *Alcohol and Crime.* Proceedings of a conference held 4–6 April 1989. Canberra: Australian Institute of Criminology.

Brady, M. (1991a) Drug and alcohol use among Aboriginal people, in J. Reid and P. Trompf (eds) (1991) *The Health of Aboriginal Australia.* Sydney: Harcourt Brace Jovanovich.

Brady, M. (1991b) Psychoactive substances among young Aboriginal Australians, *Contemporary Drug Problems* 18(2):273–329.

Brady, M. (1992a) Ethnography and understandings of Aboriginal drinking, *Journal of Drug Issues* 22(3):699–712.

Brady, M. (1992b) *Heavy Metal: The Social Meaning of Petrol Sniffing in Australia.* Canberra: Aboriginal Studies Press.

Brady, M. (1993) Giving away the grog: an ethnography of Aboriginal drinkers who quit without help, *Drug and Alcohol Review* 12(4):401–11.

Brady, M. (1994) *Liquor licensing laws – Aboriginal needs*. Paper presented at the National Liquor Licensing Policy Forum, Canberra, 11 July.

Brady, M. (1995a) *Giving Away the Grog: Aboriginal Accounts of Drinking and Not Drinking*. Canberra: Australian Institute of Aboriginal and Torres Strait Islander Studies.

Brady, M. (1995b) *The Prevention of Drug and Alcohol Abuse Among Aboriginal People: Resilience and Vulnerability*. Research Section Occasional Paper No. 2/1995. Canberra: Australian Institute of Aboriginal and Torres Strait Islander Studies.

Brady, M. (1995c) *Broadening the Base of Interventions for Aboriginal People with Alcohol Problems*. Technical Report No. 29. Sydney: National Drug and Alcohol Research Centre, University of New South Wales.

Brady, M. and Palmer, K. (1984) *Alcohol in the Outback: A Study of Drinking in an Aboriginal Community*. Darwin: Australian National University, North Australia Research Unit.

Brady, M. and Torzillo, P. (1994) Petrol sniffing down the track, *Medical Journal of Australia* 160:176–7.

Brant, C.C. (1990) Native ethics and rules of behaviour, *Canadian Journal of Psychiatry* 35:534–9.

Braroe, N.W. (1975) *Indian and White: Self-Image and Interaction in a Canadian Plains Community*. Stanford: Stanford University Press.

Bray, D.L., and Anderson, P.D. (1989) Appraisal of the epidemiology of fetal alcohol syndrome among Canadian Native peoples, *Canadian Journal of Public Health* 80:42–5.

Brewers Association of Canada (1993) *International Survey: Alcoholic Beverage Taxation and Control Policies*, 8th edn. Ottawa: Brewers Association of Canada.

Broadhurst, R.G., Ferrante, A., Loh, N., Reidpath, D. and Harding, R.W. (1994) *Aboriginal Contact with the Criminal Justice System in Western Australia: A Statistical Profile*. Perth: Crime Research Centre, University of Western Australia.

Brody, H. (1975) *The People's Land: Eskimos and Whites in The Eastern Arctic*. Harmondsworth: Penguin.

Brody, H. (1977) Alcohol, change and the industrial frontier, *Etudes/Inuit/Studies* 1(2):31–47.

Brooks, C.R. (1994) Using ethnography in the evaluation of drug prevention and intervention programs, *International Journal of the Addictions* 29:791–801.

Broughton, W. (1991) Qualitative methods in program evaluation. Primer on evaluation methods, *American Journal of Health Promotion* 5:461–5

Bruun, K. (1963) Outcome of different types of treatment of alcoholics, *Quarterly Journal of Studies on Alcohol* 24:280–8

Burchell, G. (1996) *Foucault and Political Reason: Liberalism, neo-Liberalism and Rationalities of Government*. Chicago: University of Chicago Press.

Burk, J. and Sher, K. (1990) Labelling the child of an alcoholic: negative stereo-typing by mental health professionals and peers, *Journal of Studies on Alcohol* 51(2):156–63.

Burns, C.B., d'Abbs, P. and Currie, B.J. (1995) Patterns of petrol sniffing and other drug use in young men from an Australian Aboriginal community in Arnhem Land, Northern Territory, *Drug and Alcohol Review* 14:159–69.

Cain, R., Davidson, R. and McGrath, M. (1981) *Report of the Review of Adult Aboriginal Education Section (Education Department of Western Australia)*. Perth: Education Department of Western Australia, Technical Education Division.

Canada, Department of Indian Affairs and Northern Development (1995) *1991 Census Highlights on Registered Indians: Annotated Tables.* Ottawa: Indian and Northern Affairs Canada.

Canada, Development Indicator Project Steering Committee (1991) *Using Development Indicators for Aboriginal Development.* Ottawa: Department of Indian and Northern Affairs.

Canada, House of Commons Standing Committee on Health (1995) *Towards Holistic Wellness: The Aboriginal Peoples.* Report, Issue No. 31, July. Ottawa: House of Commons Standing Committee on Health.

Canada, Health and Welfare (1987) *Suicide in Canada: Report From the Task Force on Suicide in Canada.* Ottawa: Health and Welfare Canada.

Canada Health and Welfare (1989) *Alcohol in Canada.* Ottawa: Ministry of Supply and Services.

Canada, Health and Welfare (1990a) Eliany, M., Geisbrecht, N., Nelson, M., Wellman, B. and Wortley, S. (eds) *National Alcohol and Other Drugs Survey (1989): Highlights Report.* Ottawa: Ministry of Supply and Services.

Canada, Health and Welfare (1990b) *Health Status of Canadian Indians and Inuit.* Ottawa: Health and Welfare Canada.

Canada, Health and Welfare (1991) *National Native Alcohol and Drug Abuse Program: A Progress Report.* Ottawa: Minister of National Health and Welfare Canada, in cooperation with the National Native Advisory Council on Alcohol and Drug Abuse.

Canada, Health and Welfare (1993) *Prevention: Prevention Framework for First Nations Communities.* Ottawa: Health and Welfare Canada.

Canada, Health and Welfare (1993) Stephens, T., Fowler G. D. (eds) *Canada's Health Promotion Survey 1990: Technical Report.* Ottawa: Ministry of Supply and Services.

Canada, Health (1994) *Smoking Among Aboriginal People in Canada, 1991.* Ottawa: Minister of Supply and Services.

Canada, National Native Alcohol and Drug Abuse Program (1995) *Treatment Activity Reporting Systems (TARS).* Quarterly report. April 1994 – March 1995.

Canada, Royal Commission on Aboriginal Peoples (1996) *Report of the Royal Commission on Aboriginal Peoples.* Ottawa: Royal Commission on Aboriginal Peoples.

Canada, Statistics (1993) *Language, Tradition, Health, Lifestyle and Social Issues: 1991 Aboriginal Peoples Survey.* Cat. No. 89–533. Ottawa: Statistics Canada.

Canada, Task Force on Program Review (1985) *Improved Program Delivery: A Study Team Report to the Task Force on Program Review.* Ottawa: Canadian Government Publishing Centre.

Carr, D.J. and Carr, S.G.M. (1981) *People and Plants in Australia.* Sydney: Academic Press.

Carr-Hill, R.A. (1985) The evaluation of health care, *Social Science and Medicine* 21(4):367–75.

Casswell, S. (1992) Alcohol and other recreational drug issues in New Zealand, *Journal of Drug Issues* 22(3):797–805.

Casswell, S. (1995) Public discourse on alcohol: implications for public policy, in H. Holder and G. Edwards (eds) *Alcohol and Public Policy: Evidence and Issues.* Oxford: Oxford University Press.

Casswell S., Cullen, C. and Gilmore, L. (1984) Review of alcohol-related statistics comparing Maori and non-Maori, in D. Awatere, S. Casswell, H. Cullen, L. Gilmore and D. Kupenga (eds) *Alcohol and the Maori People.* Auckland: Alcohol Research Unit, School of Medicine, University of Auckland.

Cavanagh, J., Clairemonte, F. and Room, R. (eds) (1985) *The World Alcohol Industry with Special Reference to Australasia and Oceania.* Transnational Corporations Research Project. Sydney: University of Sydney.

Cawte, J. (1982) Disulfiram effective, but doctor–patient relationship must prevail, *Medical Journal of Australia* December 2:606

Centre for Education and Information on Drugs and Alcohol (1986) *An Australian Guide to Drug Issues.* Canberra: Australian Government Publishing Service.

Chalmers, E.M. (1991) Volatile substance abuse, *Medical Journal of Australia* 154(4):269–74.

Chen, H.T. and Rossi, P.H. (1983) Evaluating with sense: the theory-driven approach. *Evaluation Review* 7:283–302.

Clarke, P.A. (1988) Aboriginal use of subterranean plant parts in southern South Australia, *Records of South Australian Museum* 22(1):73–86.

Cleland, J.B. (1957) Our natives and the vegetation of southern Australia, *Mankind* 5(4):149–62.

Cobbin, D.M. and Barlow, A.R. (eds) (1993) *Tertiary Access and Equity Initiatives: A Handbook for Evaluative Research.* Canberra: Australian Government Publishing Service.

Collmann, J. (1979) Social order and the exchange of liquor: a theory of drinking among Australian Aborigines, *Journal of Anthropological Research* 32(2):208–24.

Comeau, P. and Santin, A. (1995) *The First Canadians: A Profile of Canada's Native People Today.* Toronto: James Lorimer & Co.

Communicado Film, New Zealand Film Commission, Avalon Studios and New Zealand On Air (1994) *Once Were Warriors.* Story by Alan Duff, screenplay by Riwia Brown, produced by Robin Scholes, directed by Lee Tamahori.

Cooper, M., Corado, R., Karlberg, A.M. and Peletier Adams, L. (1992) Aboriginal suicide in British Columbia: an overview, *Canada's Mental Health* September: 19–23.

Crawford, A. (1993) Much ado about nothing, commentary on Sinclair, J.D. and Sillanaukee, P. 'The preventive paradox: a critical examination', *Addiction* 88(5):595–8.

Craze, L. and Norberry, J. (1995) The objectives of liquor licensing laws in Australia, in Stockwell, T. (ed.) *Alcohol Misuse and Violence: An Examination of the Appropriateness and Efficacy of Liquor Licensing Laws across Australia.* Report 5 in a series of reports prepared for the National Symposium on Alcohol Misuse and Violence. Canberra: Australian Government Publishing Service.

Cullen, H. (1984) Alcohol and the Maori people: a history, in D. Awatere, S. Casswell, H. Cullen, L. Gilmore and D. Kupenga (eds) *Alcohol and the Maori People.* Auckland: Alcohol Research Unit, School of Medicine, University of Auckland.

Cutter, T. and Perkins N. (1976) Drinking patterns of Aborigines in the Northern Territory, *Australian Journal of Alcoholism and Drug Dependence* 3(3):74–6.

d'Abbs, P. (1989) *The Prevention of Petrol Sniffing on Aboriginal Communities: A Review of Interventions.* Darwin: Drug and Alcohol Bureau, Department of Health and Community Services.

d'Abbs, P. (1990) Restricted areas and Aboriginal drinking, in J. Vernon (ed.) *Alcohol and Crime.* Proceedings of a conference held 4–6 April 1989. Canberra: Australian Institute of Criminology.

d'Abbs, P. (1991) Drinking environments, alcohol problems and research in the Northern Territory, in T. Stockwell, E. Lang and P. Rydon (eds) *The Licensed*

Drinking Environment: Current Research in Australia and New Zealand. Perth: National Centre for Research into the Prevention of Drug Abuse, Curtin University of Technology.

d'Abbs, P., Hunter, E., Reser, J. and Martin, D. (1994) *Alcohol-related Violence in Aboriginal and Torres Strait Islander Communities: A Literature Review.* Report 8 in a series of reports prepared for the National Symposium on Alcohol Misuse and Violence. Canberra: Australian Government Publishing Service.

d'Abbs, P., Togni, S. and Crundall, I. (1996) *The Tennant Creek Liquor Licensing Trial, August 1995 – February 1996: An Evaluation.* A Menzies Occasional Paper. Darwin: Menzies School of Health Research and Northern Territory Living With Alcohol Program.

Dailey, R.C. (1964) *Alcohol and the Indians of Ontario: Past and Present.* Addiction Research Foundation Substudy 1-20-64, Toronto: Addiction Research Foundation.

Daly, A. (1993) The evaluation of labour market programs: some issues for Aboriginal policy formulation from experience in the United States, *Labour Economics and Productivity* 5:45–67.

Davies, P. and Walsh, D. (1983) *Alcohol Problems and Alcohol Control in Europe.* London: Croom Helm.

Davis, A., Wanna, J., Warhurst, J. and Weller P. (1988) *Public Policy in Australia.* Sydney: Allen & Unwin.

Davis, J. (1970) *The first-born and other poems.* Sydney: Angus & Robertson.

Devanesen, D., Furber, M., Hampton, D., Honari, M., Kinmonth, N. and Peach, H.G. (1986) *Health Indicators in the Northern Territory.* Darwin: Northern Territory Department of Health.

Dingle, A.E. (1980) 'The truly magnificent thirst': an historical survey of Australian drinking habits, *Historical Studies* 19(75):227–49.

Douglas, M. (ed.) (1987) *Constructive Drinking: Perspectives on Drinking from Anthropology.* Cambridge: Cambridge University Press.

Duff, A. (1991) *Once Were Warriors.* St Lucia, Queensland: University of Queensland Press.

Duffy, J.C. and Cohen, G.R. (1978) Total alcohol consumption and excessive drinking, *British Journal of Addiction* 73:259–64.

Duigan, P. and Casswell, S. (1989) Evaluating community development programs for health promotion: problems illustrated by a New Zealand example, *Community Health Studies* XIII:74–81.

Dull, R.T. and Giacopassi, D.J. (1988) Dry, damp and wet: correlates and presumed consequences of local alcohol ordinances, *American Journal of Drug and Alcohol Abuse* 14(4):499–514.

Duncan-Kemp, A.M. (1934) *Our Sandhill Country.* Sydney: Angus & Robertson.

Duquemin, A., d'Abbs, P. and Chalmers, E. (1991) *Making Research into Aboriginal Substance Misuse Issues More Effective.* Working Paper No. 4. Sydney: National Drug and Alcohol Research Centre, University of New South Wales.

Durie, M. (1994) *Whaiora: Maori Health Development.* Auckland: Oxford University Press.

Durkheim, E. (1952) *Suicide: A Study in Sociology.* Translated by J.A. Spaulding and G. Simpson. London: Routledge and Kegan Paul.

Dyck, N. (ed.) (1985) *Indigenous Peoples and the Nation-State: 'Fourth World' Politics in Canada, Australia and Norway.* St Johns, Newfoundland: Institute of Social and Economic Research, Memorial University of Newfoundland.

Eades, D. (1992) *Aboriginal English and the Law.* Brisbane: Continuing Legal Education Department, Queensland Law Society.

Eastwell, H.D. (1988) *Aspects of Drug Use and Aboriginal Culture*. National Drug Abuse Information Centre Technical Information Bulletin on Drug Abuse No. 79. Canberra: Department of Community Services and Health.

Eckermann, A.-K. (1977) 'The binge': some Aboriginal views, *Aboriginal Health Worker* 1(4): 49–55.

Edmunds, M. (1990) *Doing Business. Socialisation, Social Relations and Social Control in Aboriginal Societies*. Royal Commission into Aboriginal Deaths in Custody, Discussion Paper No. 2. Canberra: Department of Prehistory and Anthropology, Australian National University Press and Australian Institute of Aboriginal and Torres Strait Islander Studies.

Edwards, G. *et al.* (1995) *Alcohol Policy and the Public Good*. Oxford: Oxford University Press.

Eggleston, E. (1974) Legal controls on alcohol, in B.S. Hetzel, L. Dobbin, L. Lippmann and E. Eggleston (eds) *Better Health for Aborigines?* St Lucia: University of Queensland Press.

Eggleston, E. (1976) *Fear, Favour or Affection*. Canberra: Australian National University Press.

Engels, F. (1969) *The Condition of the Working Class in England* (first published 1854). London: Grenada.

Engs, R. (1995) Do traditional western European drinking practices have origins in antiquity?, *Addiction Research* 2(3):227–39.

Evans, R., Saunders, K. and Cronin, K. (1975) *Exclusion, Exploitation and Extermination: Race Relations in Colonial Queensland*. Sydney: ANZ Book Company.

Fenna, D., Mix, L., Schaefer, O. and Gilbert, J.A.L. (1971) Ethanol metabolism in various racial groups, *Canadian Medical Association Journal* 105:472–5.

Fiddler, S. (1985) *Suicides, Violent and Accidental Deaths Among Treaty Indians in Saskatchewan: Analysis and Recommendations for Change*. Regina, Saskatchewan: Federation of Saskatchewan Indian Nations.

Fisher, A.D. (1986) Alcoholism and race: the misapplication of both concepts to North American Indians, *Canadian Review of Anthropology and Sociology* 24:81–98.

Fleras, A. and Elliot, J.L. (1992) *The 'Nations Within': Aboriginal–State Relations in Canada, the United States, and New Zealand*. Toronto: Oxford University Press.

Flood, J. (1995) *Archaeology of the Dreamtime: The Story of Prehistoric Australia and its People*, revised edn. Pymble, New South Wales: Angus & Robertson.

Flores, P.J. (1985) Alcoholism treatment and the relationship of Native American cultural values to recovery, *International Journal of the Addictions* 20:1701–26.

Foucault, M. (1980) *Power/Knowledge: Selected Writings and Other Interviews*. New York: Pantheon.

Franks, C. (1989) Preventing petrol sniffing in Aboriginal communities, *Community Health Studies* XIII(1):14–22.

Garbutcheon Singh, M. (1990) Aboriginal education, program evaluation and public accountability: response (to Keefe, K., Bridge to Nowhere), *Discourse* 11(1):103–6.

Garmezy, N. (1991) Resiliency and vulnerability to adverse developmental outcomes associated with poverty, *American Behavioural Scientist* 34(4):416–30.

Gfellner, B.M. and Hundlelby, J.D. (1995) Patterns of drug use among native and white adolescents, 1990–1993, *Canadian Journal of Public Health* March–April:95–7.

Gibson, M. (1991) A contemporary Aboriginal viewpoint, in J. Reid and P. Trompf (eds) *The Health of Aboriginal Australia*. Sydney: Harcourt Brace Jovanovich.

Giddens, A. (1992) *Sociology*. Cambridge: Polity Press.

Gilbert, K. (ed.) (1988) *Inside Black Australia: An Anthology of Aboriginal Poetry*. Ringwood, Vic: Penguin.

Gluckman, L.K. (1974) Alcohol and the Maori in historic perspective, *New Zealand Medical Journal* 79(506):553–5.

Goodheart, R.S. and Dunne, J.W. (1994) Petrol sniffer's encephalopathy, *Medical Journal of Australia* 160:178–81.

Gossop, M. (1993) *Living with Drugs*, 3rd edn. Aldershot, Hants: Ashgate.

Gracey, M., Sullivan, H., Burke, V. and Gracey, B. (1989) Factors which affect health, growth and nutrition in young children in remote Aboriginal communities, *Australian Paediatric Journal* 25:322–3.

Graves, T. (1967) Acculturation, access and alcohol in a tri-ethnic community, *American Anthropologist* 69:306–21.

Graves, T.D. (1970) The personal adjustment of Navajo Indian migrants to Denver, Colorado, *American Anthropologist* 72:35–54.

Gray, A. (1990) *A Matter of Life and Death: Contemporary Aboriginal Mortality*. Canberra: Aboriginal Studies Press.

Gray, A. and Hogg, R. (1989) *Mortality of Aboriginal Australians in Western New South Wales 1984–1987*. Sydney: New South Wales Department of Health.

Gray, D., Drandich M., Moore L., Wilkes T., Riley R. and Davies S. (1995) Aboriginal well-being and liquor licensing legislation in Western Australia, *Australian Journal of Public Health* 19(2):177–85.

Gray, D. and Morfitt, B. (1996) Harm minimisation in an indigenous context (Australia), in *Cultural Variations in the Meaning of Harm Minimisation: The Implications for Policy and Practice in the Drugs Arena*. Proceedings of a conference convened by the World Health Organisation Collaborating Centre for Prevention and Control of Drug Abuse. Perth and Sydney: National Centre for Research into the Prevention of Drug Abuse, and National Drug and Alcohol Research Centre, University of New South Wales.

Gray, D., Morfitt, B., Ryan, K. and Williams, S. (1997) Use of tobacco, alcohol and other drugs by young Aboriginal people in Albany, Western Australia, *Australian and New Zealand Journal of Public Health* 21(1):71–6.

Gray, D., Morfitt, B., Williams, S., Ryan, K. and Coyne, L. (1996) *Drug Use and Related Issues Among Young Aboriginal People in Albany*. Perth: National Centre for Research into the Prevention of Drug Abuse, Curtin University of Technology and Albany Aboriginal Corporation.

Gray, D. and Saggers, S. (1994) Aboriginal health: the harvest of injustice, in C. Waddell and A. Petersen (eds) *Just Health*. Sydney: Churchill Livingstone.

Gray, D., Saggers, S., Drandich, M., Wallam, D. and Plowright, P. (1995) Government health and substance abuse programs for indigenous peoples: a comparative review, *Australian Journal of Public Health* 19(6): 567–72.

Gray, D., Saggers, S., Plowright, P. and Drandich, M. (1995) *Monitoring and Evaluation Models for Indigenous Peoples: A Literature Review for the Western Australian Aboriginal Affairs Department*. Perth: National Centre for Research into the Prevention of Drug Abuse.

Greeley, J. and Gladstone W. (1989) *The Effects of Alcohol on Cognitive, Psychomotor and Affective Functioning: Report and Recommendations Prepared by an Expert Working Group for the Royal Commission into Aboriginal Deaths in Custody*. Sydney: National Drug and Alcohol Research Centre, University of New South Wales.

Greeley, J. and McDonald, D. (eds) (1992) Alcohol and human behaviour, research paper No. 14 in D. Biles and D. McDonald (eds) *Deaths in Custody Australia*, 1980–1989. Canberra: Australian Institute of Criminology.

Grob, C. and de Rios, M.D. (1992) Adolescent drug use in cross-cultural perspective, *Journal of Drug Issues* 22(1):121–38.

Gross, E.R. (1989) *Contemporary Federal Policy Toward American Indians.* New York: Greenwood Press.

Gruenewald, P.J. (1993) Alcohol problems and the control of availability: theoretical and empirical issues, in M.E. Hilton and G. Bloss (eds) *Economics and Prevention of Alcohol-Related Problems.* NIAAA Research Monograph No. 25. Bethesda, Maryland: US Government Printing Office.

Gruenewald, P.J., Millar A.B. and Treno A.J. (1993) Alcohol availability and the ecology of drinking behavior, *Alcohol Health & Research World* 17(1):39–45.

Gruenewald, P.J., Ponicki, W. and Holder, H.D. (1993) The relationship of outlet densities to alcohol consumption: a time series cross-sectional analysis, *Alcoholism: Clinical and Experimental Research* 17:591–7.

Gusfield, J. (1981) *The Culture of Public Problems: Drink-Driving and the Symbolic Order.* Chicago: University of Chicago Press.

Haebich, A. (1988) *For Their Own Good: Aborigines and Government in the South-West of Western Australia, 1900–1940.* Nedlands: University of Western Australia Press.

Hall, W., Hunter, E. and Spargo, R. (1993) Alcohol-related problems among Aboriginal drinkers in the Kimberley region of Western Australia, *Addiction* 88:1091–1100.

Hallowell, A.J. (1955) *Culture and Experience.* Philadelphia: University of Pennsylvania Press.

Hallowell, R.A. and Coggins, K. (1991) Native American alcoholics, *Focus* 14(5): 30–2.

Hancock, L., Walsh, R., Redman, S., Henrikus, D., Sanson-Fisher, R. and Gibberd, R. (1992) Psychotropic drug use in the Australian community. Benzodiazapines, in J. White (ed.) *Drug problems in Our Society. Dimensions and Perspectives.* Parkside, South Australia: Drug and Alcohol Services Council.

Hanna, J.M. (1978) Metabolic responses of Chinese, Japanese and Europeans to alcohol, *Alcoholism: Clinical and Experimental Research* 2:89–92.

Harawira, W. (1996) The battle of the booze, *Mana Magazine* No. 13, Winter: 54–6.

Harding, R.W., Broadhurst, R., Ferrante, A. and Loh, N. (1995) *Aboriginal Contact with the Criminal Justice System and the Impact of the Royal Commission into Aboriginal Deaths in Custody.* Annandale, New South Wales: The Hawkins Press.

Hardy, F. (1968) *The Unlucky Australians.* Sydney: Rigby.

Harris, M. (1968) *The Rise of Anthropological Theory.* New York: Thomas Crowell.

Harris M. (1979) *Cultural Materialism: The Struggle for a Science of Culture.* New York: Random House.

Harris, M.F., (1989) Alcohol and physical disease in Bourke Aborigines, *Australian Drug and Alcohol Review* 8:79–82.

Harris, M.F., Sutherland, D., Cutter, G. and Ballangarry, L. (1987) Alcohol-related admissions in a country town, *Australian Drug and Alcohol Review* 6(3):195–8.

Hartz, L. (1964) *The Founding of New Societies.* New York: Harcourt, Brace and World.

Hasluck, P. (1970) *Black Australians: A Survey of Native Policy in Western Australia,* 1829–1897, 2nd edn. Melbourne: Melbourne University Press.

Hawkes, D.C. (ed.) (1991) *Aboriginal Peoples and Government Responsibility.* Ottawa: Carelton University Press.

Hawks, D.V. (1992) The prevention paradox revisited, *Drug and Alcohol Review* 11(3):227–8.

Hazlehurst, K.M. (1986) Alcohol, outstations and autonomy: an Australian Aboriginal perspective, *Journal of Drug Issues* 16:209–20.

Hazlehurst, K.M. (1994) *A Healing Place. Indigenous Visions for Personal Empowerment and Community Recovery*. Rockhampton: Central Queensland University Press.

Healy, B., Turpin, T. and Hamilton, M. (1985) Aboriginal drinking: a case study in inequality and disadvantage, *Australian Journal of Social Issues* 20(3):191–208.

Heath, D.B. (1962) Drinking patterns of the Bolivian Camba, in D.J. Pittman and C.R. Snyder, *Society, Culture and Drinking Patterns*. New York: John Wiley & Sons.

Heath, D.B. (1983) Alcohol use among North American Indians: a cross-cultural survey of patterns and problems, in R.G. Smart, F.B. Glaser, Y. Israel, H. Kelent, R.E. Popham and W. Schmidt (eds), *Research Advances in Alcohol and Drug Problems* 7:343–96.

Heath, D.B. (1987) Anthropology and alcohol studies: current issues, *Annual Review of Anthropology* 16:99–120.

Heather, N. and Tebbutt, J. (eds) (1989) *The Effectiveness of Treatment for Drug and Alcohol Problems*. National Campaign Against Drug Abuse Monograph Series No. 11. Canberra: Australian Government Publishing Service.

Hébert, Y.M. (1986) Naturalistic evaluation in practice: a case study, in D.D. Williams (ed.) *New Directions for Program Evaluation: Naturalistic Evaluation* 30:3–21.

Hennessy, M. and Sullivan, M.J. (1989) Good organisational reasons for bad evaluation research, *Evaluation Practice* 10:41–50.

Hertzman, C. and Ayers W. (1993) *Environment and Health in Central and Eastern Europe*. Report for the World Bank, No. 12270–ECA. Washington, DC: World Bank.

Hicks, D. (1985) *Aboriginal Mortality Rates in Western Australia 1983*. Perth: Health Department of Western Australia.

Holder, H.D. (1994) Public health approaches to the reduction of alcohol problems, *Substance Abuse* 15(2):123–38.

Holman, C.J.D. (1994) The science and ethics of low alcohol consumption. Paper presented at the Annual Scientific Meeting of the Royal Australasian College of Physicians (Western Australia). Perth, October 1994.

Holman, C.J.D., Armstrong, B.K., Arias, L.N., Martin, C.A., Hatton, W.M., Hayward, L.D., Salmon, M.A., Shean, R.E. and Waddell, V.P. (1990) *The Quantification of Drug Caused Morbidity and Mortality in Australia: Parts I and II*. Canberra: Department of Community Services and Health.

Holmes, M. (1994) The Halls Creek initiative: restrictions on alcohol availability, *Pro-Ed* 10(1), 21–2.

Holt, A. (1992) Everybody's business: 1st National Aboriginal HIV/AIDS Conference, *Connexions* 12:13–17.

Holyfield, L., Ducharme, L. and Martin, J.K. (1995) Drinking contexts, alcohol beliefs, and patterns of alcohol consumption: evidence for a comprehensive model of problem drinking, *Journal of Drug Issues* 25(4):783–98.

Homel, R., Tomsen, S. and Thommeny, J. (1992) Public drinking and violence: not just an alcohol problem, *Journal of Drug Issues* 22:679–97.

Honigmann, J.J. (1979) Alcohol in its cultural context, in M. Marshall (ed.) *Beliefs, Behaviors and Alcoholic Beverages*. Ann Arbor: University of Michigan Press.

Horton, D (ed.) (1994) *Encyclopaedia of Aboriginal Australia: Aboriginal and Torres Strait Islander History, Society and Culture.* Canberra: Aboriginal Studies Press.

House, J.S., Landis, K.R. and Umberson, D. (1988) Social relationships and health, *Science* 241 (July 29):540–5.

Howard, M.C. (ed.) (1978) *'Whitefella Business': Aborigines in Australian Politics.* Philadelphia: Institute for the Study of Human Issues.

Huggins, J., *et al.* (1991) Response to Bell, *Women's Studies International Forum* 14(5):506–7.

Hunt, H. (1981) Alcoholism among Aboriginal people, *Medical Journal of Australia – Special Supplement* 1(2), 2 May:1–3.

Hunter, E. (1989) Changing patterns of Aboriginal mortality in the Kimberley region of Western Australia, *Aboriginal Health Information Bulletin* 11:27–32.

Hunter, E. (1990) Resilience, vulnerability and alcohol in remote Aboriginal Australia, *Aboriginal Health Information Bulletin* 14:16–24.

Hunter, E. (1991a) Out of sight, out of mind – 1. Emergent patterns of self-harm among Aborigines of remote Australia, *Social Science and Medicine* 33(6):655–9.

Hunter, E. (1991b) Out of sight, out of mind – 2. Social and historical contexts of self-harm among Aborigines of remote Australia, *Social Science and Medicine* 33(6):661–71.

Hunter, E. (1991c) The social and family context of Aboriginal self-harmful behaviour in remote Australia, *Australian and New Zealand Journal of Psychiatry* 25:203–9.

Hunter, E. (1992) Aboriginal alcohol use: a review of quantitative studies, *Journal of Drug Issues* 7:13–31.

Hunter, E. (1993a) *Aboriginal Health and History.* Melbourne: Cambridge University Press.

Hunter, E. (1993b) Demographic factors contributing to patterns of violence in Aboriginal communities, *Australasian Psychiatry* 4:152–3.

Hunter, E., Hall, W. and Spargo, R. (1991) *The Distribution and Correlates of Alcohol Consumption in a Remote Aboriginal Population.* Monograph No. 12. Sydney: National Drug and Alcohol Research Centre, University of New South Wales.

Hunter, E., Hall, W. and Spargo R. (1992) Patterns of alcohol consumption in the Kimberley Aboriginal population, *Medical Journal of Australia* 156:764–8.

Jackson, M. (1988) *Locking Up Natives in Canada: A Report of the Canadian Bar Association Committee on Imprisonment and Release.* Typescript. Vancouver: University of British Columbia.

Jarvis, G.K. and Boldt, M. (1982) Death styles among Canada's Indians, *Social Science and Medicine* 16:1345–52.

Jock, R., Jorgenson, R., Sillito, J., Wilde, W., Collette, D. and Barrett, R. (1996) *Visions, Nechi Review 1996.* Edmonton: Nechi Training, Research and Health Promotions Institute.

Johnson, C. (1979) *Long live Sandawara.* Melbourne: Quartet Books.

Johnson, P. (1978) *A Shopkeeper's Millennium.* New York: Hill & Wang.

Jull, P. (1992) *The Constitutional Culture of Nationhood, Northern Territories and Indigenous Peoples.* Discussion Paper No. 6. Darwin: Australian National University, North Australia Research Unit.

Jurd, S. (1996) Addiction as a disease, in C. Wilkinson and B. Saunders (eds) *Perspectives on Addiction: Making Sense of the Issues.* Perth: William Montgomery.

Kahn, M., Hunter, E., Heather, N. and Tebbutt J. (1990) Australian Aborigines and alcohol: a review, *Drug and Alcohol Review* 10: 351–66.

Kamien, M. (1975) Aborigines and alcohol: intake, effects and social implications in a rural community in western New South Wales, *Medical Journal of Australia* 1:291–8.

Kamien, M. (1978) The measurement of alcohol consumption in Australian Aborigines, *Community Health Studies* II(3):149–51.

Kamien, M. (1986) Alcohol and drug problems in minority groups, *Australian Drug and Alcohol Review* 5:59–61.

Karasek, R.A. and Theorell, T. (1990) *Healthy Work: Stress, Productivity, and the Reconstruction of Working Life*. New York: Basic Books.

Karp, R.W. (1992) D. or not D., *Alcoholism: Clinical and Experimental Research* 16(4):786–7.

Keefe, K. (1990) Rejoinder: a reply to Garbutcheon Singh, *Discourse* 11(1):107–9.

Keen, I. (1988) Introduction, in I. Keen (ed.) *Being Black: Aboriginal Cultures in 'Settled' Australia*. Canberra: Aboriginal Studies Press.

Kendell, R.E., de Roumaine, M. and Ritson, E.B. (1983) Effect of economic changes on Scottish drinking habits 1978–82, *British Journal of Addiction* 78(4):365–79.

Khoury P. (1989) Aborigines and the politics of alcohol, in R. Kennedy (ed.) *Australian Welfare: Historical Sociology*. Melbourne: Macmillan.

Kivlahan, D.R., Walker, R.D., Donovan, D.M. and Mishke, H.D. (1985) Detoxification recidivism among urban American Indian alcoholics, *American Journal of Psychiatry* 142(12):1467–70.

Knowles, S. and Woods, B. (1993) *The Health of Noongar People in the Great Southern Health Region*. Perth: Health Department of Western Australia.

Kreitman, N. (1986a) Loss of control and other matters: comment on Robin Room's 'Dependence and Society', *British Journal of Addiction* 81:55–8.

Kreitman, N. (1986b) Alcohol consumption and the preventive paradox, *British Journal of Addiction* 81:353–63.

Kumpfer, K.L., Sher, G.H., Ross, J.G, Bunnell, K.K., Librett, J.J. and Millward, A.R. (1993) *Measurements in Prevention: A Manual on Selecting and Using Instruments to Evaluate Prevention Programs*. Rockville, Maryland: Centre for Substance Abuse Prevention.

Kunitz, S.J. (1994) *Disease and Social Diversity: The European Impact on the Health of Non-Europeans*. New York: Oxford University Press.

La Barre, W. (1969) *The Peyote Cult*. New York: Schoken.

Lang, E., Stockwell, T., Rydon, P. and Gamble, C. (1991) Community survey of patterns and places of drinking, in *Reports on Patterns and Places of Drinking of 16–29 year olds in the Perth Metropolitan Area*. Technical Report. Perth: National Centre for Research into the Prevention of Drug Abuse, and Curtin University of Technology.

Langton, M. *et al.* (1991) 'Too much sorry business' (Report of the Aboriginal Issues Unit of the Northern Territory), Appendix D (I) in *Royal Commission into Aboriginal Deaths in Custody: National Report*. Canberra: Australian Government Publishing Service.

Langton, M. (1992) 'Too much sorry business', *Aboriginal and Islander Health Worker Journal* March/April:10–23.

Langton, M. (1993) Rum, seduction and death: 'Aboriginality' and alcohol, *Oceania* 63(3):195–206.

Larkins, K. and McDonald D. (1984) Recent Northern Territory liquor control initiatives, *Australian Alcohol/Drug Review* 3(1):59–64.

Larsen, K.S. (1979) Social crisis and Aboriginal alcohol abuse, *Australian Journal of Social Issues* 14(2):31–45.

Leary, J., Dodson, P., Tipolura, B. and Bunduk, L. (1975) *Alcoholism and Aborigines. A Report to the Interdepartmental Committee on Alcoholism and Aborigines.* Typescript.

Lederman, S. (1956) *Alcohol, Alcoholism, Alcoholisation,* Vol. 1, Connées Scientifiques de Caractère Physiologique, Economique et Social, Institute National d'Etudes Demographique, Travas et Documents, Cah. No. 29. Paris: Presses Universitaires de France.

Leland, J. (1976) *Firewater Myths: North American Indian Drinking and Alcohol Addiction.* New Brunswick, New Jersey: Rutgers Centre of Alcohol Studies.

Levine, H.G. and Reinarman, C. (1993) From prohibition to regulation: lessons from alcohol policy for drug policy, in R. Bayer and G.M. Oppenheimer (eds) *Confronting Drug Policy.* Cambridge: Cambridge University Press.

Levy, J.E. and Kunitz, S.J. (1971) Indian reservations, anomie, and social pathologies, *Southwest Journal of Anthropology* 27:97–128.

Levy, J.E. and Kunitz, S.J. (1974) *Indian Drinking: Navajo Drinking and Anglo-American Theories.* New York: Wiley-Interscience.

Lewis, M. (1992) *A Rum State: Alcohol and State Policy in Australia 1788–1988.* Canberra: Australian Government Publishing Service.

Little Bear, L., Boldt, M. and Long, J.A. (eds) (1984) *Pathways to Self-determination: Canadian Indians and the Canadian State.* Toronto: University of Toronto Press.

Lloyd, P.J. (1985) The economics of regulation of alcohol distribution and consumption in Victoria, *Australian Economic Review,* 1st Quarter:16–29.

Long, J.A., Boldt, M. and Little Bear, L. (eds) (1988) *Governments in Conflict? Provinces and Indian Nations in Canada.* Toronto: University of Toronto.

Long, J. and Vaillant, G. (1989) Escape from the underclass, in T. Dugan and R. Coles (eds) *The Child in Our Times: Studies in the Development of Resiliency.* New York: Brunner/Mazel.

Lurie, N. (1979) The world's oldest on-going protest demonstration: North American Indian drinking patterns, in M. Marshall (ed.) *Beliefs, Behaviors and Alcoholic Beverages.* Ann Arbor: University of Michigan Press.

Lyon, P. (1990) *What Everybody Knows About Alice: A Report on the Impact of Alcohol Abuse on the Town of Alice Springs.* Alice Springs, Northern Territory: Tangentyere Council.

Lyon, P. (1991) Liquor licensing, Aborigines and take-away alcohol in Central Australia, *Aboriginal Law Bulletin* 51:11–13.

MacAndrew, C. and Edgerton, R.B. (1969) *Drunken Comportment: A Social Explanation.* Chicago: Aldine.

McCarthy, F.D. (1957) *Australia's Aborigines: Their Life and Culture.* Melbourne: Colorgravure Publication.

McCorquodale, J. (1987) *Aborigines and the Law: A Digest.* Canberra: Aboriginal Studies Press.

McEvoy, C. and Rissel, C. (1992) Fourth generation evaluation and its appropriateness for evaluating Aboriginal health programs, *Evaluation Journal of Australasia* 4(1):23–31.

McInnes, S. and Billingsley, P. (1992) Canada's Indians: norms of responsible government under federalism, *Canadian Public Administration* 35(2): 215–36.

McKenzie, D. (ed.) (1993) *Aboriginal Substance Use: Research Issues.* Proceedings of a Joint Research Advisory Meeting, Canadian Centre on Substance Abuse and National Native Alcohol and Drug Abuse Program. Ottawa: Canadian Centre on Substance Abuse.

McKeown, T. (1979) *The Role of Medicine: Dream, Mirage or Nemesis?*, 2nd edn. Oxford: Basil Blackwell.

Macknight, C.C. (1976) *The Voyage to Marege*. Melbourne: Melbourne University Press.

McLaughlin, K.L. and Harrison-Stewart, A.J. (1992) The effect of a temporary period of relaxed licensing laws on the alcohol consumption of young male drinkers, *International Journal of the Addictions* 27(4):409–23.

McLennan, W. (1996) *Australian Social Trends*. Canberra: Australian Bureau of Statistics.

McLennan, W. and Madden R. (1997) *The Health and Welfare of Australia's Aboriginal and Torres Strait Islander Peoples*. Canberra: Australian Bureau of Statistics and Australian Institute of Health and Welfare.

Madden, R. (1995) *National Aboriginal and Torres Strait Islander Survey 1994*. Canberra: Australian Bureau of Statistics.

Mandelbaum, D.G. (1965) Alcohol and culture, *Current Anthropology* 6:281–93.

Manderson, D. (1993) *From Mr Sin to Mr Big. A History of Australian Drug Laws*. Melbourne: Oxford University Press.

Marinovich, N., Larsson, O. and Barber, K. (1976) Comparative metabolism rates of ethanol in adults of Aboriginal and European descent, *Medical Journal of Australia*, Special Supplement 1:44–6.

Mark, S. and Hennessy N. (1991) Alcohol-free zones in NSW, *Aboriginal Law Bulletin* 51:16–17.

Marmot, M.G. (1986) Social inequalities in mortality: the social environment, in R.G. Wilkinson (ed.) *Class and Health: Research and Longitudinal Data*. London: Tavistock, 21–33.

Marmot, M.G. and Smith, G.D. (1989) Why are the Japanese living longer?, *British Medical Journal* 299:1547–51.

Mars, G. (1987) Longshore drinking, economic security and union politics in Newfoundland, in M. Douglas (ed.) *Constructive Drinking: Perspectives on Drinking from Anthropology*. Cambridge: Cambridge University Press.

Marshall, M. (1979) Introduction, in M. Marshall (ed.) *Beliefs, Behaviors and Alcoholic Beverages*. Ann Arbor: University of Michigan Press.

Martin, A. (1988) *Evaluation of Statewide Programme July 1987 – June 1988*. Adelaide: Youth Initiatives Unit, South Australia College of Technical and Further Education.

Martin, C., Wylie, A. and Casswell, S. (1992) Types of New Zealand drinkers and their associated alcohol-related problems, *Journal of Drug Issues* 22:773–96.

Mathews, J.D. (1984) The biological basis of susceptibility to alcohol, in K. Larkins, D. McDonald and C. Watson (eds) *Alcohol and Drug Use in a Changing Society: Proceedings of the 2nd National Drug Institute, Darwin, Northern Territory*. Canberra: Alcohol and Drug Foundation.

May, P.A. (1977) Explanations of Native American drinking: a literature review, *Plains Anthropologist* 22:223–32.

May, P.A. (1982) Substance abuse and American Indians: prevalence and susceptibility, *International Journal of the Addictions* 17:1185–1209.

May, P.A. (1986) Alcohol and drug misuse prevention programs for American Indians: needs and opportunities, *Journal of Studies on Alcohol* 47(3):187–95.

May, P.A. and Smith, M.B. (1988) Some Navajo American Indian opinions about alcohol abuse and prohibition: a survey and recommendations for policy, *Journal of Studies on Alcohol* 49:324–34.

Merton, R.K. (1968) *Social Theory and Social Structure*, enlarged edn. New York: Free Press.

Midford, R., Daly, A. and Holmes, M. (1994) The care of public drunks in Halls
    Creek: a model for community development, *Health Promotion Journal of
    Australia* 4(1):5–8.
Mill, J.S. (1859) *On Liberty.* London: J.W. Parker.
Millar, C.J. and Leung, J.M.S. (1974) Aboriginal alcohol consumption in South
    Australia, in R.M. Berndt (ed.) *A Question of Choice: An Australian Aboriginal
    Dilemma.* Perth: University of Western Australia Press.
Miller, K. and Rowse, T. (1995) *CAAAPU: An Evaluation.* A Menzies Occasional
    Paper, Issue No. 1/95. Darwin: Menzies School of Health Research.
Miller, W.R. and Hester R.K. (1986) The effectiveness of alcoholism treatment:
    what research reveals, in W.R. Miller and N. Heather (eds) *Treating Addictive
    Behaviours: Process of Change.* New York: Plenum Press.
Moncher, M.S., Holden, G.W. and Trimble, J.E. (1990) Substance abuse among
    Native-American youth, *Journal of Consulting and Clinical Psychology* 58:
    408–15.
Moodie, R. (1989) The politics of evaluating Aboriginal health services,
    Community Health Studies XIII(4):503–9.
Moore, D. (1992) Beyond the bottle: introducing anthropological debate to
    research into Aboriginal alcohol use, *Australian Journal of Social Issues* 27(3):
    173–93.
Moore, M.H. and Gerstein, D.R. (1981) *Alcohol and Public Policy: Beyond the Shadow
    of Prohibition.* Washington, DC: National Academy Press.
Moss, J. and Higgins, D. (1986) *Drug Information Series for Professionals.* Perth:
    Western Australian Alcohol and Drug Authority.
Mustard, C. (1993) *The Utilisation of Prenatal Care and Relationship to Birthweight
    Outcome in Winnipeg, 1987–88.* Winnipeg: Manitoba Centre for Health Policy
    and Evaluation.
Myers, F. (1986) *Pintupi Country, Pintupi Self.* Canberra and Washington:
    Australian Institute of Aboriginal Studies and Smithsonian Institute.
Nathan, P. and Japanangka, D. (1983) *Health Business: A Report for the Central
    Australian Aboriginal Congress.* Melbourne: Heinemann.
National Centre for Research into the Prevention of Drug Abuse (1989) *Our
    Place? Your Place?* Proceedings of a Conference on Social and Psychological
    Health Issues in the Aboriginal People. Perth: National Centre for Research
    into the Prevention of Drug Abuse.
New Zealand, Manatu Hauroa, Ministry of Health (1995) *He Taura Tieke:
    Measuring Effective Health Services for Maori.* Wellington: Ministry of Health.
New Zealand, Manatu Hauroa, Ministry of Health (1996) *Progress on Health
    Outcome Targets 1996: The State of Public Health in New Zealand.* Wellington:
    Ministry of Health.
New Zealand, Te Puni Kokiri and Alcohol Advisory Council of New Zealand
    (1995) *Te Maori me te Waipiro: Maori and Alcohol.* Wellington: Te Puni Kokiri
    and Alcohol Advisory Council of New Zealand.
New Zealand, Te Tari Tatau, Statistics New Zealand (1997) *New Zealand Official
    Year Book.* Wellington: Statistics New Zealand.
Nicholson, D. (1984) Indian government in federal policy: an insider's view, in
    Little Bear, L., Boldt, M. and Long, J.A. (eds) (1984) *Pathways to Self-
    determination: Canadian Indians and the Canadian State.* Toronto: University of
    Toronto Press.
Nieuwenhuysen, J. (1986) Liquor control policy and alcohol; availability–
    consumption relationships: reflections on the Victorian debate, *Australian
    Drug and Alcohol Review* 7(3):263–72.

Noble, E.P. (1992) The association of the D_2 dopamine receptor gene with alcoholism and cocaine dependence. Paper presented at the Drug Awareness Relief and Education Symposium, Perth, Western Australia, 22 October 1992.

Northern Territory Drug and Alcohol Bureau (1984) *Smoking, Drinking, Marijuana and 'Sniffing' Behaviour Among Northern Territory School Children.* Darwin: Northern Territory Department of Health and Community Services.

O'Connor, R. (1984) Alcohol and contingent drunkenness in Central Australia, *Journal of Social Issues* 19(3):173–83.

O'Connor, R. and Associates Pty Ltd (1988) *Report on the Aboriginal Alcohol Treatment/Rehabilitation Programmes Review and Consultation.* Typescript. Perth: Western Australian Alcohol and Drug Authority.

O'Connor, J. and Saunders, B. (1992) Drug education: an appraisal of a popular preventive, *International Journal of the Addictions* 27(2):165–85.

O'Donoghue, L. (1995) *Aboriginal Health: An ATSIC Perspective.* Research Section, Occasional Paper No. 1/1995. Canberra: Australian Institute of Aboriginal and Torres Strait Islander Studies.

Oetting, E.R., Edwards, R.W., Ruth, W. and Beauvais, F. (1989) Drugs and Native-American Youth, *Drugs and Society* 3(12):1–34.

Okwumabua, O.J. and Duryea, E.J. (1987) Age of onset, periods of risk, and patterns of progression in drug use among American Indian high school students, *International Journal of the Addictions* 22(12):1269–76.

Owen, J. (1993) *Program Evaluation: Forms and Approaches.* Sydney: Allen & Unwin.

Owston, R.D. (1983) A cooperative model for the evaluation of Indian community schools, *Canadian Journal of Native Education* 10(3):1–4.

Palfrey, C. (1992) *Policy Education in the Public Sector: Approaches and Methods.* Brookfield, Vermont: Avebury.

Parker, L. (1990) The missing component in substance abuse prevention efforts; a native American example, *Contemporary Drug Problems* 7(2):251–70.

Patton, M. (1980) *Qualitative Evaluation Methods.* Los Angeles: Sage.

Peele, S. (1991) What works in addiction treatment and what doesn't: is the best therapy no therapy?, *International Journal of the Addictions* 25:1409–19.

Perkins, J.J., Sanson-Fisher, R.W., Blunden, S., Lunnay, D., Redman, S. and Hensley, M.J. (1994) The prevalence of drug use in urban Aboriginal communities, *Addiction* 89:1319–31.

Plomley, N.J.B. (1966) *Friendly Mission: The Tasmanian Journals and Papers of George Augustus Robinson 1829–1834.* Hobart: Tasmanian Historical Research Association.

Pols, R.G. and Hawks, D.V. (1987) *Is There a Safe Level of Daily Consumption of Alcohol for Men and Women: Recommendations Regarding Responsible Drinking Behaviour.* A Report prepared at the request of the National Health and Medical Research Council for the Health Care Committee. Canberra: Australian Government Publishing Service.

Poundmaker's Lodge Philosophy and Guiding Principles (n.d.) Brochure.

Powderface, S. (1984) Self-government means biting the hand that feeds us, in J.A. Long, M. Boldt, in association with L. Little Bear (eds) (1988) *Governments in Conflict? Provinces and Indian Nations in Canada.* Toronto: University of Toronto.

Powell, K. (1988) *Drinking and Alcohol in Colonial Australia 1788–1901 for the Eastern Colonies.* National Campaign Against Drug Abuse, Monograph 3. Canberra: Australian Government Publishing Service.

Rathje, W. (1978) Archaeological ethnography . . . because sometimes it is better to give than to receive, in R.A. Gould (ed.) *Explorations in Ethnoarchaeology.* Albuquerque, New Mexico: University of New Mexico Press.

Rebach, H. (1992) Alcohol and drug use among American minorities, *Drugs and Society* 6(1/2): 23–58.

Reed, T.E., Kalant, H., Gibbins, R.J., Kapur, B.M. and Rankin, J.G. (1976) Alcohol and acetaldehyde metabolism in Caucasians, Chinese and Amerinds, *Canadian Medical Association Journal* 115:851–5.

Reid, J. and Trompf, P. (eds) (1991) *The Health of Aboriginal Australia.* Sydney: Harcourt Brace Jovanovich.

Reser, J. (1989) Aboriginal deaths in custody and social construction, *Australian Aboriginal Studies* 2:43–50.

Reser, J. (1991) Aboriginal mental health, in J. Reid and P. Trompf (eds) (1991) *The Health of Aboriginal Australia.* Sydney: Harcourt Brace Jovanovich.

Reynolds, H. (1981) *The Other Side of the Frontier: Aboriginal Resistance to the European Invasion of Australia.* Ringwood, Victoria: Penguin.

Rhoades, E.R., Mason, R.D., Eddy, P., Smith, E.M. and Burns, T.R. (1988) The Indian Health Service approach to alcoholism among American Indians and Alaskan Natives, *Public Health Reports* 103(6):621–7.

Richardson, B. (1993) *People of Terra Nullius: Betrayal and Rebirth in Aboriginal Canada.* Vancouver: Douglas and McIntyre.

Riley, M., Lee, A., Davis, R. and Mathews, J. (1988) Nutrient status and food intake in a kava using community, in *Annual Report 1987/88,* Menzies School of Health Research. Darwin: Menzies School of Health Research.

Ronin Films, Australian Film Commission and Australian Broadcasting Corporation (1989) *State of Shock.* Producer and director David Bradbury, editor Stewart Young.

Room, R. (1984a) Alcohol control and public health, *Annual Review of Public Health* 5:293–317.

Room, R. (1984b) Alcohol and ethnography: a case of problem deflation? *Current Anthropology* 25(2):169–78.

Room, R. (1985) Dependence and society, *British Journal of Addiction* 80:133–9.

Room, R. (1988) The dialectic of drinking in Australian life: from the Rum Corps to the wine column, *Australian Drug and Alcohol Review* 7:413–37.

Room, R. (1990) Recent research on the effects of alcohol policy changes, *Journal of Primary Prevention* 11(1):83–94.

Roseberry, W. (1988) Political economy, *Annual Review of Anthropology* 17:161–85.

Rowell, R.M. (1990) Warning signs: intravenous drug abuse among American Indians/Alaskan Natives, *Drugs and Society* 5(1/2): 21–35.

Rowley, C.D. (1974) *The Destruction of Aboriginal Society.* Harmondsworth: Penguin.

Rowse, T. (1993) The relevance of ethnographic understanding to Aboriginal anti-grog initiatives, *Drug and Alcohol Review* 12: 393–9.

Rowse, T. (1994) *Make a Better Offer: The Politics of Mabo.* Leichhardt, New South Wales: Pluto.

Rowse, T. (1996) *Traditions for Health.* Darwin: Australian National University, North Australia Research Unit.

Royal College of Physicians (1987) *A Great and Growing Evil: The Medical Consequences of Alcohol Abuse.* London: Tavistock.

Rubel, A.J. and Kupferer, H.J. (1968) Perspective on the atomistic-type society: Introduction, *Human Organisation* 27:189–90.

Rutter, M. (1979) Protective factors in children's responses to stress and disadvantage, in M.W. Kent and J.E. Rolf (eds) *Primary Prevention of*

Psychopathology, Vol 3: Social Competence in Children. Hanover, New Hampshire: University Press of New England.

Rydon, P. and Stockwell, T. (1997) Local regulation and enforcement strategies for licensed premises, in M. Plant, E. Single and T. Stockwell (eds) *Alcohol: Minimising the Harm.* London: Free Association Books.

Rydon, P., Stockwell, T., Lang, E. and Beel, A. (1996) Pseudo-drunk patron evaluation of bar-staff, *Australian and New Zealand Journal of Public Health* 20(3):290–5.

Sackett, L. (1977) Liquor and the Law: Wiluna, Western Australia, in R.M. Berndt (ed.) *Aborigines and Change.* Canberra: Australian Institute of Aboriginal Studies.

Sackett, L. (1988) Resisting arrests: drinking, development and discipline in a desert context, *Social Analysis* 24, December:66–77.

Sackett, L. (1993) A post-modern panopticon: The Royal Commission into Aboriginal Deaths in Custody, *Australian Journal of Social Issues* 28(3):228–43.

Saggers, S. (1994) 'But that was all in the past'. The relevance of history to contemporary Aboriginal health, *Australian Journal of Occupational Therapy* 40(4):153–6.

Saggers, S. and Gray, D. (1991) *Aboriginal Health and Society.* Sydney: Allen & Unwin.

Saggers, S. and Gray, D. (1997) Supplying and promoting 'grog': the political economy of alcohol in Aboriginal Australia, *Australian Journal of Social Issues* 32(3):215–37.

Saggers, S. and Gray, D. (1998) Alcohol, risk and liberty: a comparative analysis of interventions in indigenous communities in Australia and Canada, in C. Waddell and A. Petersen (eds) *Health Matters.* Sydney: Allen & Unwin.

Sanders, W. (1993) *Reconciling Public Accountability and Aboriginal Self-determination/Self-management: Is ATSIC Succeeding?* Centre for Aboriginal Economic Policy Research Discussion Paper No. 51. Canberra: Australian National University.

Sansom, B. (1980) *The Camp at Wallaby Cross: Aboriginal Fringe-dwellers in Darwin.* Canberra: Australian Institute of Aboriginal Studies.

Sargent, M. (1979) *Drinking and Alcoholism in Australia: A Power Relations Theory.* Melbourne: Longman Cheshire.

Saunders, B. and Phillips, M. (1993) Is 'alcoholism' genetically transmitted? And are there any implications for prevention?, *Drug and Alcohol Review* 12:291–8.

Schaefer J. (1981) Firewater myths revisited: review of findings and some new directions, in D. Health, J. Waddell and M. Topper (eds) *Cultural Factors in Alcohol Research and Treatment of Drinking Problems, Journal of Studies on Alcohol* Supplement No. 9:99–117.

Schaffer, H.J. and Jones, S.B. (1989) *Quitting Cocaine: The Struggle Against Impulse.* Lexington, Massachusetts: Lexington Books.

Schweinhart, L. *et al.* (1985) *A Report on the High/Scope Preschool Curriculum Comparison Study: Consequences of Three Preschool Curriculum Models Through Age 15.* Ypsilanti, Michigan: High/Scope Educational Research Foundation.

Scott, K.A. (1993) Substance use among indigenous Canadians, in D. McKenzie (ed.) *Aboriginal Substance Use: Research Issues.* Proceedings of a Joint Research Advisory Meeting, Canadian Centre on Substance Abuse and National Native Alcohol and Drug Abuse Program. Ottawa: Canadian Centre on Substance Abuse.

Scott, K. (1996) Indigenous Canadians, in *Canadian Profile 1996.* Ottawa: Health and Welfare Canada.

Schuckit, M.A. (1995) *Drug and Alcohol Abuse: A Clinical Guide to Diagnosis and Treatment.* New York: Plenum Medical Book Company.

Seidman, S. (1994) *Contested Knowledge.* Cambridge: Blackwell.

Singer, M. (1986) Toward a political economy of alcoholism: the missing link in the anthropology of drinking, *Social Science and Medicine* 23(2):113–30.

Single, E. (1988) The availability theory of alcohol-related problems, in C.D. Chaudron and D.A. Wilkinson (eds) *Theories on Alcoholism.* Toronto: Addiction Research Foundation.

Single, E. (1995) Harm reduction and alcohol, *International Journal on Drug Policy* 6(1):26–30.

Single, E., Brewster, J., MacNeil, P., Hatcher, J. and Trainor, C. (1995) *Alcohol and Drug Use: Results from the 1993 General Social Survey.* Report prepared for the Studies Unit, Health Promotion Directorate, Health Canada. Ottawa: Health Canada.

Single, E., Morgan, P. and deLint, J. (eds) (1981) *Alcohol, Society and the State. 2: The Social History of Control Policy in Seven Countries.* Toronto: Addiction Research Foundation.

Single, E., Williams, B. and McKenzie, D. (1994) *Canadian Profile: Alcohol, Tobacco & Other Drugs.* Toronto: Addiction Research Foundation.

Single, E. and Wortley, S. (1993) Drinking in various settings as it relates to demographic variables and level of consumption: findings from a national survey in Canada, *Journal of Studies on Alcohol* 54(5):590–600.

Skog, O.-J. (1985) *The Distribution of Alcohol Consumption Part III: Evidence of a Collective Drinking Culture,* Oslo: National Institute for Alcohol Research.

Smart, R.G. (1979) A note on the effects of changes in alcohol control policies in the Canadian north, *Journal of Studies on Alcohol* 40:908–13.

Smart, R.G. and Adlaf, E.M. (1986) Banning happy hours: the impact on drinking and impaired driving charges in Ontario, Canada, *Journal of Studies on Alcohol* 47:256–8.

Smart, R.G. and Ogborne, A.C. (1986) *Northern Spirits. Drinking in Canada Then and Now.* Toronto: Addiction Research Foundation.

Smith, D.I. (1989a) Effect on liver cirrhosis and traffic accident mortality of changing the number and type of alcohol outlets in Western Australia, *Alcoholism: Clinical and Experimental Research* 13(2):190–5.

Smith, D.I. (1989b) Effectiveness of legislative and fiscal restrictions in reducing alcohol related crime and traffic accidents, in Vernon, J. (ed.) *Alcohol and Crime: Conference Proceedings.* Canberra: Australian Institute of Criminology.

Smith, D.I. (1990) Effectiveness of restrictions on availability as a means of reducing the use and abuse of alcohol, *Australian Alcohol and Drug Review* 2(2):84–9.

Smith, D.I. and Burvill, P.W. (1986) Effect on traffic safety of lowering the drinking age in three Australian states, *Journal of Drug Issues* 16(2):183–98.

Soulier, M.J. (1984) *Counselling Parallel of Indian/non-Indian Clients: The Anishinabe Way Workshop Module IV.* Spooner, Wisconsin: Ain Dah Ing.

Spenser, D.J. (1988) *Transitional Alcoholism: The Australian Aboriginal Model.* National Drug Abuse Information Centre Technical Information Bulletin on Drug Abuse No. 79. Canberra: Department of Community Services and Health.

Stewart, L. and Casswell, S. (1992) Community control and liquor licensing: a public health issue in New Zealand, *Journal of Drug Issues* 22:743–55.

Stockwell, T. (1995) Do controls on the availability of alcohol reduce alcohol problems?, in T. Stockwell (ed.) *Alcohol Misuse and Violence: An Examination of the Appropriateness and Efficacy of Liquor Licensing Laws Across Australia.* Report 5 in a series of reports prepared for the National Symposium on Alcohol Misuse and Violence. Canberra: Australian Government Publishing Service.

Stockwell, T. (ed.) (1995) *Alcohol Misuse and Violence: An Examination of the Appropriateness and Efficacy of Liquor Licensing Laws Across Australia.* Report 5 in a series of reports prepared for the National Symposium on Alcohol Misuse and Violence. Canberra: Australian Government Publishing Service.

Stockwell, T. (1997) Regulation of the licensed drinking environment: a major opportunity for crime prevention, in R. Homel (ed.) *Policing for Prevention: Reducing Crime, Public Intoxication and Injury.* Crime Prevention Studies Vol. 7. Monsey, New Jersey: Criminal Justice Press.

Stockwell, T., Lang, E. and Rydon, P. (1993) High risk drinking settings: the association of serving and promotional practices with harmful drinking, *Addiction* 88:1519–26.

Stockwell, T. and Single, E. (1997) Standard unit labelling of alcohol containers, in M. Plant, E. Single and T. Stockwell (1997) *Alcohol Minimising the Harm: What Works?* London: Free Association Books.

Stoddart, G. (1996) Toward an understanding of the determinants of health – together, *Population Health Promotion: Bringing Our Visions Together.* Typescript.

Stone, A.C. (1911) The Aborigines of Lake Boga, Victoria, *Proceedings of the Royal Society of Victoria* 23 (NS), Part 2.

Sugarman, J.R., Warren, C.W., Oge, L. and Helgerson, S.D. (1992) Using the behavioral risk factor surveillance system to monitor year 2000 objectives among American Indians, *Public Health Reports* 107(4):449–56.

Sulkunen, P. (1976) Drinking patterns and the level of alcohol consumption, an international review, *Research Advances in Alcohol and Drug Problems* 3:223–81.

Sullivan, H.M., Gracey, M. and Hevron, V. (1987) Food costs and nutrition of Aborigines in remote areas of northern Australia, *Medical Journal of Australia* 147:334–7.

Sumner, M. (1995) Substance abuse and Aboriginal domestic violence, *Aboriginal and Islander Health Worker Journal* 19(2):16–17.

Swan, P. and Raphael, B. (1995) *'Ways forward' National Consultancy Report on Aboriginal and Torres Strait Islander Mental Health,* Part 1 & 2. Canberra: Australian Government Publishing Service.

Swensen, G. and Unwin, E. (1994) *A Study of Hospitalisation and Mortality Due to Alcohol Use in the Kimberley Health Region of Western Australia.* Perth: Health Department of Western Australia.

Thomson, D. (1939) Notes on the smoking pipes of North Queensland and the Northern Territory of Australia, *Man* 76:81–91.

Thomson, D. (1949) *Economic Structure and the Ceremonial Exchange Cycle in Arnhem Land.* Melbourne: Macmillan.

Thomson, N., Paden, F. and Cassidy, G. (1990) The identification of Aborigines in hospital admissions in the North Coast Health Region, New South Wales, *Aboriginal Health Information Bulletin* 13:28–32.

Tobler, N. (1986) Meta-analysis of 143 adolescent drug prevention programs: quantitative outcome results of program participants compared to a control or comparison group, *Journal of Drug Issues* 16(4):537–67.

Tonkinson, R. and Howard, M. (eds) (1990) *Going it alone? Prospects for Aboriginal Autonomy.* Canberra: Aboriginal Studies Press.

Trigger, D. (1992) *Whitefella Comin'*. Cambridge: Cambridge University Press.

Trigger, D.S., Anderson, C., Lincoln, R.A. and Matis, C.E. (1983) Mortality rates in 14 Queensland Aboriginal reserve communities: association with socio-environmental variables, *Medical Journal of Australia* 16(1):361–5.

Trimble, J.E. (1984) Drug abuse prevention research among American Indians and Alaskan Natives, *White Cloud Journal* 3:22–34.

United States, National Clearinghouse for Alcohol Information (1985) Alcohol and Native Americans, *Alcohol Topics Research Review*. Rockville, Maryland: National Institute on Alcohol Abuse and Alcoholism.

United States Senate, Select Committee on Indian Affairs (1992) Bureau of Indian Affairs and Indian Health Service Inspector General reports on Indian alcohol and drug abuse programs: hearing before the Select Committee on Indian Affairs, United States Senate, One Hundred and Second Congress, second session, 30 July 1992. Washington, DC.

Unwin, E., Gracey, M. and Thomson, N. (1995) The impact of tobacco smoking and alcohol consumption on Aboriginal mortality in Western Australia, 1989–91, *Medical Journal of Australia* 162(9):475–8.

Unwin, E. and Serafino, S. (1995) *A Study of Hospitalisation and Mortality Due to Alcohol Use in the Pilbara Region and Western Australia, 1989–1993*. Perth: Health Department of Western Australia.

Unwin, E., Thomson, N. and Gracey, M. (1994) *The Impact of Tobacco Smoking and Alcohol Consumption on Aboriginal Mortality and Hospitalisation in Western Australia: 1983–1991*. Perth: Health Department of Western Australia.

Vaillant, G. (1986) Deconstruction deconstructed: comment on Robin Room's 'Dependence and Society', *British Journal of Addiction* 81:58.

Veroni, M., Gracey, M. and Rouse, I. (1994) Patterns of mortality in Western Australian Aboriginals, 1983–1989, *International Journal of Epidemiology* 23(1): 73–81.

Veroni, M., Swensen, G. and Thomson N. (1993) *Hospital Admissions in Western Australia Wholly Attributable to Alcohol Use: 1981–1990*. Perth: Health Department of Western Australia.

von Stürmer, J. (1981) Talking with Aborigines, *Australian Institute of Aboriginal Studies Newsletter* 15:13–30.

Wagenaar, A.C. (1993) Research affects public policy: the case of the legal drinking age in the United States, *Addiction* 88, Supplement:75–81.

Waldram, J.B., Herring, D.A. and Young, T.K. (1995) *Aboriginal Health in Canada: Historical, Cultural, and Epidemiological Perspectives*. Toronto: University of Toronto Press.

Walker, R.D., Benjamin, G.A., Kivlahan, D. and Walker, P.S. (1985) American Indian alcohol misuse and treatment outcome, in D. Spiegler, D. Tate, S. Aitken and C. Christian (eds) *Alcohol Use Among US Ethnic Minorities*. DHHS Publication No ADM 89–1435. Washington, DC: US Government Printing Office.

Ward, J. (1978) Aborigines and alcohol, in A.P. Diehm, R.F. Seaborn and G.C. Wilson (eds) *Alcohol in Australia: Problems and Programmes*. Sydney: McGraw Hill.

Ward, R. (1981) *The Australian Legend*. Melbourne: Oxford University Press.

Wardlaw, G. (1992) Overview of National Drug Control Strategies, in *Comparative Analysis of Illicit Drug Strategy*. National Campaign Against Drug Abuse Monograph Series No. 18. Canberra: Australian Government Publishing Service.

Warner, W.L. (1969) *A Black Civilisation: A Social Study of an Aboriginal Tribe.* Gloucester, Massachusetts: Peter Smith.

Watson, C., Fleming, J. and Alexander, K. (1988) *A survey of drug use patterns in Northern Territory Aboriginal Communities: 1986–1987.* Darwin: Northern Territory Department of Health and Community Services.

Watson, P. (1991) *Pituri:* an Aboriginal drug, *International Journal on Drug Policy* 2(4):32–3.

Watts, T.D. and Lewis, R.G. (1988) Alcoholism and native American youth: an overview, *Journal of Drug Issues Special Issue: Alcohol Problems and Minority Youth* 18(1):69–86.

Weatherburn, D. (1990) Sources of confusion in the alcohol and crime debate, in J. Vernon (ed.) *Alcohol and Crime: Proceedings of a Conference Held 4–6 April 1989.* Canberra: Australian Institute of Criminology.

Weaver, S.M. (1984) Indian government: a concept in need of a definition, in Little Bear, L., Boldt, M. and Long, J.A. (eds) (1984) *Pathways to Self-determination: Canadian Indians and the Canadian State.* Toronto: University of Toronto Press.

Weeramanthri, T., d'Abbs, P. and Mathews, J. (1994) Towards a definition of an alcohol-related death: an analysis in Aboriginal adults, *Australian Journal of Public Health* 18(1):71–8.

Weibel-Orlando, J.C. (1985a) Indians, ethnicity and alcohol: contrasting perceptions of the ethnic self and alcohol use, in L.A. Bennett and G.M. Ames (eds) *The American Experience with Alcohol: Contrasting Cultural Perspectives.* New York: Plenum Press.

Weibel-Orlando, J.C. (1985b) Pass the bottle Bro!: A comparison of urban and rural Indian drinking patterns, in D. Spiegler, D. Tate, S. Aitken and C. Christian (eds) *Alcohol Use Among US Ethnic Minorities.* DHHS Publication No ADM 89–1435. Washington, DC: US Government Printing Office.

Weibel-Orlando, J.C. (1987) Drinking patterns of urban and rural American Indians, *Alcohol Health and Research World* 11: 8–12.

Weibel-Orlando, J.C. (1989) Hooked on healing: anthropologists, alcohol and intervention, *Human Organisation* 48:148–55.

Weibel-Orlando, J.C. (1990) American Indians and prohibition: effect or affect? Views from the reservation and the city, *Contemporary Drug Problems* 17(2): 293–322.

Welborn, S. (1987) *Swan: the History of a Brewery.* Perth: University of Western Australia Press.

Weller, A. (1981) *The Day of the Dog.* Sydney: Allen & Unwin.

Werner, E.E. and Smith, R.S. (1989) *Vulnerable but Invincible: A Longitudinal Study of Resilient Children and Youth,* 2nd edn. New York: Adams, Bannister and Cox.

Westermeyer, J. (1979) 'The drunken Indian': myths and realities, in M. Marshall (ed.) *Beliefs, Behaviors, and Alcoholic Beverages.* Ann Arbor: University of Michigan Press.

Western Australia, Innovation and Technology and Aboriginal Affairs Department (1995) *Aboriginal Contact With The Criminal Justice System in Western Australia: Royal Commission into Aboriginal Deaths in Custody,* Vol. 2. Perth: Aboriginal Affairs Department.

Western Australia, Crime Research Centre and Aboriginal Affairs Department (1995) *Aboriginal Youth and the Juvenile Justice System in Western Australia: Royal Commission into Aboriginal Deaths in Custody,* Vol. 3. Perth: Aboriginal Affairs Department.

Western Australia, Task Force on Aboriginal Social Justice (1994) *Report of the Taskforce on Aboriginal Social Justice*, 2 Vols and Summary. Perth: Government of Western Australia.

Wette, H., Zhang, J., Berg, R. and Casswell, S. (1993) The effect of prices on alcohol consumption: New Zealand 1983–1991, *Drug and Alcohol Review* 12:153–60.

Wilkinson, R.G. (1994) The epidemiological transition: from material scarcity to social disadvantage?, *Daedalus*: 61–77.

Wodak, A. (1994) What I would most like to know: how do communities achieve reductions in alcohol- and drug-related harm?, *Addiction* 89:147–50.

Wolfson, M., Rowe, G., Gentleman, J.F. and Tomiak, M. (1993) Career earnings and death: a longitudinal analysis of older Canadian men, *Journal of Gerontology* 48(4):S167–79.

Workman, K. (1996) Achieving the Crown's goals for Maori health. Paper presented at the IRR Conference 'Bringing together Strategies to Improve Maori Health', Wellington, 12 March 1996. Typescript

Wyllie, A., Zhang, J.F. and Casswell, S. (1993) Comparison of six alcohol consumption measures from survey data, *Addiction* 89:425–30.

Wynter, J. (1991) Central Australian Aboriginal Alcohol Planning Unit: A challenge for change, *Aboriginal Law Bulletin* 2(51):7.

Wynter, J. and Hill, J. (1988) Discussion paper on alcohol-related problems in the Alice Springs town camps. Alice Springs: Tangentyere Council.

York, G. (1992) *The Dispossessed: Life and Death in Native Canada*. Toronto: Little Brown.

Young, T.J. (1988) Substance abuse among Native Americans, *Clinical Psychology Review* 8: 36–46.

Young, T.J. (1991) Native American drinking: a neglected subject of study and research, *Journal of Drug Education* 21(1):65–72.

Yukon, Government of (1990) *Yukon Alcohol and Drug Survey Fall 1990*, Vol. 1. Technical Report. Whitehorse: Executive Council Office, Bureau of Statistics.

Zinberg, N. (1984) *Drug, Set, and Setting: The Basis for Controlled Intoxicant Use*. New Haven: Yale University Press.

Index

Aboriginal and Torres Strait Islander
    Commission 178, 179
Aboriginal and Torres Strait Islanders *see*
    Australian Aborigines
Aboriginal Peoples Survey (Canada) 58–9
Aboriginals, persons identifying
    themselves as 6, 8
abstinence
    and moral authority over drinkers 66
    Australian Aborigines 56, 57, 66
    indigenous women 193–4
    Maori 58
    native Canadians 44–5, 59
    see also treatment programs
accidents and injury 20, 30
acculturative stress 74–5
acute interventions 155–6
advertising *see* alcohol promotion
alcohol 29–30
    and colonisation 17–18
    as cultural artifact 33
    historical usage 27–8
    in human society 190
    reputed benefits 30
    sociability of 13, 24, 137
alcohol availability *see* availability of
    alcohol
alcohol consumption 12–17, 51–60
    Aboriginal and Torres Strait Islanders
        14, 53, 54–6
    and alcohol control 91–3
    as learned behaviour 78–9
    as positive image 13, 15, 137
    changing patterns, factors 37–9
    decline in Australia, Canada and New
        Zealand 36–7
    indigenous accounts 15–16
    indigenous Australian rules 64, 79

    legislative restrictions, models 100–1
    Maori 57–8
    measurement 51–3, 54
    native Canadians 58–60
    social and health impacts 33–4
    worldwide comparison 34–7
    see also drinking; excessive alcohol
        consumption
alcohol control 45–51
    and Aboriginal affairs policy 96–8
    availability hypothesis 90–1, 138
    consumption levels and alcohol-related
        harm 91–3
    indigenous Australian communities
        98–102
    indigenous Australians 46, 48–50, 60–1,
        87
    legislative restrictions 100–1
    Northern Territory initiatives 94–5,
        101–2, 164–5
    preventive paradox 91
    state role 95–6
    Western Australian rural towns 117–21
    see also availability of alcohol;
        prohibition
alcohol dependence
    and availability of alcohol 90–1
    as 'disease' or dysfunction 71–3
    biological basis 69–70
    definition 71–2
    genetic predisposition 69–70, 72
alcohol industry 93–6, 137
alcohol metabolism, genetic differences
    69–70
alcohol misuse 4
    as a 'sickness' 71
    cause or consequence of social
        problems 24–5